SEEDS 2

SEEDS 2:

Supporting Women's Work around the World

Edited by Ann Leonard

Introduction by Martha Alter Chen
Afterwords by Mayra Buvinić, Misrak Elias, Rounaq Jahan,
Caroline Moser, and Kathleen Staudt

THE FEMINIST PRESS
at The City University of New York
New York

99 98 97 96 95 5 4 3 2 1

Library of Congress Cataloging-in-Publication Data

Seeds 2 : supporting women's work around the world / edited by Ann Leonard ; introduction by Martha Alter Chen ; afterword by Mayra Buvinic . . . [et al.].
    p.   cm.
    Originally published in a pamphlet series Seeds.
    Includes bibliographical references.
    ISBN 1-55861-107-X (alk. paper). — ISBN 1-55861-106-1 (alk. paper)
    1. Women in development—Developing countries—Case studies.
2. Women in business—Developing countries—Case studies. 3. Women-Employment—Developing countries—Case studies. 4. Women in community development—Developing countries—Case studies. 5. Child care services—Developing countries—Case studies. I. Leonard, Ann, 1945–   . II. Seeds (New York, N.Y.) III. Title: Seeds two.
HQ1240.5.D44S44   1995
305.4'09172'4—dc20   95-4144
                                                                         CIP

This book is an outgrowth of the Seeds booklet series on women's income-generating activities. Project direction and administrative support for Seeds are provided by the Population Council. Funding for production of this book has been made possible primarily by The Ford Foundation. Since its inception, support for the Seeds project has been provided by The Carnegie Corporation, the Canadian International Development Agency (CIDA), The Ford Foundation, the General Services Foundation, the Government of the Netherlands, the Interamerican Foundation, Oxfam America, the Population Council, the Rockefeller Foundation, UNICEF, UNIFEM, and the Women in Development Office of the United States Agency for International Development.

Cover photo: Janice Jiggins
Cover design: Lucinda Geist
Typeset by Stanton Publication Services, Inc., Saint Paul, Minnesota
Text design by Paula Martinac
Design and Production: Tina Malaney
Printed in the United States of America on acid-free paper by McNaughton and Gunn, Inc.

Contents

AFTERWORDS

Preface

It has now been almost twenty years since the ground-breaking first International Women's Conference in Mexico City launched the official United Nations Decade for Women (1975–1985). The decade ended in Nairobi in 1985, with a jubilant celebration of women's achievements, endurance, creativity, and hope for the future. But today, as we look toward the 1995 International Women's Conference, to be held in Beijing, it is clear that a great deal remains to be done. The increasing "feminization of poverty" in countries of both the North and the South testifies to the fact that, despite increased attention to women's livelihoods, the economic responsibilities imposed on women in most parts of the world to maintain not only themselves but their families are increasing more rapidly than their earning opportunities.

The Seeds booklet series on women's income-generating activities was begun in the late 1970s in response to the dearth of information available on successful efforts by and for women to earn an income. The series commissions and publishes case studies of economic development projects that focus on women. When the series was launched, it was our belief that by the end of the decade, women's economic conditions and perceptions of women would have changed to such an extent that documentation efforts such as Seeds would no longer be needed.

That this is not the case is evident not only from the world situation noted above, but also from the continually increasing interest in Seeds among new as well as previous generations of readers. As this book goes to press, seventeen case studies have been documented in the series; nine have been translated into Spanish, eight into French; and a local language program established with colleagues in developing countries has resulted in publication of Seeds booklets in Arabic, Bahasa (Indonesia), Hindi (India), Kiswahili (East Africa), Nepali, Thai, Urdu (Pakistan), and Vietnamese.

In 1989, the first Seeds book, *Seeds: Supporting Women's Work in the Third World,* was published by The Feminist Press. This volume brings together nine case studies and four original essays that set them within the broader context of women's economic development from both international and regional perspectives. Having the case studies available in book format has made this material accessible to an entirely new audience of general readers and scholars alike.

As we entered the 1990s, the Seeds Steering Committee realized that there had been enough significant changes in the field of women's economic development to warrant revising the introduction that accompanies each case study. The text was emended to broaden the concept of women's work from simply earning income to encompassing their need to "generate livelihoods and to improve their economic status"; and for selection of projects that serve "not only to strengthen women's productive roles, but also to integrate women into various sectors of development, both social and economic."

The seven new case studies included in this second *Seeds* volume illustrate this change in direction. They also focus attention on the similarity of the economic problems women face in all parts of the world (as evidenced by publication in 1993 of the first booklet to feature a project in the United States) and highlight the organizational requirements of success—such as the significant role of training and experience in mounting an effective project, the vital links between women's family and work roles, and the importance of political consciousness in forging economic change.

The introduction to this edition, written by Martha Chen, of the Harvard Institute of International Development, and afterwords by Mayra Buvinić, Misrak Elias, Rounaq Jahan, and Caroline Moser address the changes that are taking place in this field—particularly in the decade between Nairobi and Beijing— from a variety of perspectives and outline issues that will need to be addressed as we approach the dawn of a new century. We have also asked Kathleen Staudt to update her excellent essay, "Planting *Seeds* in the Classroom," for this volume to include a discussion of the new material and how it can be used in a variety of academic settings.

For all of us involved in its development, the Seeds project remains a rewarding effort. We are pleased that, through this book, we are able to share with you the reality of women's lives from cultures around the world in a way that, while illustrative of the problems they face, focuses on women's strength, courage, and ingenuity in meeting challenges and bringing about change.

Ann Leonard
for the Seeds Steering Committee

Acknowledgments

On the copyright page of this volume are listed all the donors who have made the Seeds project possible over the years. We are grateful to all of them for their support. However, we would like to note here the special role that The Ford Foundation has played, as the first home base for the project and, subsequently, by providing continued financial support and program expertise over the years.

The role of the Steering Committee in setting editorial policy and developing individual case studies has been pivotal to the success of the project. Special thanks go to both current and former members: Kristin Anderson, Betsy Campbell, Marilyn Carr, Martha Chen, Margaret Clark, Misrak Elias, Adrienne Germain, Anne Kubisch, Cecilia Lotse, Karen McGuinness, Katharine McKee, Kirsten Moore, Jill Sheffield, William Sweeney, Anne Walker, and Mildred Warner.

As it has since the early 1980s, the Population Council continues to provide project direction and administrative support for Seeds and to serve as the project's home base. Administrative and editorial oversight are carried out by Ann Leonard, project coordinator/editor, with the assistance of Judith Bruce, project advisor. Margaret Catley-Carlson, Council President, and George Brown, Vice President of the Programs Division, are to be acknowledged for their stalwart support of this project; special thanks also go to Tim Thomas, Executive Assistant, for his continuing interest in the Seeds project.

And finally, we acknowledge the people who truly made it all possible—the grassroots women whose stories are told in these case studies.

Introduction

Martha Alter Chen

I. Looking Back

Twenty years ago, when the international women's movement was officially launched, there was a common belief that if women could obtain a job for wages outside the home, or otherwise earn an independent income, they would be able to exercise control over the income they earned and thus to exercise increased bargaining power within their homes. This, in turn, would lead to improvements in their own and their family's well-being. Twenty years later, this belief has been challenged by a wide cross-section of women in the movement. What happened to challenge these initial beliefs? What brought about this change in thinking?

Certainly, the international women's movement has become more sophisticated in its thinking and operation. In 1975, most of the scholars, activists, planners, and advocates involved in the women's movement thought the tasks at hand were to increase the visibility of women (particularly as workers); to increase women's access to the processes of development (especially economic development); and to develop special offices, special mechanisms, and special projects for women (at both the local and national levels). We therefore undertook detailed descriptive studies of women's work, designed innovative income-generating projects for women, and lobbied for women's integration into the development process.

By 1985, however, most of us had begun to question some of these assumptions. Did we, in fact, want to integrate women into the existing development models? Were separate (but seldom equal) offices and mechanisms for women really useful? Did isolated, local income-generation projects for women produce the intended benefits? We asked these questions because we had become increasingly aware that the root causes of women's problems are not economic (in the narrow sense of jobs and income) but structural and political. Women everywhere began to call for a redefinition of economic development. And we called for collective organization and empowerment of women. But, at the same time, we found it difficult to translate this new way of thinking into actual, specific programs and policies. This was partly because we were asking women to challenge age-old as well as modern structures while, at the same time, these structures were themselves changing in ways that often proved contradictory for women.

In 1975, the economic orthodoxy of the 1950s and '60s was just beginning to be challenged. And while concern for basic needs had been voiced, the promise that continued economic growth would lead to development for all seemed assured. By 1985, however, the persistence of widespread poverty, the failure of growth policies in numerous countries, and an international economic recession had precipitated a reassessment of economic development. One result was the adoption of corrective economic measures, known as structural adjustment policies (SAPs), by many developing nations at the insistence of the International Monetary Fund and the World Bank. The focus of such policies is economic stabilization, increased privatization, and debt refinancing.

One aspect of this reassessment was the recognition that the economic crises of debt, trade, and the environment have global dimensions and that solutions to these crises must be negotiated on the global stage. Meanwhile, certain political crises also gained momentum, intensity, and global proportions—religious fundamentalism, civil strife within nations, and ethno-nationalistic movements—all having concomitant effects on both economic and human development. By the early 1990s, the collapse of communism had unleashed a new wave of ethno-nationalism and created a global political climate of unprecedented uncertainty, as well as promise.

While the world as a whole was visibly shaken by these global crises, women (and their children) were being buffeted by a less visible but equally consequential, and not unrelated, local crisis—within the family itself. While marriage remains almost universal across most regions and social groups in developing countries, the number of years an adult woman is likely to live without a partner in residence, and the number of women who are likely to raise children without a partner, are surprisingly high. Due to the death of an older spouse, the migration of a working spouse, desertion and divorce, or polygamy (a feature of family life still evident in many parts of the world), many women today are maintaining families virtually on their own (Bruce et al. 1995).

II. Taking Stock

What has been the impact of these global and domestic forces on the lives and work of women? The evidence is somewhat contradictory. In the developing world, women have made considerable progress over the last thirty years. Life expectancy, literacy, educational attainment, and political participation of women have all improved, yet the gap between men's and women's achievement continues. Although women's average life expectancy now exceeds men's in some developing countries, women lag behind men in terms of other measures of human development. The following table shows the number of women achieving a variety of development goals as measured against every 100 men attaining the same level (UNDP 1991, 30, 139), as follows:

	Women	Men
Adult Literacy	66	100
Mean Years of Schooling	53	100
Labor Force Participation	52	100
Election to Parliament	15	100

And throughout most of the world—including developed countries—women continue to earn, on average, two-thirds of what men do.

In addition to this human development gap, other indicators reveal that poverty is increasingly a female problem—indicators of what can be, and has been, called in both developing and developed world settings the "feminization of poverty."[1] To set the stage, it is important to note that the large majority of the world's women (62 percent) live in countries with very low per-capita gross domestic production (GDP)—less than US $1,000 per year—and very low or declining economic growth—less than US $10 per year and declining (UN 1991, 96). Of course, so do the large majority of the world's men. But within poor countries, women are more impoverished than men. In most developing countries, households supported by women are often economically disadvantaged: that is, the poorest households often include large numbers of female-headed households.

For example, in Brazil, female-headed households make up 10 percent of all households but account for 15 percent of all households that are poor (WDR 1990, 31). And within most poor households, women (and girls) are economically deprived, usually receiving less food, medical care, and education than men (and boys).

Why has this gender gap in human development persisted (or even increased in some areas), despite the efforts of the international women's movement? In addition to the aspects of the recent economic situation, noted above, that have generated pervasive insecurity for poor men and women alike, there are continuing aspects of traditional systems—discriminatory customs and norms regarding the sexual division of work, marriage and family, inheritance and property—which serve to perpetuate gender inequality. In addition, many gender inequalities deeply embedded in traditional marriage and kinship systems are, in turn, reinforced by modern law. Among the more notable examples is the fact that in many countries, women are denied the same rights as men, under both customary and modern law, to own or inherit property.

In addition, there is discrimination within governmental structures—including differential access to public sector services and discriminatory policies and regulations—which perpetuates gender inequality. In many countries in the developing world, social services (health and education), development services (credit, extension, technology), and the institutional structures that support development (local government, cooperatives, trade unions) are universally open to men but either closed or inaccessible to women.

Furthermore, patterns of economic development and their associated impact on women's employment have proved to be more complex than had been predicted. Economists have long been divided as to whether industrialized development in third-world countries would push women out of or pull them into wage work. In the 1960s, Ester Boserup, among others, argued that women were prominent as workers in traditional forms of production but that the growth of the modern sector in developing countries threatened to displace and thereby marginalize them as workers (Boserup 1970). For example, in Bangladesh, the husking of "paddy" (pounding the harvested rice husks to separate the grain) traditionally was the work of women. However, when this task was mechanized, it became the work of men—and not even the work of male relatives of the displaced women workers but men from higher-status families.

An alternative hypothesis put forward was that trade liberalization and export-led industrialization would lead to many new jobs, which would favor an increase in female employment. But over the next three decades, as noted above, the impact of economic development on women's employment proved more complex than the early theorists had predicted.

Take, for example, the phenomenon commonly referred to as the "feminization" of the labor force: a term that is used in different ways. For some scholars it refers to the fact that, since the 1960s, women's share in the labor force has increased around the world, both in absolute numbers and relative to men. However, other scholars use the term to refer to the fact that many jobs and activities traditionally dominated by men have recently been "feminized," meaning that they have been downgraded into the type of work traditionally geared to women—i.e., low-paid or "flexible" (Standing 1989). The fact that both forms of "feminization"—the increased use of female labor, and the informalization, such as lower wages, and less regulation of working conditions—often go hand in hand captures the complexity of the development process and its contradictory impact on women's employment.

Although since 1950 women's official labor-force participation[2] in the developing world has increased dramatically, the trend between 1970 and 1990 was uneven (UN 1991, 83). During that time, women's share in the labor force increased in Latin America, North Africa, and the Middle East; stayed constant in Asia;[3] and declined in sub-Saharan Africa.[4] In Africa, principally due to severe economic conditions, the growth in female labor force participation has actually fallen well behind the growth in population (UN 1991, 83). These uneven trends in women's labor force participation rates reflect uneven patterns of economic development—due either to economic recession, economic privatization and liberalization, or economic globalization—which became particularly pronounced during the 1980s. These uneven patterns of growth affected women's work in a variety of ways, including:

1. *Fewer Jobs in General.* In much of the world, women continue to be the last to benefit from job expansion and the first to suffer from job contraction. Across most countries, the lower the per-capita income, the lower the proportion of women employed in the formal sector. This is why so many women around the world are forced to create their own jobs or enterprises in order to gain access to cash income—usually with few resources and little support (UN 1991, 93).

2. *Working at Home, Minus Labor Benefits.* Many of the "jobs" created by recent industrial expansion actually represent a shift to decentralized and more flexible labor relations whereby labor-intensive, lower-paid, more informal tasks are subcontracted out, usually to women workers (Standing 1989, 1080). In southeast Asia, for example, women factory workers are often excluded from assembly lines when they marry and

have children. Frequently, their only option then is to become engaged in industrial subcontracting within their own homes, which usually pays at a significantly lower rate and offers no benefits (Pongpaichit 1988).

3. *Pursuit of Lower Wages: Substituting Women for Men.* The pursuit of lower wages by businesses and industries often leads to the substitution of women workers for men because men are less likely to work for sub-minimal wages. This practice is most notable in the export-oriented manufacturing sector (Standing 1989).

4. *Loss of Benefits.* The deregulation of labor markets associated with privatization and liberalization affects women in various ways, including undermining whatever protective effect regulations might have had on wages, worker benefits, job security, and working hours. For example, women workers in the export-oriented, labor-intensive "free trade zones" (for example, electronic assembly and garment manufacturing plants located in areas such as along the U.S.-Mexico border) tend to enjoy fewer rights and benefits than women workers in the private formal sector outside the zones (Standing 1989; Elson 1991).

The crucial point is that although in some ways women may be gaining economically by their increased share in the labor force,[5] the "feminization" of the labor force, as noted above, has also led to pervasive insecurity. As Standing (1989) has noted, "Traditionally, women have been relegated predominantly to more precarious and low-income forms of economic activity." The fear now is that their increased economic role reflects a spread of those forms of economic activity to many other sectors of the economy.

III. Response of the International Women's Movement: Research and Theory

These contradictory trends for women and the persistent gender inequality associated with recent economic development (in both the developing and developed worlds) have forced women scholars to reexamine existing models of the household, the current understanding of how markets function, and orthodox theories about the links between economic forces and gender inequality. As a result, research and action over the last decade have had quite a different focus than they did between 1975 and 1985.

Over the past decade, women scholars have contributed to our understanding of the "feminization" of the labor force by highlighting the fact that women's entry into the paid labor force often represents a "distress sale" of their labor; that women work long hours for a "pittance"; that women work long hours at both paid and unpaid work; that certain low-paid occupations have always been stereotyped as female; and that recent economic forces have converted some "male" occupations into "female" occupations because they now offer lower wages and fewer benefits (Elson 1992).

In terms of women's roles within households, women scholars have moved beyond documenting age and gender hierarchies within the household to further conceptualize intrahousehold relationships in terms of the interplay of divergent male/female interests. This has meant going beyond both the neoclassical and Marxian paradigms of households—which assume equality and harmony within the household unit—to models that acknowledge that different members have different needs, rights, and responsibilities and that both conflict and cooperation exist within households (Folbre 1988; Sen 1990).

Moreover, women scholars are now faced with the challenge of reconceptualizing what actually constitutes a household. That is, they have found that they can no longer afford to focus only on the crisis *within* the household but must address the crisis *of* the household itself. For example, we now know that while marriage remains nearly universal across most regions and social groups, women in many settings will spend a considerable portion of their reproductive lives without a spouse in residence—e.g., in some West African countries, from one-third to one-half of their reproductive years.[6] Furthermore, in many countries, the number of families and households supported by women is increasing.[7]

In terms of the gender division of work, scholars have moved beyond documenting women's relative time burden—the "double" or "triple" day's work—to analyzing the root causes of that burden, as well as its implications for women's ability to achieve physical well-being, social status, and political power. In this regard it has become apparent that whereas the gender division of the labor force has been changing—more women are spending longer hours at paid work—the gender division of family responsibilities has not changed. Despite growing discussion and debate, men in almost all cultures continue to devote a relatively small proportion of their time to household tasks and child care.

Therefore, while many women today are spending longer hours in paid work, they continue to spend long hours in unpaid work as well. It is apparent that entry into the paid labor force will not bring the expected benefits to women as long as their work is underpaid, hazardous, unprotected, and insecure, and as long as women are not able to control the income or resources generated by their employment.

In terms of our understanding of women's roles in household livelihood and survival strategies, studies have highlighted that many poor households are no longer coping only with known local conditions such as seasonality, droughts, or floods. Rather, they are now having to cope with broader, often unknown forces related to economic restructuring and the global economic crisis.

Finally, with regard to our understanding of women's subordination to men, we now know that the early assumption that modern capitalist development would loosen patriarchal control has proved false. Growing evidence reveals that while recent economic development has served to undermine traditional systems of reciprocity and sharing based on kinship and community ties, it has not loosened men's control over women's labor and mobility or reduced the degree to which women's access to markets (land, labor, and credit) is negotiated or controlled by men. The conclusion, therefore, is that loosening traditional forms of social security based on relationships among family and kin, in the absence of some form of social security provided by the state, has in fact generally served to disadvantage women.

In brief, over the past two decades, those of us concerned with issues of women's economic development have had to interpolate into our analysis how the traditional path of economic development and the traditional family and gender systems affect women (in contrast to men) and to consider the specific short-term impacts of acute political and economic crises on women. And we have had to strengthen our capacity to address the various forces that shape the structure of women's lives. These forces include: chronic, long-term forces such as the traditional structures of the family and the marketplace; persistent development crises such as poverty and uneven patterns of growth; the quiet but alarming crisis of family and broader social disintegration; and the more recent global crises in the political arena (militarism, fundamentalism, and ethno-nationalism) and in the economic arena (debt, trade, economic restructuring, and environment).

IV. Response of the International Women's Movement: Policy and Action

But have increased knowledge and understanding translated into action? At the level of policy and program design, women planners have developed an approach which takes into account the fact that women and men play different roles and have different needs and that women face both practical everyday basic needs as well as more strategic long-term needs. As Caroline Moser, a leading gender planner, describes the situation, women face practical needs which derive from the specific conditions under which they live and work, as well as strategic needs which derive from the structure and nature of their relationship with men (Moser 1989, 1799).

But how do these gender planning concepts translate into action? To illustrate with an example from this volume, the women in India who were organized by SARTHI could have met their practical needs for fuel and fodder by joining the existing men's groups engaged in reforestation. However, in order to address their strategic needs for equal political participation (i.e., equal to men's) in local development organizations and for equal land rights (again, equal to men's), the women found it was necessary to form their own representative institutions and to negotiate their own independent rights to land. In this way, they gained not only access to and control over resources but a degree of personal empowerment and political influence that they have been able to carry over into other aspects of their lives.

The projects documented in this volume illustrate both the potential for and the difficulties of translating such increasingly sophisticated understanding (and rhetoric) into specific, actionable projects for women. All of the projects documented in this volume began by addressing the immediate practical needs that women themselves had expressed; several were then able to move on to help the women analyze the interconnection between their practical needs and their longer-term strategic interests. Women need to analyze the difference between, for example, receiving credit from project funds and negotiating access to formal institutional sources of credit. However, as a group, the projects illustrate the range of strategies necessary to translate theories into reality, including:

- Increasing women's access to land, labor, markets, and credit (for example, the Port Sudan project that helped women gain access to credit and other services);
- Increasing women's access to growing sectors of the economy (for example, the Thailand project enabling women to capture a place for themselves in the new and dynamic dairying sector);
- Overcoming structural barriers to women's full productivity and income (for example, WomenVenture's business development program, which has helped women entrepreneurs in the United States overcome the numerous hurdles they faced competing in the marketplace);
- Increasing women's participation in community institutions that guide development (for example, the SARTHI project, in India, which organized women into their own representative organizations able to negotiate effectively with male-dominated village councils);
- Mainstreaming women into bureaucratic systems (for example, in Zambia, where women were mainstreamed within a large agricultural bureaucracy);
- Providing childcare, health care, and other support services (as women in various countries are involved in both receiving and delivering child care); and, most importantly,

• Organizing women for collective action in order to change and expand the terms of trade and enterprise, thereby increasing their power (most notably as was done in the SARTHI case, where women who needed access to natural resources were able to influence the institutions that controlled those resources).

Several important lessons emerge from these projects. Many are not new. Some, in fact, build on and expand upon the lessons and challenges identified in the first *Seeds* (Germain 1989, 8–10):

Upscaling* and *Leveraging. There is a need to increase the number of women who have direct access to specific projects designed to benefit women, and to leverage greater benefit for the large numbers of women who remain outside discrete projects by pursuing strategic interventions that have the potential for widespread impact.

Diversifying* and *Deepening. It is important to support women in multiple ways that address their needs throughout the whole of their lives (for example, the need for child care) and that support women in ways that can help them address increasingly complex structural constraints (such as laws that deny women the right to own and control land).

Mainstreaming* and *Positioning. We need to ensure that both projects for women, and women themselves, are central to overall development efforts and that women are positioned to gain access to or challenge existing structures.

Perhaps the lesson that has emerged most clearly from these and other projects in recent years is the critical need to organize women for empowerment through collective action. A related recognition, however, is that earlier forms of organizing women for such purposes often fell short of empowering women because they failed to transform the larger arena of women's economic concerns. In this regard, it is possible to distinguish among four types of collective action for women:

Self-Help: when women organize themselves (or are organized) to help one another meet their mutual needs, often through mobilizing the unpaid labor of women (Elson 1992, p. 40);

Receiving Benefits: when women are organized by project staff into local groups to receive project inputs, such as loans;

Collective Production or Marketing: when women are organized to undertake collective production or marketing; and

Collective Demand-Making or Resistance: when women are organized to make strategic demands, to address structural issues, and to resist exploitation.

We now recognize that whereas women may need to organize themselves for mutual self-help in periods of crisis, this type of collective action should not be used as an excuse or substitute for providing women with the support they need and deserve. In addition, while women may need to come together in groups in order to receive various project inputs, organizing women should be seen as an important end in and of itself, not merely a means of achieving project objectives. On the other hand, whereas women workers may need to organize for purposes of collective production or marketing (e.g., the dairy farmers in Thailand), calling for the pooling of individual women's resources (money or goods) generally proves to be impractical, if not divisive, actually undermining the value of collective action in other, often more important areas, such as joint lobbying and negotiating. In the final analysis, we have recognized that the kind of collective action which will truly empower women is collective action to demand public services, to demand access to development institutions and services, to demand political participation, and to address structural barriers: in effect, to demand change.

Low-income women in both the developing and the developed world want and need change. They need help to close the gap between North and South, between rich and poor, between different races, between men and women, and (most importantly for the future) between girls and boys. They are fighting for change at many levels: within their families and communities; within government and public services; within national political arenas; and on the global stage. But as the women in the projects documented in this book have taught us, there are three prerequisites to effective change: First, that grassroots women themselves should be involved in defining and determining both the pace and the direction of change; second, that grassroots women should be organized to negotiate and demand change; and, third, that it is difficult for grassroots women to organize around the longer-term issues that frame their lives—and inevitably those of their daughters and sons—unless their day-to-day requirements for economic livelihoods are first addressed.

Notes

1. The term "feminization of poverty" was coined by Diana Pierce to describe the worsening economic position of female-headed households in the United States.

2. The official labor force participation rate of women, as accounted for in official national censuses, typically includes their participation in the paid labor force. While it sometimes includes women's participation in family production as unpaid labor, it seldom includes their domestic work and their subsistence activities (for example, collecting fuel, fodder, and water.)

3. Women's share in the labor force stayed at high levels in east and southeast Asia and stayed at low levels in south Asia.

4. Women's share in the labor force (i.e., average percentage of total labor force who are women) increased from 24 to 29 percent for Latin America; from 12 to 17 percent in northern Africa and western Asia; stayed at 40, 35, and 20 percent, respectively, for east, southeast, and south Asia; and fell from 39 to 37 percent in sub-Saharan Africa. A similar trend emerges for women's economic activity rates (i.e., average percentage of women aged 15 and over economically active) between 1970 and 1990.

5. For instance, the female proportion of productive wage workers rose in all countries that set up large Export Processing Zones (Standing 1989, 1080).

6. Demographic and Health Surveys data reported in Bruce, Lloyd, and Leonard, 1995.

7. For example, from the 1970s to the 1980s, the proportion of households headed by women rose from 11.5% to 17.3% in Morocco, 12.5% to 21.6% in Thailand, 20.7% to 26.1% in the Dominican Republic, and 14.7% to 19.5% in Peru. Report by K. Ono, United Nations, as cited in Bruce, Lloyd, and Leonard, 1995.

References

Boserup, Ester. 1970. *Women's Role in Economic Development*. New York: St. Martin's Press.

Bruce, Judith, Cynthia B. Lloyd, and Ann Leonard. 1995. *Families in Focus: New Perspectives on Mothers, Fathers and Children*. New York: The Population Council.

Elson, Diane. 1991. "Structural Adjustment: Its Effect on Women." In T. Wallace and C. March, eds. *Changing Perceptions: Writings on Gender and Development*. Oxford, U.K.: Oxfam.

____. 1992. "From Survival Strategies to Transformation Strategies: Women's Needs and Structural Adjustment." Chapter 3 in Lourdes Beneria and Shelley Feldman, *Unequal Burden: Economic Crises, Persistent Poverty, and Women's Work*. Boulder, CO: Westview Press, pp. 26–48.

Folbre, Nancy. 1988. "The Black Four of Hearts: Toward a New Paradigm of Household Economics." In D. Dwyer and J. Bruce, eds., *A Home Divided: Women and Income in the Third World*. Stanford, California: Stanford University Press.

Kristoff, Nicholas D. 1991. "Stark Data on Women: 100 Million Are Missing." *New York Times*. 5 November.

Moser, Caroline. 1989. "Gender Planning in the Third World: Meeting Practical and Strategic Gender Needs." *World Development* 17 (11): 1799–1825.

Pongpaichit, P. 1988. "Two Roads to the Factory: Industrialisation Strategies and Women's Employment in South East Asia." In Bina Agarwal, ed. *Structures of Patriarchy: The State, the Community and the Household*. London: Zed Books.

Sen, Amartya. 1990. "More than 100 Million Women are Missing." *New York Review of Books*. 20 December: 60–66.

_____. 1990. "Gender and Cooperative Conflicts." In I. Tinker, ed. *Persistent Inequalities*. New York: Oxford University Press.

Sen, Gita, and Caren Grown. 1987. *Development, Crises and Alternative Visions: Third World Women's Perspectives*. New York: Monthly Review Press.

Standing, Guy. 1989. "Global Feminization through Flexible Labor," in C. Grown and J. Setstad, eds. *Beyond Survival: Expanding Income-Earning Opportunities for Women in Developing Countries*. In *World Development*, 17 (7) (Special Issue), pp. 1077–1095.

United Nations. 1991. *The World's Women 1970–1990: Trends and Statistics*. New York: United Nations.

United Nations Development Programme. 1991. *Human Development Report 1991*. New York: United Nations.

World Bank. 1990. *World Development 1990*. New York: Oxford University Press.

I

AFRICA

1
Breaking New Ground: Reaching Out to Women Farmers in Western Zambia

Janice Jiggins
with Paul Maimbo and Mary Masona

In sub-Saharan Africa as a whole, it is estimated that women produce more than 60 percent of the food grown for consumption and sale, as well as a large proportion of nonfood cash crops. However, even though women play a major role in agricultural production, crop processing, and trading, in Africa (as in other parts of the world), they have received little support from mainstream government agricultural services. Over the last few decades, small-scale projects have been developed throughout Africa to help incorporate women farmers into the mainstream of agricultural extension services. However, only a handful of ministries of agriculture have drawn upon that experience thus far. In this chapter, we present one interesting example from Zambia's Western Province. This program is working to change a government agricultural bureaucracy from within by redefining mandates, encouraging attitude change through staff training, broadening village-level opportunities and perceptions, and widening technical and economic research agendas. The experience of this program emphasizes the importance of using a variety of approaches in order to reach women farmers and meet their needs effectively.

Background

Zambia is a poor, landlocked country in central-southern Africa. From the perspective of Lusaka, the nation's capital, the Western Province is a remote place lacking the essentials of modern life. Mongu, the provincial capital, is over 600 km. from Lusaka and can be reached by bus or car over partly unpaved roads during the dry season. But the journey becomes pro-gressively more difficult as the rains set in, and the weekly air service is too expensive for most Zambians.

Traveling east to west, the landscape slowly changes from the lightly forested sandy plateau to the escarpment at Mongu, where the land drops abruptly to the floodplain of the Zambezi River. During the rains, the only way to cross the plain is by boat or canoe. The fertility of the land ranges from the relatively prosperous Kaoma area on the plateau, a center of maize production, to the famine-stricken districts of Senanga West in the far south.

In recent years, smallholder agriculture in the Western Province has been undermined by Zambia's ailing national economy. Hardly anything works well, and many things, from water pumps to clinics, operate below capacity due to the collapse of public services and lack of spare parts, maintenance, and supplies. The availability of food subsidies and agricul-tural inputs, such as fertilizer, also has declined steeply in recent years. Many employees receive some assistance in the form of food rations and other allowances to supplement their salaries, but employment in the for-mal and government sectors is limited. Women in particular—at all income levels—are coming under increasing stress as a result, since they must care for the sick, feed the unemployed, and try to eke out enough cash to send their children to school in the midst of economic chaos.

Women of the Western Province

Like almost all women in rural Zambia, the majority of women in the Western Province are farmers:

- *By Custom.* It is a woman's duty to produce food to feed herself and her children and to sell farm produce to meet basic cash needs. She must also serve as a major source of labor in support of the farming activities of her husband and relatives.
- *By Necessity.* Women head over one-third of all households in Zambia, in law or in fact. Census data suggest that the number of female-headed households is largest in the poorer, more remote rural areas, where agri-culture is the sole basis of survival; in some districts, women head more than 60 percent of all households.
- *By Choice.* In areas with good soil, efficient agricultural advisory ser-vices, access to markets and inputs such as fertilizer, and an adequate road or rail network, the introduction of crops, such as confectionery groundnuts, for commercial sale can provide women as well as men with worthwhile income-generating opportunities.

As in many African societies, in Western Zambia a woman's status and her access to land and other resources is based on marriage, lineage, and her ability to bear children. In the Western Province, about one-fifth to one-quarter of all married women are in polygamous unions. Co-wives typically live in different villages and are visited by their husband in rotation. Villages tend to be scattered and small, with fewer than 100 residents, and perhaps fewer than twenty households per village. Many men are absent in search of paid employment. Many adult women head their own households, and a large proportion of these household heads are divorcees.

One of the implications of this situation is that traditional community support for the most vulnerable families is becoming weaker, and women raising children alone are particularly vulnerable; they become more isolated socially and have fewer relatives on whom to call for help with immediate needs, such as cash, labor, or help with household chores. Under such circumstances, women often experience a sense of abandonment and despair. As a woman from Kweseka village in Mongu District laments, "We have been forgotten by the world."

Land use in the Western Province is controlled by community leaders. As the province is sparsely populated, it is easy for both men and women to obtain land for cultivation and grazing, but there is localized competition for plots in the best and most accessible areas. In this part of Zambia, the basic constraint to farm production is labor—particularly women's labor—not land. Women make up the main agricultural work force in the Western Province, and men and other family members usually have a priority on the use of their labor. While some men do help women to clear land for food cropping, they spend most of their time tending their cattle, fishing, looking after their own food plots, and cash cropping.

According to case studies, during the short rainy season, women spend over ten hours a day on domestic and field work, whereas men generally spend considerably less time working on the farm. Because of this traditional division of labor, a married woman farmer may still face a labor shortage even when her husband is in residence. In order to cope at all, women often form mutual aid work parties, because relatively few earn enough cash to hire labor. In fact, most of the women who work as hired laborers head their own households; but the little cash they earn must be balanced against the lower yield they get by neglecting their own crops.

Food preparation also takes up a great deal of women's time. The staple food—whether maize, millet, sorghum, or cassava—is pounded into flour and then generally consumed as a thick porridge. Because hammer mills are rare and hand-pounding is arduous, whenever possible, households prefer to sell their own crops and buy milled breakfast meal (a refined

Tending vegetable crops in Western Province, Zambia. *(Janice Jiggins)*

maize flour). Because of the time required for processing by hand, rice is rarely consumed at home; the whole crop is usually sold. Women must also devote time to other domestic chores, such as collecting water and fuel, and to child care.

Few sources of income besides farming are available to women in Western Zambia. The sale of mats and baskets, wild fruits and mushrooms, bananas, and mangoes, and small-scale fishing activities provide occasional income for some. Studies show that women spend their income on, in order of importance, food, clothing, and schooling for their children.

By far the most common source of cash for women is in brewing and selling beer. Surveys suggest that three-quarters of all women brew regularly, mainly for sale but also to mobilize and reward hired labor. On average, women brew four to five times a year, mainly in the dry season. Net profits vary a great deal but 100 kwacha (about U.S. $3) for each batch brewed is not uncommon.

In Western Zambia, constraints on the amount of time women can devote to their own crops, together with a lack of cash, limit their ability to purchase food. This situation is leading to increased cultivation of cassava as a food crop, and, when converted to beer, as a cash crop. Cassava is a relatively hardy crop that needs little attention once it has been planted, and the roots can be stored in the ground until needed. Although it is rich in carbohydrates, it is poor in protein and minerals. Thus, with the increased cultivation of cassava added to the undernutrition already widespread in the region, malnutrition is reportedly increasing, especially among children, who find it difficult to eat enough of the bulky, starchy cassava to gain sufficient nutrients.

Agricultural Extension and Women Farmers

In Zambia, as is the case throughout Africa, policymakers and service providers have neglected the role of women in agriculture because large, conservative, male-dominated bureaucracies have regarded women's work on farms as simply "what women do." The real contribution that women's farming makes to family welfare and national food security has remained virtually invisible. In addition, because of the underlying assumption of governments and technical assistance agencies that modern farming means "male" farming, large-scale agriculture and livestock surveys have rarely captured data on factors such as women's labor input, women's management practices, or the crops that typically only women grow.

While women continue to be neglected by mainstream agricultural development efforts, their role in farming is becoming more critical. Complex changes in social and economic life are leaving more and more rural women as sole providers for their families. While not all female heads of households have the same problems, the excessive demands on their time and energy often leave women socially isolated as well as economically marginalized. The competing demands of farm work and the care of children and other dependents can lead to the rapid deterioration of family welfare and security.

Although numerous rural women somehow do manage to prosper, the majority experience hardships that mainstream agricultural services have been slow to recognize or respond to. Among the most important are:

- Heavy work loads, long working days, and little access to the cash needed to hire labor;
- Lack of access to credit and financial services, usually related to problems of mobility, women's status under the law, and the type of financial services offered;
- The gender of agricultural extension agents (mostly male), their reluctance to break cultural taboos about working with women who are not family members, and their tendency to hold stereotypic views of what women can and should do;

- Lack of access to training (particularly in critical agricultural activities such as ox plowing) and to fertilizer and other inputs, again often related to the gender of agricultural extension personnel; and
- Women's own lack of confidence in asserting themselves, taking on new roles, and challenging attitudes, despite the major changes taking place in the customary organization of life around them.

Although the government of Zambia broadly supports special efforts to promote women's development, agricultural policy still does not explicitly recognize the role of women farmers. Since the mid-1980s, women researchers at the University of Zambia, "Women and Development" project staff, and the Senior Home Economics Officer in the Ministry of Agriculture and Water Development have joined together to develop ideas and strategies to: (1) identify desired policy changes; (2) bring relevant experience to the attention of policymakers; and (3) stimulate official recognition of women's contribution to agriculture and greater access to government agricultural services. They are closely watching the work of the Women's Extension Program (WEP) in Western Zambia, because, unlike many other women's extension projects, its primary task is not to provide services directly to women farmers; rather, it is designed as a strategic intervention of limited duration that will bring about change *within the mainstream* of the Department of Agriculture's programs through advocacy, training, information, statistics, persuasion, and liaison.

Origins of the Women's Extension Program

The Women's Extension Program (WEP) is located within the Home Economics Section of the Department of Agriculture, although operationally it falls under the overall direction of the Provincial Agricultural Officer (PAO). The authority of the PAO, in turn, opens access for the WEP to the training and extension activities of the department and to the Research Section. The program's location in Home Economics and its design are the result of earlier experiments to find the right point of leverage to enable the program to build linkages within the Department and initiate effective methods for changing attitudes.

The Home Economics Section had been providing training to women on topics such as food preservation and storage, nutrition, and child care since 1971, but as far as women's farming activities were concerned, it faced two handicaps: reliance on specialists in other sections for technical advice and the need to use the department's existing extension field staff in order to reach women. To achieve its own goals, the section thus had to develop effective mechanisms for working with and through other people, the majority of whom are men.

In the Western Province, most of the department's 200 extension field staff, called agricultural assistants (AAs), are male. The Provincial Home Economics Officer, Elizabeth Kazungo, notes: "Really, it has always been a struggle. The men feel that anything to do with women farmers and home economics is not their concern."

Moreover, in a system based on individual farm visits, there are far too few agricultural assistants to provide adequate coverage. The ratio of AAs to farm households is around 1:450. A survey in five areas of the Western Province revealed that while an AA had never visited at least 40 percent of male household heads, more than 80 percent of female heads of households had never received a visit. The AAs tend to excuse their neglect of women farmers by hiding behind tradition. They say: "We do not feel comfortable talking to a woman. It is not our custom. Husbands and boyfriends might accuse us."

A real breakthrough occurred in the early 1980s when the department launched a special rice-growing project with support from the Dutch government. The project soon recognized that it would have to involve women more closely if it was to succeed. A Dutch female extension officer was recruited to conduct a survey of local women: their workloads, contribution to rice production, attitudes toward agricultural education, and access to the male AAs. Her report provided the hard data needed to open up discussion of women farmers and their needs. In addition, the presence of a female "expert" helped legitimize issues of "women in farming" among the male provincial staff, both expatriate and local.

Following the survey, the Dutch expert was asked to form the women living in the project area into groups in order to provide them more easily with training and extension services. She began by enlisting the help of female technical officers working on the project, such as Mary Masona, who was later to head the WEP. Mary Masona was then working as an animal husbandry officer, advising the project on the draft oxen needed to plow the rice fields. Together with other female project staff, these women began to mobilize the women farmers into groups. It was also felt that male AAs would be less reluctant to work with groups of women than with individuals.

The group approach proved to be very successful. As Elizabeth Kazungo says: "It fits our way of doing things here. Soon we learn to feel comfortable together. There is so much support from one another." But the experience also convinced the department that it needed a more strategic intervention that could address both the attitudinal barriers among male staff and some of the practical difficulties. After further analysis and discussion, the Women's Extension Program—while located within the Home Economics Section—was attached to the ongoing Extension Training Program, since the link with training would strengthen WEP's ties with the mainstream agricultural extension program.

The new program had two main training objectives. The first was internal and involved adding a short course to the training program for the male agricultural assistants in order to make them aware of women's roles in agriculture in the Western Province. The second was external: to develop and run mobile courses for women that relate directly to women's farming. In 1986, Mary Masona was appointed the first WEP Coordinator.

> It was a challenge but I am always running—I like to get things done! What's more, I come from this area and I know the traditions. I have ten children and I know the hardships of women here.—*Mary Masona*

The WEP set the following goals:

• To collect data on women in agriculture and related issues;
• To help members of the department appreciate the importance of reaching women farmers;
• To advise the department on how to reach women farmers effectively;
• To sensitize field staff to the importance of women's farming;
• To assist in the planning and implementation of development projects and to assess their effects on women; and
• To provide assistance in setting up and running women farmers' groups.

Putting Women on the Agenda

The WEP operates primarily through the existing structures, staff, and projects of the Department of Agriculture. Apart from the coordinator, the WEP has no staff of its own. Its influence is based on persuasion and cooperation rather than formal power, and bureaucratic context shapes the way the program works. Mary Masona defines the WEP as a "strategic booster," to help get women into the mainstream.

The coordinator, therefore, works through her provincial and district colleagues to build networks of understanding and support with other sections. An important first step has been helping district and field-level colleagues become aware of the importance of women's involvement in agriculture within the province.

Departmental Coordinating Committee

The Departmental Coordinating Committee (composed of section heads and project coordinators) is an important forum for maintaining interest in the goals of the WEP. The committee tries to meet regularly to coordinate transport, share ideas, and revise plans. Initially, the committee relied on the women members for ideas about how to reach women farmers. But, as

It used to be considered taboo for women to plow.
(Janice Jiggins)

Elizabeth Kazungo notes, male colleagues are now gaining the confidence to contribute their own suggestions. By avoiding confrontation and by concentrating on the presentation of data and results of field studies, the WEP has been able to offer some subtle gender training within the committee meetings themselves. The WEP coordinator adds, "Now they come to us when they need our help or have an idea. They can see that we have something to contribute to their work, too."

Mobile Training

The WEP also encourages colleagues within the department to deliver field-level training in ways that are compatible with women's time constraints, domestic responsibilities, and educational experience. Mobile training programs offer an alternative to more traditional residential courses and are proving to be successful with both staff and farmers. The mobile training is run by the AAs, with support from district or provincial specialists, over a two- or three-day period, at a time and place convenient to the participants. Each course deals with a specific topic, such as fertilizer application or row planting of hybrid maize. Unlike the formal, lecture-style training offered in residential courses, the on-site courses use a mixture of methods, including practical instruction, question-and-answer, discussion, and on-the-spot trial of what has been learned.

At first the WEP emphasized women-only courses because women were reluctant to attend classes where men were also present. But the aim has always been to integrate women more fully. As Mary Masona says: "If women are separated, they will always be on their own." Nevertheless, the WEP has also recognized that women-only courses are needed on topics of special concern to women, such as food preservation, and on skills that men already possess and women want to learn, such as ox-plowing.

Monitoring

The WEP encourages agricultural assistants to monitor women's participation in residential training, mobile training courses, field days, and demonstrations. A target of 50-percent female participation has been set for mixed courses (i.e., those with both male and female participants), field days (opportunities for farmers and AAs to review progress on a host farmer's field), and demonstrations; the results are quite encouraging. During the 1989 to 1990 season, women's participation in all courses reached close to 40 percent.

As a Mongu-based AA explains, "Now women are coming willingly for courses, and there are no suspicions of me, even if I meet a woman farmer in her field. And the women accept me because they see I have knowledge that is useful to them."

Breaking Through Traditional Barriers

A real success for the WEP has been to provide women with access to training in ox-plowing. In the past, women did not plow themselves; it was a man's skill, and a woman's touch was thought to bring bad luck and sickness. Today, with more women being sole providers, there is a growing recognition that women must also learn this skill.

Use of oxen for plowing is critical to increase crop yields from rainfed farming, but a number of cultural, practical, and financial barriers have barred women from use of draft animals. Although women rarely herd or corral cattle, almost one-third of all women in the province probably own cattle at some point in their lives through inheritance or as payment of "bride price." Nevertheless, it is a widely held belief among men that women have little to do with the care and management of cattle and that they are not interested in keeping them.

One of the difficulties in women's ownership of cattle is the cost of caring for them (hiring herd boys and people to shift the corrals, buying medicines, and so on). Women who can afford to plow are usually forced to enter into complex borrowing or hiring arrangements to get the work done.

As a result, women's fields are usually plowed after the men's—which typically means poorly and late—with commensurate low returns in terms of yields.

To help women learn to plow, the WEP has had to leverage and guide coordination among a number of department sections, including animal draft training officers, the agricultural assistants, and the women farmer groups (described below).

The First Step

At first, the very idea seemed a joke. An ox-plowing training center had been established in the province in 1983, but no one ever thought about training *women* farmers. The expatriates involved in the ox center were afraid of breaking cultural taboos, and the agricultural assistants simply thought that women would not be able to learn such a skill. However, when the rice growing project began in the area, it created a great deal of extra work for women.

A survey of women's work in rice production carried out by the Dutch advisor had revealed that a number of women already owned an ox, or even a team, or had access to one through relatives. However, they had no control over the use of the oxen and lacked the skill to plow themselves. Quietly, a few women farmers involved in the rice project got together with Mary Masona and her colleagues and began to practice plowing. When the next agricultural show came along, the women demonstrated their skill, to the great surprise of the onlookers! The first step had been taken toward training women in ox-plowing.

Growing Recognition

The department also realized that special ox-drawn implements, especially cultivators and ridgers, were needed, or weeds would halt the spread of rice production. In October 1989, work began to test and introduce low-cost ox-drawn implements. Through liaison with the WEP, women's groups are becoming involved in the testing program. Today, ox-plow training is routinely provided to women's groups through mobile courses and by the agricultural assistants. Increasingly, women are being hired as teams to plow for others. These women's plowing teams are establishing a good reputation as conscientious and effective handlers of oxen.

Changing Attitudes and Aspirations

The women themselves are enthusiastic; they are proud that they have acquired this "difficult" male skill. They also recognize it as a break-through in the way they are regarded within the community. Although many local women lack access to oxen and equipment, and are unable to take out the large loan needed to buy them, they attended the courses because "Maybe one day I will buy an ox," or "Perhaps my daughter will do better than I in life and then I can help her to plow," or "If the maize is good this year, maybe my group will decide, after all, to buy a team and the necessary equipment."

Women's participation in ox-plowing and other changes have not come about solely as a result of training and persuasion. They have been reinforced by two other operational innovations within the Department: the People's Participation Project and the Adaptive Research Planning Team.

Building Women's Confidence and Organizational Strengths

One of the lessons of the rice-growing project was that group mobilization and support are essential to: (a) provide a culturally acceptable point of contact between women and the male agricultural assistants; (b) encourage women to make use of existing services; and (c) develop women's organizational skills and leadership capacity at the village level.

Initially, activities of the women's groups were coordinated directly by the WEP program. Later, they were formalized as part of a centrally supervised People's Participation Project (PPP), with support from the Food and Agriculture Organization (FAO) and the Dutch government. However, coordination of the PPP proved difficult within the WEP framework, in large part because the WEP has neither staff nor a mandate to become directly involved in field activities.

The department, therefore, seconded Lydia Ndulu from within the provincial department to serve as the Provincial Coordinator of the PPP. She also works within the Home Economics Section. With training in nutrition, home economics, and horticulture, and considerable experience in the department, Lydia Ndulu had sufficient standing among her male colleagues to be accepted as an agricultural professional, not just the leader of a special "women's project."

Group Development
Lydia Ndulu is convinced that women's best option is to get access to existing services and support structures through the mechanism of group development. But before this can happen, the women have to become aware of their rights, develop organizational strengths and leadership ability, and overcome feelings of ignorance and shyness.

The PPP began in February 1984. By 1988, twenty-four groups had been established in the three districts of Kaoma, Mongu, and Kalabo. By mid-1990, there were 130 groups with 1,144 women members and 507 men. In some groups, all the members are women, but most also include men. Village men initially resented the emphasis on women: "Why are you segregating us?" they demanded. As Lydia Ndulu says, "It was quite a bit tough to explain." But PPP has found that, in the long run, the inclusion of men helps the groups because, for one thing, it assures the AAs that they are not breaking cultural taboos when they work with the group. Male members can also defend the groups to others and, because they have better access to male officials, they can even advance women's causes more effectively. But the PPP has been careful to ensure that men do not take over: no male member can be a group office holder.

Women Speak to Women

At the village level, local women have been recruited to work as group promoters. They support the women farmer groups and mobilize more women to join. One group promoter from Limulunga, who joined the PPP right from the start, recalled that, at first, she found it very difficult: "When we went to a village to talk to the Village Headman and the Party Section Chairman, I felt shy and did not know how to explain what it was we wanted to do. We told them that the project was for 'women who are lame,' but they were suspicious of our motives. We also did not know at first how to go about mobilizing the women and supporting them."

Now she is sure that village women would always prefer to speak first to another woman, one from the same background as themselves. "They have many problems they feel shy to discuss with a man. They can ask me questions about feeding their children, about tools and skills in farming, without feeling ignorant and stupid. If men had been running this project, we wouldn't have progressed so far."

Lydia Ndulu confesses that, although it was difficult at first, the men in the department have come around. Initially, they regarded the group approach and the emphasis on women as "FAO ideas," but: "They have come to realize that it benefits the department's work and makes it easier for everyone to work with the people."

Impact: "We Don't Want to Starve"

Rosemary Ntoka is the leader of a group in Lilu village in Limulanga area of Mongu District. She is a farmer with two children and pregnant with her third. Is she happy with the PPP? "Yes, of course! To survive, we women have to learn new ideas and methods. We don't want to starve! And I am interested in the group because this way we share our problems, we share ideas, and we learn together."

Some Successes

In Kweseka village, one of the earliest groups is now thriving. It began in 1984 with nine women members. Their first group savings came from cultivating a maize plot together. Then they tried wheat, maize again, sweet potatoes, and cashew seedlings. For the first time in their lives, they received help from the agricultural assistant and learned how to plow with oxen.

In 1988, the Kweseka group opened a consumer shop, investing 200 kw. from the group's savings account. By 1990, the shop had generated a profit of 4,000 kw. (about U.S. $100). The group also makes and sells brooms, baskets, and knitted berets. Group savings are deposited in a post office account reserved for future investments and working capital. (Group members are also encouraged to establish separate accounts of their own.) The group plans to begin buying and selling breakfast meal (refined maize) as soon as they have enough saved.

Some Difficulties

Ishekendo, another group in the area, is struggling. The village lacks water, and agricultural opportunities are fewer. The women tried to grow rice, but it became infested with black maize beetles. They, too, have been taught how to plow, but they have no opportunity to borrow oxen and equipment, and they are afraid to buy their own animals because they fear the thieves who prowl along the nearby road at night. However, with the help of their group promoter, they have improved the marketing of their craft products. The extra income has helped them to buy the supplies need-ed to grow maize, and, when the rains are good, they have produced good harvests. Though their gains have been modest so far, the women are pos-itive: "We get a lot of strength from being together. The agricultural assis-tant here is a lady, and she gives us a lot of encouragement. She taught us how to make *gari* (the name of a West African dish made of dry cassava flakes). We feel good about learning new things. Nobody talked to us before."

Taking Up Women's Agricultural Priorities

An increasing number of studies have demonstrated that a lack of under-standing of how small farmers, both men and women, actually operate their farms lessens the efficiency and effectiveness of agricultural research. To develop this understanding, an Adaptive Research Planning Team (ARPT) has been established in the Western Province as part of a national program under the Research Section of the Department of Agri-culture (see Figure 1). ARPT's mandate is: (a) to work with small and emergent farmers to provide them with the technical and economic infor-mation needed to improve production; and (b) to carry out adaptive research with farmers on their own fields.

The team works closely with experimental trial assistants (all men) based in the field and with the agricultural assistants. From its inception in

1985, part of ARPT's mandate has been to include women farmers in its work and to pay special attention to farm households headed by women. It was recognized that women might be farming under a different set of constraints or with different priorities than men. However, despite this mandate, team sociologist Gerben Vierstra notes that the concept of "women as an issue, or as our collaborators, did not really receive any attention in the Western Province until around 1987."

Including Women in Surveys and Trials
One of the first steps taken, with the encouragement of the WEP, has been to ensure that ARPT surveys interview both female household heads and married women. A related, but more difficult, effort is to encourage the agricultural assistants to identify more women willing to participate in field trials. Knowledge of women's role in farming in many cases remains limited. For example, many agricultural assistants still remain totally unaware that there are households where women are farming alone. And for their part, women farmers are often reluctant to risk experimentation with their main food crops because their family's survival often depends

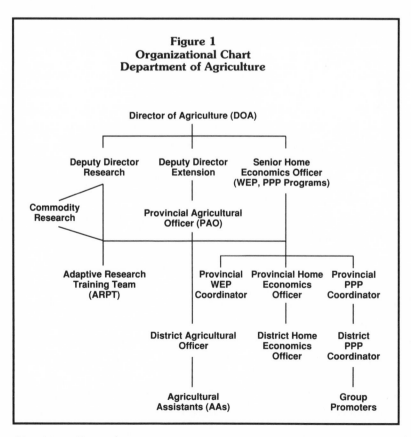

Figure 1
Organizational Chart
Department of Agriculture

on getting at least one good crop from their land. Women are most inter-ested in experiments on crops that make the most money (both modern and traditional vegetables), but these crops have not been the focus of ARPT's work to date.

Professional Bias

Charles Kapekele Chileya, ARPT's socioeconomist, confesses that when he began working with other scientists, "I was blind. I just went along with what the biological scientists saw. But then I did my master's degree in the U.K., where we had an international group with a number of strong women students and teachers and an interdisciplinary approach. The women there convinced me I should pay attention to this aspect of rural life."

On his return to Zambia, he was at first disappointed at the reaction of his male colleagues to his new insight. His closest friend, an agricultural economist, argued with him: "We can't be doing this. Within any category of farmers, men and women are the same." But then, Kapekele Chileya adds with a laugh, "My friend showed his true colors when he said, 'Any-how, women farmers are not useful in economic analysis. You don't get good results because they don't plant in time!'"

Taking the Lead

By the end of 1987, the Provincial ARPT Coordinator, an agronomist, had learned enough to be convinced that women's participation was an issue to be considered. He asked Kapekele Chileya to prepare a position paper that was well received within the department. Now, more emphasis is given to the benefits that women farmers might receive from ARPT's work; for example, crops typically grown only by women, such as bambara nuts, beans, cowpeas, and groundnuts, have begun to receive some attention. "This is a good move, and we should do much more in this direction," states Kapekele Chileya. "Crops like these fetch a high price and have excellent nutritional value. And any time the woman needs money, she can sell a small amount in the market or even to her neighbors."

Kapekele Chileya works closely with WEP to change attitudes within the department. He makes sure, for example, that when the team lists the crops grown by farmers, the "minor" crops of importance to women do not get overlooked. And, if he cannot attend a staff meeting, he invites Mary Masona or Lydia Ndulu to take his place. If an agricultural assistant invites the team to attend a field day, he insists that ARPT will show up only if women farmers are going to be present.

Kapekele Chileya also encourages ARPT and the trial assistants to work with the PPP groups. Doing experimental trials with a women's group not only benefits ARPT but the group as well, increasing the strength of their organization and increasing the profits earned from the sale of their crop.

Recognizing Diversity
Still, Kapekele Chileya feels that if ARPT is going to take women farmers seriously, it will have to stop speaking of "the small farmer" as a man, or even of "female-headed households." "The ARPT has to recognize that the majority of its (potential) clients are women. But they are not all farming in the same way with the same resources. We have to be much more careful about defining who is doing what, and finding out what their needs and possibilities really are. We have to recognize that 'women' are not one thing: their needs are diverse."

The Bureaucratic Change Process
Advocacy
A key element in changing attitudes and developing special activities to help women farmers within the Department of Agriculture was the support of the Provincial Agricultural Officer (PAO) serving when the WEP program began. He defended and protected the concept and helped to establish "women farmers" as a legitimate professional concern. "Without him, we never could have opened the door," says Mary Masona. Promoted to a senior Ministry position in Lusaka, the former Provincial Agricultural Officer now provides an open channel for communicating about the successes and difficulties of the WEP and the needs of women farmers at the national policy level.

The Importance of Data
On the other hand, the Assistant Provincial Agricultural Officer confesses that he worked in agricultural extension for a long time without considering special programs for women to be necessary or worthwhile. However, in 1985, he attended staff seminars on women in agriculture and was persuaded that some special effort was needed. "I thought at first the seminars would just be about somebody's opinions. But the survey data convinced me. It was the first time we had anything concrete to go on. I now read everything from the WEP or the ARPT that tells me more about women in farming in the province."

In April 1990, the Assistant Provincial Agricultural Officer conducted a small, random sample survey in two local government areas of Mongu District to investigate the work of the agricultural assistants. He found that none of the "contact farmers" selected by the AAs as their primary links with the farming community were women. "The criteria for farmer selection probably account for this," he comments. "Most women farmers don't have the indicators necessary to be selected. Maybe we should look at the indicators again." But, he adds: "Personally, I believe that the group approach is the right way to go." Not only do groups help make the work of the agricultural assistants "cheaper per contact hour," but he speculates that, in the light of the fragile resources of the department, women will have a better chance of sustaining their hard-won gains if they have a structure through which they can become somewhat self-reliant.

The Group Approach

The effectiveness of the group approach to extension and training has impressed WEP's colleagues at every level within the department. The District Agricultural Officer for Mongu affirms: "We have seen so far that the idea of a group promoter is very effective. Now we see every day that women, and men, are forming groups among themselves and that the AAs are encouraging them, even without a promoter to help them. In the old days, it was the women who did the work but the men who got the training."

Seeing Is Believing

The District Agricultural Officer's own ideas changed from 1982 to 1983 when he was working as an animal husbandry officer and saw women plowing for the first time. Today he is convinced: "If they have access to oxen and equipment, especially the women without husbands, they can plant on time and get a better crop. . . . Now, when we have shows, others are impressed when such women come with their groups to display what they have grown. They win a lot of prizes! This has a good effect on the thinking of the *indunas* (traditional leaders) and the people."

Networking

The WEP knows it needs the support of a wider group of colleagues. Often women's activities are marginalized, even within a supportive bureaucracy. Therefore, it is necessary to build personal relationships with senior civil servants and to provide channels through which experiences can be exchanged and reviewed. Two network initiatives are of particular importance in legitimizing the issue of women in agriculture within the government bureaucracy: (1) establishment of Women Development Committees which draw together concerned women from various aspects of government service throughout the country; and (2) government-sponsored workshops for professional and technical staff at the provincial and district levels that share information and experiences related to women's roles in agriculture.

Women's plowing teams have shown that they are up to the job. *(Janice Jiggins)*

Counting the Cost

The provincial Department of Agriculture's own financial resources are meager. The government spends on average between US $100,000-130,000 each quarter to cover the recurrent costs of the department's extension work. Projects financed by external donors contribute perhaps five times as much to the department's total budget. Nevertheless, the success of any project depends on its being able to draw on the core resources of the department itself.

The total budget for the PPP project, from 1986 to the end of 1990, was U.S. $248,000. The department contributes the salaries of the district and provincial coordinators, part of the petrol and training costs, and daily subsistence allowances for the AAs and a driver.

The annual costs of the PPP per district are modest. For example, the expenditure in Mongu District from January to December, 1989, was 257,169 kwacha (under U.S. $7,000). Although the project has supplied motorbikes to each of its district coordinators, the bikes are not really suitable transportation, especially in the rainy season. PPP staff are often dependent on hitching rides on the district agricultural officer's vehicles, but when none is in operating condition, the PPP's own work gets stalled.

The department contributes the coordinator's salary and an office for the WEP. Between 1983 and 1988, the costs of what became the WEP were absorbed under the Extension Training Program and ran at about U.S. $120,000 per year. From 1989 through 1991, the budget totaled about U.S. $550,000 to 600,000. This sum included the costs of expatriate researchers and consultants.

The PPP and WEP each have provided both female and male staff of the department with opportunities to gain wider experience and training regarding women in agriculture within the region and internationally. The provincial agricultural officer says that it has helped the department press for change because it now realizes that neglecting women holds back the development of agriculture—a problem shared by many countries—and that practical solutions are possible.

Facing the Future

Last in Line when Resources Are Scarce

Contrary to initial expectations, the major problems facing the program have been logistical rather than attitudinal. Problems relating to custom, attitude, male-female relations, and so forth, are proving to be manageable, more so than the crippling budgetary limitations facing the department as a whole. When resources are scarce, the WEP and its related activities receive the lowest priority. For example, there are not enough vehicles, fuel is expensive and sometimes scarce, and maintenance is difficult. Support of groups and of agricultural assistants is thus less frequent or reliable than desired. The transport problem has constrained expansion to new areas, or to a larger number of groups, and has also limited the number of times AAs and other staff have received training on issues relating to "women in agriculture."

Staffing Concerns

Sustaining group development also poses a difficult staffing problem. The group promoters currently mobilizing and organizing the women farmer groups cannot be absorbed into the government structure because of their low educational qualifications, yet they are essential to the whole approach. The assistant provincial agricultural officer points to another staffing issue that he has often discussed with women at headquarters: too few women apply for jobs in the department, partly because few women enroll at the agricultural training colleges. Mary Masona notes: "This is where the WEP comes in. We just have to convince our male colleagues to work with women farmers and provide them with the skills to do so."

Reviewing What Has Been Accomplished

The main achievement of the WEP has been to launch a process of internal change within a conservative agricultural bureaucracy. It has relied largely on bringing about voluntary change in the behaviors and attitudes of male staff working in the mainstream units of the Department of Agriculture (Animal Husbandry and Engineering, Training, Agricultural Extension, and Research). The experience shows that, with a dedicated staff and a clear vision of the strategic objectives, leverage is possible, even when the locus is within a relatively powerless and marginalized unit such as the Home Economics Section.

———————————————— Lessons ————————————————

1. **Incorporating the needs of women farmers into the mainstream of a traditional (male-dominated) agricultural bureaucracy requires a multifaceted approach.** Persuasion, leverage, liaison, and demonstration are all required to redefine mandates, incorporate gender perspectives in training, broaden research agendas, extend technical services to women, and encourage and support female farmers to expand their opportunities and perceptions.

2. **When there is sufficient support within the higher echelons of large bureaucracies, even a small staff operating out of a relatively marginalized unit can be an effective agent for change.** The leadership of the provincial agricultural officer for the Western Province, along with the dedication and determination of key female staff in the Home Economics Section and the WEP and PPP programs, created a climate conducive to the establishment and nurturing of positive working relationships with other units carrying out mainstream agricultural extension activities. The experience of the WEP program demonstrates that neither a large budget nor the hiring of new cadres of personnel is required to make a significant difference when sufficient institutional support is present.

3. **Although change from within is a slow and sometimes cumbersome process, it is essential to encourage evolution within a large bureaucracy while also creating a demand for change from outside.** Incorporation of women as a focus was something the Department of Agriculture itself identified as a concern. Thus, it could take pride in its leadership role in attempting to better address the needs of women farmers. Particularly in times of scarce resources, using an approach that encourages openness to change, rather than defensiveness, may be a

more appropriate way to effect change. At the same time, building up demand at the grassroots level is critical to ensuring appropriate and effective delivery of services once the bureaucracy accepts the idea that such services are warranted.

4. **In addition to training and liaison, hard data and demonstrable results are persuasive ammunition that can do a great deal to convince a traditional, male-dominated bureaucracy to take women's farming seriously. Seeing is believing!** This underscores the importance of including women farmers in research design, experimental field trials, and data collection, so that the results clearly demonstrate, in black and white, what women farmers are already doing, what they are capable of doing, and how their needs differ from those of male farmers.

5. **Bringing women together in groups can be an effective way of helping them gain access to extension services, empowering them to take initiatives and demand access to resources, and providing them with a network of mutual support**—particularly important as more and more women become the sole support of families and traditional family/community bonds continue to erode. The group process creates a supportive environment that helps women to better define and effectively articulate the type of assistance they require, even when their perceptions differ from what male extension staff think they need!

6. **Given that agricultural extension agents are predominantly male and few resources exist that would allow for the training and hiring of female agents, male agents can effectively provide services to women farmers if they are given proper, gender-sensitive training; if they receive encouragement from respected colleagues (particularly other men); and if they can see for themselves what women are actually capable of doing.** The establishment of farmers' groups also makes it easier for male field staff to work with women farmers, as working with a group overcomes their reluctance to interact on a one-to-one basis with a woman who is not a member of their family.

7. **Although women's primary role as farmers requires a focus on access to mainstream agricultural extension services, development of non-farming, income-generating activities, such as craft production and marketing, can be a culturally acceptable strategy for getting women involved in groups, as well as providing a needed source of cash income that can be used to fund farm investments.** While such a strategy may be beneficial, and is non-threatening to both women and the community, it must *not* overshadow women's primary role as farmers.

8. **Women can readily learn important, non-traditional skills—such as ox-plowing—if they are given the necessary support and training.** Once a core group of women have demonstrated their mastery of formerly "male-only" tasks, and it becomes clear that access to these skills will substantially increase their productivity (and thus the welfare of the entire family) and does not threaten the role of men, the old prejudices and taboos about what women can and should do will begin to fade away.

9. **Minimal reliance on expatriate funding and personnel may facilitate internal ownership of the change process within a bureaucracy.** However, outside validation of an innovative concept, such as recognizing and supporting the role of women farmers, can be a critical factor that lends legitimacy to early efforts at the local level. In the Western Province, this was emphasized by the initial presence of a female expatriate expert and by Kapekele Chileya's exposure to new ideas during his tenure in the U.K. and his return to Zambia as an advocate for change. Awareness of the existence of a broad body of literature and experience on women's role in agriculture can provide support to programs seeking to address the needs of women farmers and help them to learn from experiences in other settings.

Further Information

The following publications document various aspects of integrating the needs of women farmers within agricultural extension programs. Please contact the publishers directly regarding costs of publications and shipping.

(1) *Working Together: Gender Analysis in Agriculture*, vol. 1, Case Studies; vol. 2, Teaching Notes, by Hilary Sims Feldstein and Susan V. Poats, eds.; (2) *Women's Roles and Gender Differences*, series of seven African and two Asian case studies for planners; (3) *The Impact of Male Outmigration on Women in Farming,* by Ingrid Palmer. The Kumarian Press, 630 Oakwood Ave., Suite 119, West Hartford, CT 06110-1529, USA. Telephone: (203) 953-0214; FAX (203) 953-8579.

Women in Agriculture: What Development Can Do, by Mayra Buvinic and Rekha Mehra, 1990. ICRW, 1717 Massachusetts Ave., N.W., Suite 302, Washington, DC 20036.

The Gender Variable in Agricultural Research, by H. S. Feldstein, C. B. Flora and S. V. Poats. Women in Development Unit, IDRC, Ottawa, Canada.

Using Male Research and Extension Personnel to Target Women Farmers, by Anita Spring, 1987. Women in International Development, Michigan State University, Working Paper No. 144.

Agricultural Extension for Women Farmers in Africa, by Katrine A. Saito and

C. Jean Weidemann. World Bank Discussion Papers, No. 103, 1990. World Bank Publications, Building 424, Raritan Center, 80 Northfield Ave., Edison, NJ 08818-7816, USA. Telephone: (908) 225-2165; FAX: (908) 417-0482.

Women and Livestock Production in Asia and the South Pacific Region, by Alexandra Stephens. RAPA Publication No. 1990/5. Regional Office for Asia and the Pacific, FAO, Bangkok, Thailand.

Gender Issues in Farming Systems Research and Extension, ed. M. Schmink, S. Poats, and A. Spring. Boulder, Colorado: Westview Press, 1988.

2
Supporting Women Farmers in the Green Zones of Mozambique

Ruth Ansah Ayisi

Women throughout much of the developing world are farmers, not only producing the food crops needed to feed their families, but seeking to generate the cash income necessary to gain access to education, health care, and a better way of life in today's world. However, in many countries—particularly in sub-Saharan Africa—women farmers must deal not only with the inherent difficulties of gender inequities, poverty, and the vagaries of nature, but with the consequences of war and civil strife as well. This case study focuses on efforts that are helping women farmers to survive and prosper in the Green Zones of Mozambique—and to provide desperately needed foodstuffs for the local market—despite years of brutal warfare in what is currently one of the poorest countries in the world.

Background

For the first time in over a decade and a half, Mozambicans are enjoying peace—a peace that was a long time coming.

For over 500 years, Mozambique (a nation of 16 million people situated on Africa's southeastern coast and bordering on Malawi, Zimbabwe, and South Africa) suffered under Portuguese colonial rule. This was a time of virtual slave labor, when Mozambicans were forced to neglect their own food crops to grow cash crops for export, primarily to neighboring Rhode-

This case study is a result of a collaboration with UNICEF/Mozambique and UNICEF's Development Programme for Women in New York.

41

sia and South Africa. Then, in 1975, after ten years of armed struggle, Mozambique gained its independence. The Portuguese finally departed, but they left bitterly, taking with them all their belongings and destroying much of what they could not carry off. The economy was in shambles and social services were all but nonexistent. At independence, less than 10 percent of the population had received any formal education and over 90 percent could not read or write. Adequate health care could only be found in the capital, Maputo, and potable water was available in or around urban areas where only about 30 percent of the population reside.

Worse still, the euphoria that accompanied independence proved to be short-lived. Fighting soon recommenced between the new Government of the Mozambique Liberation Front (FRELIMO) and rebels of the Mozambique National Resistance (RENAMO). Sixteen years of civil strife were to follow, resulting in the killing of hundreds of thousands of people, including many women and children. The country's already precarious economy was further crippled, reducing Mozambique to one of the world's poorest nations.

Estimates of the conflict's costs, in the 1980s alone, go as high as U.S. $15 billion. The country's infrastructure was devastated, and agriculture—the country's backbone—declined as people fled to the safety of urban areas and coastal districts. Some 1.7 million Mozambicans crossed into neighboring countries while another four million were displaced. In the countryside, women and children were the main victims of atrocities, and hundreds of thousands of people were cut off from the basic means of survival. It is estimated that almost one million people were killed during the war and that over 500,000 children were torn from their families.

Then, as if the war were not enough, in the early 1990s, Mozambique experienced its worst drought in seventy years. As there were huge food shortages, even more people left the fertile lands that still remained under cultivation. Fortunately, the drought did not result in mass famine, because the people have developed survival strategies for dealing with drought. Many managed to flee to areas where food aid was being distributed, or they survived by eating unusual foods, like wild roots.

The coming of the rains coincided, in 1992, with the signing of a general cease-fire between the government and RENAMO. Slowly, those who had fled to neighboring countries or had been internally displaced began to return to their homes. Now the government, RENAMO, aid agencies, and the communities themselves have begun the massive task of repairing roads and rebuilding the bridges, wells, schools, and health centers that were destroyed. And agriculture is slowly being revitalized as previously unsecured areas and roads are opening up.

Conflict, drought, and, in a different way, peace have all combined to put Mozambique in a chronic emergency situation. Between mid-1992 and the end of 1994, a United Nations force was in place to keep the peace. The task was relatively easy given the desire on the part of Mozambicans themselves for peace.

The peace process culminated in the holding of the country's first multi-party election October 27–29, 1994. President Joaquim Chissano and his ruling FRELIMO party were announced as the victors on November 19th, receiving 43.3 percent of the 4.95 million votes cast, as opposed to 33.7 percent for his rival, Alfonso Dhlakama and the RENAMO party. The elections were hailed as free and fair with almost 90 percent of registered voters turning out at the polls—a significant feat as many voters had to travel for as long as a whole day just to reach the polling station.

The newly elected government faces a truly difficult task. Mozambique's debt burden is one of the world's highest and represents four times the country's Gross Domestic Product. Over 80 percent of the population live in absolute poverty, and UNICEF estimates that death from disease or lack of food continues to threaten as many as three million, or more than one-third of all children in Mozambique.

While times are hard for everyone, one of the most vulnerable groups in Mozambique is the urban poor, who possess little or no land to grow crops. Many urban dwellers are people who once lived off the land but fled to the safety of the cities during the war. For them, food is no longer something to grow, but something to buy. Prices have risen dramatically since the introduction of the Economic Structural Recovery Program sponsored by the International Monetary Fund and the World Bank in 1987, and unemployment is high. Even for those few who are formally employed, life is tough. Wages have lagged well behind price hikes, and the minimum monthly wage in 1994 was only about U.S. $13. This makes wages in Mozambique among the lowest in Africa.

The "Green Zones" Initiative

"Green Zones" is the name frequently given to suburban farm land that surrounds large cities, such as Mozambique's capital, Maputo. Here most of the produce, chicken, eggs, and other foodstuffs found in the urban marketplace are grown. Before independence, the Green Zones were primarily underutilized areas not under cultivation. When the Portuguese left, Mozambican farmers moved onto the land and, over the years, many were able to legalize possession through local authorities. However, these farmers knew little about agricultural production techniques.

At about the same time, in an attempt to stimulate agricultural production, the government forced many farmers to work on large, state-run farms. But, these unmanageable "cooperatives" were not highly productive, primarily because the people themselves received few of the benefits and thus were not committed to the movement. They continued to live off their own personal plots, which they farmed after putting in their required hours on the "people's" farms. Not surprisingly, many Mozambicans today are wary of any attempts at collectivization until they can clearly see the benefit of participation.

The Maputo Green Zones Project

After the failure of the "people's" farms, the government sought other means to increase productivity. In 1980, a *Gabinete des Zonas Verdes* (Green Zones Cabinet) was established to provide administrative and technical support to both cooperative and private farms within the Green Zones. Administratively attached to the Maputo City Council, the cabinet was also a part of the Ministry of Agriculture (MOA) and worked through the seven MOA agricultural centers located throughout the Maputo area. These centers were designed to offer technical assistance through the services of extension workers and provision of transport, seeds, fertilizer, and the like.

As in most African countries, women in Mozambique traditionally are responsible for most agricultural work and, therefore, make up the majority of farmers working in the Green Zones. Many of these women are widowed or divorced; others are married to men who have migrated to work in South African mines, making them the essential source of support for their households and families. It was in 1984 that twenty-one Green Zones agricultural cooperatives, operated by about five hundred women, were selected to participate in a special project funded by UNICEF. The project would attempt not only to improve agricultural production, but to upgrade the overall standard of well-being of the women and their children.

Operating under the auspices of the Green Zones Cabinet, the project was designed to:

• Increase and improve means of production;
• Provide social infrastructure such as crèches, training centers, and sanitary facilities;
• Offer more training courses in such areas as agriculture, and increase knowledge about basic health, nutrition, and child care; and
• Provide higher compensation for workers in cash or kind.

Immediate goals were to:

• Improve water supply and irrigation systems;
• Establish eleven crèches;

- Provide social infrastructure (stores, latrines, offices, etc.);
- Strengthen training structures and provide didactic materials;
- Increase profitability of co-ops to allow payment of at least minimum wage; and
- Improve the nutritional value of agricultural produce.

The Green Zones area is rich in groundwater, but at the time of the project only a few of the farms were irrigated. Therefore, the sinking of boreholes and the provision of pumps were considered of primary importance in boosting production. As few of the cooperatives had any buildings—even sheds—each group was given assistance to construct a storehouse and a protected site for cooking.

Because most of the women had no source of child care and few could afford to send their children to school, the construction of crèches and literacy centers accessible to each cooperative was also a priority. Mini-crèches were established within each individual co-op and are run by the co-op members themselves. They are built right in the fields to facilitate breast feeding. And because most of the women themselves were illiterate, classes in basic Portuguese (the national language) were to be provided to all co-op members. To carry out these social programs, nineteen women from the Green Zones were trained by the Ministry of Health as crèche monitors while another group was trained as nutrition monitors. The Ministry of Education trained literacy monitors to conduct two-hour classes daily and supplied the literacy centers with basic equipment.

As malnutrition was still a problem at the time, arrangements were made for the World Food Programme to provide a minimal food basket to each co-op member and her family until the level of production on the farms could be improved. Local dairies supplied milk to the crèches and the government food distributor in Maputo made sure the child-care centers received basic foods such as cereal, oil, sugar, etc.

Through the participation of the People's Development Bank, the cooperatives were able to take out bank loans to cover the cost of constructing buildings and developing other infrastructures. Co-op members also provided the labor needed for construction as well as farming. Thus, the cooperative members were, from the outset, partners in this development effort.

———

The co-ops in Matola Gare, about 20 kilometers from the city, are approachable up a sandy track, far from the main road. Plots of neatly cultivated maize lie on either side.

It was the hottest day of the summer during my visit to the Maputo

Green Zones. Some women sat on a cane mat under the patchy shade of a fruit tree. They had started in the fields very early in the morning to avoid the full force of the sun. It was now calm, with a hot breeze blowing gently. Maputo City's chaos of around two million people seemed far away.

The only constant noise was the clucking of chickens, but they too were quieter than normal. Temperatures had soared to over 40 degrees Celsius and many of the chickens were dying. Despite the discomfort, the women (mostly dressed in bright-colored cotton wraps, barefoot, and with scarves on their heads) chatted comfortably.

Christine Malecko, a 45-year-old divorcée, is in charge of the finances of one of six cooperatives that are part of a union named Josina Machel, after the first wife of the late president Samora Machel. Since joining the co-op, her life has improved dramatically. Ms. Malecko now earns 100,000 meticais (approximately U.S. $15) from the cooperative, which is about 25 percent above the minimum wage.

Before joining the cooperative in 1987, she had lived with her husband. "Then, suddenly, my husband left me after ten years of marriage because I could have no children," said Ms. Malecko, tenderly cradling the baby of another co-op member in her arms. She was talking in the local language, Ronga. "Before he left, my husband built me a house and gave me a plot of land so I could survive on subsistence farming. But it was very difficult. I worked on my machamba *[plot of land], but I was growing just enough food to eat. I had to work on the* machambas *of others to earn money so I could buy other basics, like soap and clothes."*

The hours of labor took their toll. Ms. Malecko would start working on other people's plots at 4:00 A.M., before working on her own plot. Then she had to trek for forty-five minutes to fetch water, and another forty-five minutes to go home with the heavy bucket on her head. "My health wasn't too good, because when your spirits are low it breaks down your health."

In the early 1980s, on hearing that a cooperative had formed in her area, Ms. Malecko jumped at the opportunity. "I thought it was better to join with others than to work by myself." Besides the chickens, she works with other women growing cabbage, carrots, tomatoes, onions, maize, and beans. "We all work well together," she reports. But she still keeps her own machamba, *where she grows cashews to sell.*

The co-op also gave Ms. Malecko the opportunity to attend literacy classes. She had only completed the first grade at primary school because she had to leave, following the death of her parents, without learning how to read or write. The classes, however, are difficult for most of the women, who not only have to master literacy skills but also have to learn what is for most a new language, Portuguese. Although Ms. Malecko is still unable

to read the daily newspaper, she can now sign her name on checks and her
new skill has assisted her with accounting tasks at the co-op.

Yet, despite joining the co-op, for a long time Ms. Malecko still feared
for her life. "During the war we suffered a lot," she said. "I was kidnapped
with my brother and nephew three times, but we managed to flee each time.
We were unable to sleep inside our homes at night. After 3:00 P.M. I would
have to leave my home, and at night I would sleep in the bush.

"My life these days is much better. I sleep at home, I can buy soap, new
capalanas *[cloth wrappers], and I can save some money aside for the hos-*
pital in case I'm sick, although my health is better now. My only plan is to
save money to construct a better house. [My house now] is only made of
cane and is too small."

———

The new Green Zones initiative was developed in response to the government's decision to provide greater support to small production units in order to meet the critical need for food in the cities. From the start, however, it was stressed that the project would take a "self-help approach" that would "encourage cooperative workers to regard the results as a fruit of their own work rather than a free gift" (UNICEF 1985).

Much of the inspiration for the Green Zones approach comes from an Italian priest, Father Prosperino Gallipoli, who has lived and worked among the peasant farmers of Mozambique since the 1950s. The priest is a modest man, reluctant to talk about his important part in the success of the Green Zones project. But his vision was to create an organization that would empower people to take charge of their own lives—"people's development," he calls it. Therefore, one of his main roles has been to secure the kind of support, from the government and donors alike, that makes such autonomy possible. To do this, he has often had to challenge both the authorities and the "educated elite." However, his faith in the ability of peasant farmers to operate new technologies and ultimately to improve their social and economic status has remained firm. His valuable contribution is now widely recognized; UNICEF, for example, pays him a modest salary and he currently serves as a consultant manager to the General Union of Cooperatives (GUC).

The General Union of Cooperatives

The GUC was established in 1983 to better serve the needs of the cooperatives operating within the Green Zones. Although it was not intended to be a "women's" organization, it has become a strong one, with women regularly holding most, if not all, of the leadership positions—the current

Christine Malecko was divorced by her husband because she could not have children. Now she is in charge of her co-op's finances. *(Ruth Ayisi)*

president, Selina Cossa, is a woman. At times, its independence has brought it into conflict with the Ministry of Agriculture, the ruling party, and even the national women's organization, but it has not only persevered, it has thrived (Urdang 1989).

All individual co-op members automatically belong to the GUC, and membership is free. By 1985, the GUC had united more than 12,000 members and was unable to accept more. However, many of the women had joined solely because membership allowed them access to food and other commodities that were in scarce supply during the height of the war years. When economic structural adjustment policies were introduced in 1987, and price controls removed, food became more readily available in the marketplace. Membership in the GUC then dropped by almost 50 percent, as those not really committed to the cooperative movement dropped out.

Today, there are about 5,400 GUC members (approximately 95 percent of them women), grouped in approximately 182 co-ops located on 700 hectares of land on the outskirts of Maputo. All of the cooperatives, except one, are headed by women. The cooperatives vary in size, but average about fifty members each. Each individual co-op determines when and if new members are admitted, but given that the average size of available plots shared by members is around 3.3 hectares, in most cases too large a membership would be uneconomical.

In 1990, the GUC was registered as a company and the individual co-ops became its shareholders, constituting its General Assembly, which meets annually. Elections take place every three years by secret ballot. The GUC has a central office responsible for all juridical and administrative matters, accounts, and technical assistance for agricultural production. It is staffed by Green Zones cooperative members, who receive their salary from their own co-op. The staff is supervised by a president, vice-president, and director, all of whom are elected by co-op members.

The GUC is run as a private enterprise. It has no institutional relationship to the Ministry of Agriculture, although it respects MOA policies, nor does it have any official relationship with the government or any NGO.

How the Individual Cooperatives Function

Most cooperatives have a democratically elected president, with different members responsible for agricultural production, marketing, social affairs, and accounting. All those in charge are elected by the cooperative members for a three-year period. Literacy and numeracy skills are not required to serve as an officer in an individual cooperative (to serve within the GUC it is necessary, however, to be able to read and write). Within each cooperative, members hold regular meetings where they discuss the current level of wages, credit repayment, and the structure of the co-op. "The members are enthusiastic about the meetings," said one of the women. "We have regular attendance, and people are no longer shy to participate. We send our proposals to the General Union, which weighs the advantages and disadvantages of what we suggest." Typically the proposals the co-ops submit are for building new installations (such as setting up a mill to grind maize) or starting new projects (such as raising pigs).

Cooperative members pay themselves a regular salary, which is just above the country's minimum wage. This basic amount can increase if profits permit: usually about 50 percent of earnings go to pay back loans from the GUC; the other 50 percent is distributed among the members. These loans are primarily to purchase equipment that the GUC has been able to buy at wholesale cost. To secure loans from the GUC, a co-op must sign an agreement to pay back the loan within a certain period of time. The rate of interest charged is lower than the commercial rate. The main advantage of the system, however, is that the women get access to credit, which would be impossible for them to obtain from a commercial bank.

Most co-op members live with their families near the plots of land they farm for the cooperative. Some have always lived there; others have returned following the peace settlement. Some hold title to their land, but this is not a requirement for co-op membership. The GUC has been able to help many of the women who want private plots to secure the title to their land from the local authorities, although the process can be long and tedious. Today, almost all of the arable land around Maputo has been claimed, which restricts the further growth of the movement in the area.

The Role of the GUC

The members of the individual co-ops relate to the GUC either directly or through local unions. Local unions represent ten to fifteen cooperatives in the same area and form the middle level of a pyramid structure that includes the individual co-ops at the bottom and the GUC at the top. The aim, however, is for the co-ops themselves to become more self-sufficient and to rely less and less on direction from the GUC.

Probably the most critical role of the GUC is marketing the produce grown by the cooperatives. As the co-ops are located about 20 kilometers outside the city and most members have no access to private transport, the GUC buys livestock and produce from the cooperatives for sale in the city. The GUC maintains its own cashier so that the women are reimbursed immediately for their goods, thus eliminating the need for them to deal with intermediaries, such as banks. "Farm women are often timid about going into big banks," said one co-op member. "They would probably get robbed. They're not used to dealing with big quantities of money."

Because most co-ops are too poor to afford even the most basic equipment, the GUC also supplies basic farm implements and a range of other goods and services. For example, it has set up two storehouses which supply seeds, fertilizers, hoes, watering cans, hose pipes, construction material, diesel pumps, and the like. Because most co-ops cannot afford the market price of basic equipment, the GUC buys farm implements in bulk, at a discount, and then sells the items at cost to the co-ops. The members can pay for the items they take on credit. The GUC also conducts workshops to teach members how to assemble and repair their equipment.

In 1991, during a meeting of the General Assembly, 145 out of the existing 182 cooperatives opted for distribution of some property and means of production among individual co-op members, while still maintaining the cooperative structure. Low-cost farming instruments (such as hoes, watering cans, etc.) also have become individual property in 145 co-ops, while more costly infrastructure items—such as poultry units, vehicles, and water pumps—continue to be collective property.

Each year the GUC organizes teams of its own members to assist in evaluating activities and drawing up plans for the coming year. Regular meetings between the cooperative members in each area are also organized, offering the women an opportunity to exchange experiences and discuss problems with members of other groups. The GUC also assists members in solving conflicts, particularly over land "ownership" (usually between private farmers and some private companies), as well as helping them solve internal conflicts such as theft, or when someone within the group usurps decision-making authority without the consent of the rest of the members.

Agricultural Production

Today, chicken breeding is the cooperatives' greatest source of income; they currently supply 60 percent of the chicken for the Maputo market. Originally the co-ops had focused on raising pigs, but they proved too difficult to care for because there was not sufficient expertise available locally on their care and feeding. The GUC was able to provide the cooperatives not only with baby chicks but with the necessary feed, vaccinations, and technical backup needed to raise chickens, as well as providing help with transportation—all on a credit basis. In addition, there is a great demand for chicken in Maputo. The GUC has also been able to secure bank loans for individual groups to enable them to build poultry units and other infrastructure items.

The GUC buys all the chickens for resale to city markets, serves as a quality-control check before resale, and assists the co-ops in maintaining their accounts. It has also constructed a modern slaughterhouse with deep-freezers to preserve chickens for sale to hotels, restaurants, and other establishments which buy in bulk. In 1993, besides supplying themselves (i.e., the co-op members), the GUC sold 822,000 chickens. Other crops, such as fruits and vegetables, have been less successful lately, due to the drought and, more recently, to plagues of insects which destroyed most produce. (While the co-ops have access to pesticides this does not protect them from certain types of plagues.) Yet, despite these setbacks, the co-ops managed to produce 3,500 tons of vegetables, 1,900 tons of cereal, and 400 tons of fruit in 1993.

———

Ms. Rosa is the mother of seven children. Her first husband was killed in the war. Today, Ms. Rosa sometimes earns more than her second husband, who is a printer. "My husband has no problem that I sometimes earn more than he does," Ms. Rosa said. "We have a lot of children, so although I earn more than most people, it's still not enough with these high prices of today."

The main activity of her co-op is chicken farming. Every forty-five days the women sell 12,000 chickens to the GUC. Members can buy chickens themselves at the subsidized price of 8,000 mt. (approximately U.S. $1.30). The market price is 25,000 mt. (approximately U.S. $4.00) per chicken. The previous month, her local union made 39 million mt. (approximately U.S. $6,000) from selling chickens.

The bumper sales should enable the women to increase their monthly salary. While members' salaries vary slightly, all earn more than the minimum wage of 75,000 mt. Ms. Rosa earns, on average, 121,000 mt.

Ms. Rosa is more formally educated than the others in her group. Speaking in Mozambique's official language, Portuguese, she stresses how important but hard it is for women to obtain formal education. She, herself, managed to attend school up to the fourth grade. "But then my father stopped me from continuing because he said I would get into trouble with boys. He wanted me to get a job. I worked in a factory making exercise books until I was sacked for being too young. Then I helped a dressmaker. But I had wanted to continue to study."

Today all of Ms. Rosa's children who are old enough attend school.

Training and Education of Cooperative Members

Training has been an important component in ensuring the development of the co-op movement—particularly leadership training. The GUC maintains its own training center and all members attend a leadership training class for one week every year (Helmore 1989). In addition, over the past three years, the GUC has trained 900 co-op members to serve as managers. To participate in the management training program, members must be able to read and write and have attended at least four years of school. Regular meetings with the GUC also help each co-op to develop budgetary plans. Most of the women have not had to deal with credit repayment before. Through this process, they are learning to look more towards the future, rather than just at immediate gains. Training has also been offered in subjects as varied as chicken breeding, agriculture, accounting, and pottery.

Tending the chickens,
Maputo Green Zones.
(Ruth Ayisi)

More Than Just Farming

As documented in the chapter "Child Care: Meeting the Needs of Working Mothers and Their Children" in this book, one of working women's primary concerns is who will care for their children while they work. With donor support, the GUC has been able to set up thirty-five day-nurseries. The nurseries, however, ran into difficulties when NGO support was terminated. Lack of parental involvement and nonpayment of fees threatened continuation of these services, but the situation is gradually being resolved by the members themselves. The GUC has provided assistance in the construction of crèches and has encouraged the co-ops to pay staff out of their profits.

Older children usually attend government primary and secondary schools. However, the GUC did build one secondary school in 1986 which is now attended by 1,000 students. A commercial institute has also been established which offers training to older children in economics and accounting. It is hoped these young people will, in turn, be able to assist their mothers in the running of the cooperatives. Enrollment has already increased from fourteen evening students when the institute opened to forty students.

Funding and Support

To be able to offer such wide-ranging support, the GUC has had to rely on the financial support of international and non-governmental organizations. To date, the GUC has received assistance from the governments of Norway, Switzerland, and Canada; private organizations such as the National Council of Negro Women in the United States; and UNICEF. Gradually, however, it is building a foundation for financial self-sufficiency, and since 1992, the GUC has received only occasional outside aid. Its chicken-breeding project, supported by a World Bank loan and credit from local banks, is currently a major source of income. With the GUC standing as collateral, the co-ops are able to obtain commercial loans through regular channels without any support from the government.

As one donor report recently stated: "The GUC has developed from a couple of illiterate women into a powerful peasant organization." At the national level, the GUC has also become active in the formation of the National Union of Peasants (UNAC). Today, the UNAC is probably the NGO most representative of rural women in Mozambique.

People's Development Is More Than Economic Development Alone

Economic power, personal development, and choice are probably the main benefits enjoyed by the women of the Green Zones, many of whom are widowed or divorced. "Women don't have to put up with bad treatment anymore," says the forty-year-old president of a group of five cooperatives in Tsalala zone. "They are earning money, some for the first time. They can survive by themselves."

Without the Green Zones initiative, most of the women—who have little, if any, formal education—would be either desperately poor, or trapped in unhappy marriages. While the co-ops cannot provide answers to all their problems, the women have been given a chance to earn a wage, most for the first time. Thus they are able to support their families, improve their skills, and contribute to the local economy.

At first, many of the married women found that their husbands were threatened by the Green Zones initiative. In the early days, men often beat up their wives or even divorced them if they joined. But gradually, as the women began to earn money, their husbands became more accepting. A few men even joined, but generally they serve as guards or "handy men."

———

Louise Fomo is president of the 29th of September co-op. A mother of three children, she chose to find another husband three years after her first spouse died. "It was my wish because I was young when my husband died and I needed support. I had serious problems. I had nobody to help me. I had to beg my kin for food."

Ms. Fomo is the second wife of her new husband. Asked whether she minds the fact that her husband has another wife, she replies, "I don't want to lie and say it's easy. But I have been a second wife before, so it is not a new thing for me. I have my own house and I have nothing to do with the first wife." And with the help of the Green Zones, which she joined ten years ago, Ms. Fomo has managed to build up a life of her own against major odds.

The war forced her to abandon her own machamba. *At that time, even the co-op was unsafe. Everybody had to leave by 2:00 P.M. to take refuge in shelters made of plastic sheeting and sticks they had built around the city. Families in her area were often kidnapped, and the co-op itself was attacked and chickens stolen. Having to leave the co-op early also disrupted her literacy classes. Ms. Fomo, who does not know her age, has had no formal education and cannot read or write.*

Even though there is now peace, Ms. Fomo still cannot work on her own plot because it is far from her home and public transport is costly. Furthermore, much of the land that was deserted during the war years was mined, as many people, particularly women and children, have found out.

———

Looking to the Future

Most co-op members are now keen to invest their profits for the future. Many of the women talk about investment plans for the co-ops if they have extra cash, rather than the immediate satisfaction of a wage increase. For example, members talk about buying a mill, so that they do not have to send their maize away to be ground, and about building pens to keep pigs and hutches for rabbits.

A Difficult Act to Follow

The Maputo Green Zones is a success story which, thus far, has proved difficult to repeat in other parts of Mozambique. After supporting the

Maputo Green Zones since 1984, UNICEF is currently directing most of its attention to the Green Zones of Beira, Mozambique's second largest city and major port. However, while the goal of the project is the same—to help women develop economically and personally—the economic activities in Beira are less geared towards agriculture. The experience in Beira thus far clearly demonstrates why trying to replicate "model" projects in other settings is often problematic.

For example, despite the existence of a local Green Zones office, the women who farm in the Beira Green Zones are very scattered and their plots are much smaller, and nearer to the city, than those in Maputo. Also, unlike Maputo, there is no existing cooperative structure on which to build. More importantly, like the other major cities in Mozambique, Beira is not nearly as large a market for produce as is the capital, Maputo. Nor does Beira possess the infrastructure, capital, or business expertise that contributed to the success of the Maputo project. The UNICEF project in Beira has, therefore, had to bring the women farmers together as individuals, helping them attain skills primarily in horticulture and non-farm-related sectors rather than being able to develop or work through a farm-based structure.

The Beira Green Zones Project

The women in this project differ from those in Maputo in that they are caught in a trap of being unable to fully exploit agricultural activities because of insufficient land, while also being unable to break into the formal employment sector because of lack of education. Typically, these women are subsistence farmers who grow one or two crops, usually rice and sweet potatoes; but last year, a plague of grasshoppers destroyed the entire rice crop. Other women in the area are now without any land because they had to flee during the war, leaving behind their plots, tools, and possessions. Many try to earn money by working on other people's farms or by brewing beer.

The Beira Green Zones project was actually established some years ago, but membership dwindled over the years due to the war when many women had to abandon their land and move into the city. Now it is growing once again. Over 300 women in three of Beira's poorest suburbs currently benefit from the project. There is no direct relationship between the Maputo and Beira projects: the former operates through the GUC while the latter is linked to the Ministry of Agriculture.

The Beira project is a center-based program. The centers are open in the afternoon to allow the women time in the morning to tackle their daily chores, fetching water and firewood, working on their *machambas*, doing

Women of the Beira Green Zones preparing to plant sweet potatoes.
(Ruth Ayisi)

their washing, and preparing meals. Activities focus on practical concerns such as horticulture and constructing improved stoves. At a demonstration of how to construct new cook stoves, a woman stamped energetically on a mixture of sand, water, and grass, while another mixed up the clay with her hands. They then placed the mixture in a mold and carried it into a shed. With good maintenance these stoves, which are safe and use little fuel, can last up to three years.

As in the Maputo project, literacy training is an important service provided at the centers. Unlike in some other parts of Mozambique, most men in Beira appear keen to have their wives learn to read and write. In fact, many women say it was their husbands who encouraged them to join the classes. It probably helps that the centers have been existence for six years and that the leaders are respected members of the community.

Especially relevant to the women farmers are the horticultural classes offered free of charge. A local extension worker gives classes once a week to improve the traditional agricultural practices used by the women. Two centers have actually set up demonstration plots for experimental purposes. The project also sells vegetable seeds to the women at subsidized prices.

Organization and Management

Given the project's limited resources, activities are now limited to three centers. Initially the project was coordinated by the Beira Green Zones office, a division of the Provincial Directorate of Agriculture, but now the women themselves are in control. Each center is run by a board made up of three women elected by the members. They manage a budget of ten million mt. (approximately U.S. $1500 at the current exchange rate) provided by UNICEF and meet weekly to discuss center activities. Any problems or suggestions for change are then put forward at a monthly meeting which is attended by a UNICEF representative and someone from the Beira Green Zones office. All decisions are made by consensus. Because the women lack management experience, a coordinating team made up of an extension worker, an accountant, and a literacy teacher from the Green Zones office assist in the management of each center.

In March 1993, the members of the centers and the coordinating team carried out a survey to assess the women's needs and expectations. The survey indicated that the following areas should be developed:

• Raising funds, mainly by selling coal and firewood and by setting up and offering the services of a diesel-operated grinding mill. The income earned will be shared among the women and used to cover the cost of running the centers;
• Training in literacy and adult education, sewing, food processing, cooking, horticulture, making improved stoves, and provision of credit;
• Promoting the centers and mobilizing more women to join because they are now operating at less than capacity and would like to serve more poor women farmers in the suburban area.

"One of the major challenges now is reaching the women," says Adelaide Alfiu, the extension worker. Ms. Alfiu and her two colleagues at the Green Zones office usually go to the fields themselves to ask women farmers to come to the centers. Sometimes women hear about the projects and come on their own accord, like Rosita Salimo.

———

Rosita Salimo first came to the "Centro De Vaz," one of the three training centers, as a last resort. Her radiant yellow cloth, wrapped around her tiny waist, and matching blouse contrast sharply with her cracked skin and

Rosita Salimo dancing,
Beira Green Zones.
(Ruth Ayisi)

*broken toenails. She enters the classroom hesitantly and begins to tell her
story in the local language, Masena.*

*"I came to Beira two years ago with my husband, who worked as a
plumber, but he is now unable to work after becoming mentally ill," says
Ms. Salimo, the mother of five children, four of whom are under thirteen
years of age. She has a small plot of land where she grows rice, but only
for the family's consumption. During the planting and harvesting season,
she sometimes has the opportunity to work on other people's farms for
about 5,000 meticais a day (approximately U.S. $1).*

*"I can't buy enough food for my family," she says. "I can bear the
hunger, but the children can't." None of her children go to school because
Ms. Salimo has no money for school books or other basic items; each child
has only one item of clothing. Ms. Salimo has her yellow* capalana, *or
wrap, for special occasions; otherwise she just has one other cloth which
she uses for farming. "Sometimes I can buy soap," she added, "but I prefer to buy food."*

Yet Ms. Salimo feels hopeful that participating in the center can help lift her out of the extreme poverty engulfing her. Before she became involved, she had heard people in her community talking about the center and its activities. As Ms. Salimo talks about her wish to participate, music can be heard. She walks out to see what is going on.

Standing in a circle, a woman blows a horn, a man drums, and a group of women clap a rhythm with blocks of wood. Others use whistles, and the rest, including some children, clap in perfect time. The women take turns entering the center of the circle, dancing barefoot to the thumping beat.

Suddenly Ms. Salimo is no longer a newcomer. Her head held high, she dances into the middle of the circle by herself, moving every part of her body, completely lost in the music, already seeming to leave her problems behind.

Of course, like that of the other women, her poverty is not going to vanish, but Ms. Salimo now has the chance to gain skills that can help her to earn more money, to learn to read and write, and, at least for a while, to forget her problems and dance.

———

Credit Opens Doors

Because agricultural production is not organized the way it is in Maputo, most of the women farmers who participate in the Beira program need other, non-farm-based opportunities to earn cash income. In July 1993, ten women from each center participated in a two-week course run by the literacy teacher on how to carry out a feasibility study and manage money. A cash credit of 200,000 meticais (about U.S. $31) was given to each participant who qualified according to the terms laid down by the group (for example, proven commitment to the group, completion of training program, up-to-date vaccination cards for her children) to develop or expand a small business. Funding was provided by UNICEF.

Most of the women used the money to invest in activities related to their farming activities, such as the sale of home-brewed beer or the resale of vegetables and maize flour in the local community. Others became engaged in the resale of dried shrimp and fish in towns and villages located further inland. With the money they have earned, these women have been able to improve their diet and buy clothes, school books, and pens for their children, as well as putting aside a small portion as savings. The women pay 3 percent interest on their loans, and so far there have been no delays in repayment.

At the end of the training course, the women performed a humorous play about the pros and cons of business life in an unpredictable market.

The play will be used in the next course to provoke discussions and draw attention to marketing problems.

———

Emilita Antonia was one of the beneficiaries of the first course. A thirty-three-year-old mother of six, Ms. Antonia runs her household pretty much by herself. Her husband has been away for years, working in South Africa. "The previous year he sent money to us, but this year he hasn't sent anything," says Ms. Antonia.

Despite being, in effect, a single parent and only having passed grade one at school, Ms. Antonia has managed to establish a small business. She was one of those who received credit of 200,000 meticais, which she used to buy wholesale bags of maize, bananas, and oranges, which she then resells. Last month she made a profit of 50,000 meticais (approximately U.S. $8).

———————————— Lessons ————————————

1. **Exporting development models, even within the same country, is a challenge which requires attention to the unique circumstances in each locale.** In many developing countries, business, government, and development assistance are all centered in one major city. Thus, as is the case in Mozambique, what worked in the capital, Maputo, could not be readily transferred to another urban site—even the second-largest city. In Maputo, the UNICEF project was able to build upon an existing cooperative structure put in place to help meet the food needs of the capital city. This infrastructure is lacking in Beira, which has resulted in the development of a more traditional intervention that is thus having, at this early stage in its development, less direct impact on women's economic productivity.

2. **People need to see how they will benefit and know they have some degree of control before they can be brought together to work productively.** Mozambicans did not naturally warm to the idea of joining cooperatives, based on their past exploitation, first by the Portuguese (who forced thousands of people to toil on large estates as virtual slaves), and then by a number of unsuccessful policies of the socialist government aimed at the collectivization of agriculture. To bring farmers together into a cooperative structure, it was necessary to demonstrate the economic advantage that they themselves would gain and to give them an active voice in operating and guiding the cooperative structure.

3. **It is important that projects be realistic about the degree of commitment that can be expected from participants and their motivation for joining a specific project.** On the other hand, many women initially joined the GUC because it offered access to goods and services that were in short supply or far too costly during the height of the war years, rather than because they were committed to the cooperative movement. Fortunately, the majority of women realized the value of working together and remained involved even when market controls were lifted and goods became more readily available.

4. **The marketing role of the GUC has been pivotal in ensuring the cooperative members an outlet for their produce.** By providing slaughterhouse facilities, cold storage, and contracts with merchants and retailers, the GUC has been able to provide a stable market for the women producers. They have removed the need to deal with middlepersons and are giving the women farmers immediate access to their profits, without the need for them to deal with banks.

5. **It is important to view mainstreaming as more than providing opportunities to earn.** It is important for women to secure assets in their own right. The GUC has also been instrumental in assisting many of the women to gain title to their land. The importance of ownership is further underscored by the decision of many of the cooperatives to make some low-cost farming equipment private property. Thus, the women are seeking to find the right balance between private and collective ownership that best serves their needs.

6. **The experience of the Green Zones projects emphasizes why women's economic needs can rarely be addressed in isolation.** Even though the women farmers in Mozambique were desperately poor, economic objectives were not their only concern. Over and over again, the women mention the value they place on literacy classes in a country that has one of the highest levels of illiteracy in the world. Offering women literacy classes and management training, helping them to reduce their heavy workloads by providing access to water, child care, and health facilities, as well as offering children a place in school, are all vital elements in the success of the Maputo Green Zones projects.

7. **The Green Zones projects have also been instrumental in empowering women to make choices in their personal lives**, in some cases offering them an alternative to abusive marriages and in others, helping them to gain greater respect and autonomy within their homes. The ability to earn income, combined with the supportive structure of the cooperatives, has been the key.

8. There is power in numbers. The GUC, in addition to supporting the cooperatives, has become influential within larger forums that affect the well-being of poor women in Mozambique. Thus, the GUC is able to provide representation for its members within the broader political arena.

References

Fehr, Irene. 1985. "Women in Agricultural Cooperatives: Green Zones Maputo." Presentation at the Workshop, "Exploring Alternative Programs for Women," in February, Comilla, Bangladesh.

Helmore, Kristin. 1989. "Grass-Roots Projects." A special report of the *Christian Science Monitor*, 1 March.

UNICEF. 1985. "Mozambique's Green Zones Cooperatives—A Challenge" (project documentation).

Urdang, Stephanie. 1989. *And They Still Dance: Women, War, and the Struggle for Change in Mozambique.* (New York: Monthly Review Press).

Youssef, Nadja. 1985. "Trip Report of Visit to the Mozambique Green Zones." (New York: UNICEF).

3
The Port Sudan
Small-Scale Enterprise Program

Eve Hall

It was the presence of desperately poor refugees that first brought Euro-Action Agency for Cooperation and Research in Development (EAA) to Port Sudan in 1980, at the request of the Sudanese Commissioner for Refugees, who asked EAA to do "something in the area of income-generating activities for spontaneously settled refugees." What resulted is The Port Sudan Small-Scale Enterprise Program. The program is not specifically a "refugee project," because it became apparent early on that the very poor of Port Sudan, both refugee and Sudanese, were facing the same problems. Nor is it a "women's project," because both women and men are poor. However, it is unusual among development projects in that it did recognize from the start that women would be an important target group, perhaps the most important. A large number of the poorest families in the slums depend on women's earnings, even when there are men in the family, and poor women, even more than poor men, find it difficult to ask for and to get help or loans for their businesses.

EAA developed a program offering training, services, and credit to poor female and male entrepreneurs, both refugee and nonrefugee. In this program, no activities are considered suitable only for women, and, in fact, while equal consideration is given to all businesses, a little "positive discrimination" is often exercised in favor of female clients. From the beginning, a goal of the program has been that at least half of the small businesses receiving help at any one time should be those run by women.

In some important ways, therefore, this is the story of a women's project because it shows how poor, illiterate women can improve and increase even the tiniest and most marginal of businesses if they are given the right kind of help in the right kind of way. It also provides an example of how women are faring in a project that sets out to make no fundamental distinction in the way self-employed men and women are assisted.

=====

Background

Port Sudan has been described as "a town of recent immigrants." In it live people of several different nationalities, many ethnic and religious groups, and refugees from drought and political conflict. In 1956 there were 50,000 people living in Port Sudan; in 1986, just 30 years later, the town had around half a million inhabitants.

There are many reasons for the sudden and enormous growth in the town's population. A port anywhere in the world lures the unemployed and the poor, who hope to find a niche in its busy economic life. For many years, Port Sudan has attracted migrant workers from as far away as West Africa. But since 1965, disasters, natural and man-made, have turned this trickle of immigrants into a flood. Drought, increasing rural poverty, and the growth of large mechanized farms have forced many Sudanese peasants and nomads to seek a living in the towns at the same time that thousands of people have fled from civil strife in Chad, Uganda, Eritrea, and Ethiopia to find refuge in the Sudan. In January 1986, there were over a million refugees in Sudan: the largest refugee population in any African nation.

Most of the newcomers live in shantytowns, the so-called "fourth-class residential areas" that surround this Red Sea port and its town. More recent arrivals have to squat illegally on the fringes of these "official" slums, building shelters made of packing crates and sacking wherever they can find space, even on rubbish dumps.

Most slum dwellers have little to do with the formal economic life of Port Sudan and receive few city services. Some men work in the port, particularly in the transport services attached to it, and some women have found employment as domestic servants. The majority, however, make a living in the "informal sector," which draws its customers mainly from the slums themselves. Petty traders, cooked food and tea sellers, carpenters, water carriers, tailors, mattress makers, bicycle repairers, blacksmiths, and a host of other entrepreneurs provide many of the slums' basic goods and services and answer a demand created by their rapidly expanding population. But just as the customers are poor, so are the businesses, which are almost always tiny and provide no more than a precarious marginal income for their operators.

The Lives of Poor Women in Port Sudan

In Sudanese society, few uneducated women take jobs outside their homes, although many rural women are active in agriculture. However, when families come to the slums, women often must find some way to earn money, even if doing so takes them outside the home. For widows and for divorced or abandoned women, Port Sudan can be a place of last resort. There are many families (their numbers are unknown, but thought to be high) with no husband or father to provide even a minimum income. It is estimated that up to 50 percent of refugee families may be headed by women whose children and other dependents rely totally on them for their survival. However, most of the women slum dwellers have little or no education. They have few marketable skills in comparison with men and are often restricted by custom and tradition as to the kind of work that is considered "acceptable" for women within their communities.

Setting Up a Program

Euro-Action ACORD is a consortium of twenty European and Canadian aid agencies. EAA had already been working in refugee farming settlements in Central and Southern Sudan, and with various rural development projects in other parts of Africa, when it responded to the request from the Sudanese Commissioner for Refugees to work in Port Sudan. This was the first time the agency considered working with poor urban people, and staff were determined from the start to do their homework very thoroughly so as to understand the economic and social forces that governed life in the slums. The project's first coordinator recalls that they were "embarking on a totally new undertaking. . . . The organization allowed for an unusual degree of research, preparation and ambiguity in the process of designing the Port Sudan Small-Scale Enterprise Program."

The program began with a three-month feasibility study initiated in 1980, which concluded that there were enough skills among the refugees in Port Sudan, and enough demand in local markets, to make a small-scale enterprise development project possible. Plans lay dormant for over a year, however, and it was only in mid-1982 that two EAA consultants, a husband-and-wife team of urban specialists with a good deal of working experience in African countries, came to Port Sudan to begin the program.

While their assignment was to design income-generating activities for refugees, from the start this team felt uncomfortable with this narrow view of who needed help most. In the context of Port Sudan, the identification of refugees as a separate, segregated group could only encourage actual segregation and lead to discrimination. The refugee influx, they felt, was only a part of the problem of rapid urbanization, and refugees were not always the poorest people in Port Sudan. To assist only refugees, they concluded, could be counterproductive; therefore, the focus of the program was broadened to include the poorest sections of the population, refugees and nonrefugees alike.

With funds guaranteed or promised by several donors, the program got under way in mid–1982. The initial research was taken very seriously, and a determined "hard-nosed" business approach became the guiding principle: assistance would be given to those who needed it most, but only for activities that made sound economic sense. The general aim of the program would be to assist the development of enterprises in the slum areas (known locally as *diems*) by:

• Stabilizing existing businesses by putting them on a more secure financial footing;
• Helping people who wanted to start new businesses; and
• Developing and improving the range of goods and services offered in the *diems*.

The first step was to recruit a team of local personnel to gather the necessary background information, to help design the program based on this information, and subsequently to implement all activities after a thorough training period. By December 1982, twenty-five staff members had been recruited through advertisements and word-of-mouth. Initially, EAA stipulated that applicants should be university graduates with working experience in one of the social sciences and a knowledge of the English, Arabic, and Sudanese languages, but there were few people available with all these high-level skills. Therefore, it was decided that it might, in fact, be better for the development of the program if men and women of different backgrounds, ages, and levels of education and experience were included. The new recruits (initially eight women and seventeen men) were a varied group: Sudanese (from Port Sudan and other parts of the country) and refugees, Moslems and Christians, university graduates and secondary school drop-outs. For some, this was their first job; others had years of experience as teachers or social workers. All in all, the staff represented many of the ethnic, religious, and national groups, and spoke all the major languages of the people of the slums.

Under the direction of the two EAA consultants, the new staff immediately began work on a four-month socioeconomic survey of six of the poorest *diems* where many refugees, mainly from Eritrea and Tigre, had settled and where approximately 63,000 families made their homes.

This wide-ranging survey primarily sought to understand the economic life of the *diems*. Staff gathered information on what services were available to the inhabitants, where different communities tended to congregate, who belonged to the most vulnerable groups, average levels of income, what kinds of businesses were carried out and by whom, and what technologies were being used. Women staff also set out specifically to assess the employment patterns and opportunities for women. They interviewed 420 women, including domestic servants, wage laborers employed in large local industries, self-employed women, and even prostitutes, in order to get an understanding of the particular social and economic situations of women in the *diems*.

Following the survey, a census of more than 5,000 businesses (266 of them run by women) was carried out. Fifty-six occupational categories were identified and studied. From these findings the staff obtained a fairly comprehensive understanding of the basic workings of the informal sector in the *diems*, which enabled them to identify what kind of help would be most useful and how it could best be given.

Halfway through the survey period, formal staff training in small-scale business development and management began. This training, which lasted for nine months, was interspersed with field assignments consisting of visitors to small businesses run by people of the *diems* to become acquainted with their operations, supply channels for raw materials, and market outlets. Staff members then shared their findings at seminars and reporting sessions, which were an important element of the training.

EAA consultants ran the training sessions, using mainly their own teaching materials developed during their years of working experience. They also used the curriculum of an expert in small enterprise development. Case studies of small businesses in many different countries were studied intensively, and role playing was used as an important part of the training. Also included was the teaching of basic methods of accounting and business analysis.

The goals of the training were three-fold:

• To familiarize staff with specific techniques and procedures, such as the analysis of a business's profit-and-loss account, the interviewing of clients, and the type of information needed to determine what assistance would be most useful in each individual case;
• To sensitize the staff to the needs and problems of small businesses and their owners and, most importantly, how to respond to the needs of different communities (refugees and Sudanese, Moslems and Christians, men and women) and help overcome the prejudices and problems that can arise from such a diversity of cultures and backgrounds; and
• To develop a team spirit among the staff members, who themselves come from many different communities and backgrounds.

During this period, all the trainees were ranked at the same level and received the same salary. Later, when the program began to work directly with clients, five trainees (including one woman) were appointed to serve as team leaders and were assigned to head five sub-offices to be opened in the *diems*. The other trainees were appointed as either consultants or assistants, according to their qualifications and experience, with different salary levels appropriate to each category.

As the training and research progressed, some of the donors became impatient at the length of time the program was taking to become operational, but EAA stuck to its belief in the need to do things slowly and carefully. The elaborate, field-oriented training not only gave the staff a sound knowledge about and confidence in their work; it brought them, early in their training, into direct contact with the people of the *diems*. They gradually became known and accepted in the slum communities so that information became progressively easier to obtain. When the program was actually ready to begin its work in January 1984, EAA staff were already familiar faces to many of the *diems'* inhabitants; and the staff, in turn, had become well acquainted with the daily pattern of social and economic life in these communities.

Towards the end of the training period, the final project strategy was drafted, with direct input from all staff members. All details were thoroughly discussed so that everyone would fully understand not only the method of operation, but also the underlying concepts. It was in this way that the aims of the program, the kinds of services it would offer, who would qualify for assistance, and how the program would be structured were finally determined.

Open for Business

In January 1984, the program opened sub-offices in five of the six *diems* that had been studied by the staff: Salalab, Dar es Salaam, El Nour, Korea, and Dar el Naeim. (The sixth *diem* was dropped from the program because it was upgraded to a "third-class residential area" by the town authorities, and plans were under way to improve official services and facilities.) The first step in implementation was to advertise the program's services and invite applicants to come in and register for assistance. Advertising to reach men was done mainly in tea shops and other popular public meeting places. To reach potential women clients, staff worked mainly with local grassroots representatives of the Sudan Women's Union (which was attached to the then-ruling party) and with the *diems'* midwives. The first months were to a large extent a trial period for both the program and *diem* residents. Initially, staff responded to every request for aid. They discussed the requests, and the businesses involved, at length during the seminars that rounded off their training sessions. Every application was painstakingly investigated. Meanwhile, residents, too, were testing the program to see what this offer of assistance had to give them. Their response was enthusiastic and initial registration brisk, as staff did not yet have the experience necessary for that first quick assessment which identifies the obviously unsuitable request.

The program, in fact, applies stringent criteria for assistance. An applicant must fulfill four basic criteria. He or she must:

• Be from among the "poorest of the poor"—defined as a family whose household head has a monthly income of less than LS 80, or approximately U.S. $25 (U.S. $1.00 = LS 3.30 in 1986);
• Be largely or totally responsible for the upkeep of the family;
• Have been resident in Port Sudan for at least two years (this is to ensure that the applicant is familiar with his or her surroundings and the basic lines of supply and demand of a business); and
• Accept the program's conditions and fees, and provide all information staff need to establish the economic situation of the household and the business.

Almost two-thirds of the initial applicants were women. This, says an EAA staff member closely involved with the program, was probably because the women were desperate, "so many wanted help even if it was obvious they couldn't qualify." Therefore, should it not be surprising that fewer than half these women applicants were found to meet the program's criteria for assistance? Only 13 percent of those who initially came forward were refugees, not only because EAA stipulated a minimum of two years' residence in Port Sudan as a qualification but also, staff believe, because "refugees have less confidence in offers of assistance and don't believe they will be included." Nevertheless, when the first loan was made, in June 1984, it was "quite by chance" to an Eritrean woman refugee who used her loan to buy handicraft material.

By the end of December 1985, the program had assisted a total of 851 businesses, 40 percent of them owned by refugees; 534 were operated by men and 317 by women. Only 72 of these clients failed to repay their loans, and only six of these "failed clients" were women. (These figures are comparable to those of other credit programs for women—see the Nicaraguan and Indian case studies in volume one of *Seeds*—which clearly demonstrates that women *do* repay loans, and that they do so to a greater extent than men.) The program also helped 142 women who had formed small groups in order to buy specially procured flour during a drought period.

Types of Credit Offered

There is no limit set as to the size of loans for business development, but each loan has a maximum repayment period. The amount loaned, therefore, is determined both by the needs of the business and the capacity of the borrower to repay within a given period. The guiding principle is that many small loans are generally a more effective way to help marginal entrepreneurs in the informal sector than a few large ones. Four different kinds of credit are offered through the program:

Hire-Purchase Loans. Loans of this type are for tools and equipment, and/or to build business premises. These loans enable businesses to cut costs and increase returns by providing tools or space that were previously leased or borrowed, and thus increase productivity. The repayment period depends on the size of the loan, but the maximum is twenty months.

Short-Term Loans for Working Capital. This type of credit enables a business person to buy raw materials in bulk and therefore more cheaply (e.g., flour for women who make and sell pancakes; wood for carpenters). The size of the loan, which must be repaid within two months, depends on the business's turnover.

Micro-Loans. These very small loans, often as little as the equivalent of U.S. $50, provide working capital. They are given to groups of two to four entrepreneurs who get together to buy stocks for their very small businesses. These loans were originally designed to meet the needs of women market vendors, but men, too, have found them useful. Micro-loans must be repaid within one month.

Home Improvement Loans. These loans are given to individuals to purchase building materials to improve or extend their houses, to build latrines, or to lay water pipes. The maximum loan is approximately LS 1200 (U.S. $364) (the current value of a typical wooden house in the *diems*). These loans must be repaid within twenty months.

No interest is charged on any of these loans, but clients must pay an initial registration fee of LS 2 (U.S. $.62) and small fixed administration charges: hire-purchase borrowers pay one percent of the value of the loan per month; those with short-term or home improvement loans pay two percent per month; and groups who receive micro-credit pay one percent per week. The charges to the clients go to offset administrative costs and losses incurred from defaulted loans.

How the Program Operates

The program has a main office in the town with a small administrative staff headed by the current coordinator, the only expatriate member of the staff, and a Sudanese deputy coordinator. Each of the five sub-offices in the *diems* has four staff members, known as "consultants"—two women and two men—one of whom is the group leader. (The sub-office in Diem el Nour is the only one headed by a woman.)

The sub-offices are simple buildings in the middle of each *diem*, almost indistinguishable from the surrounding houses except for a modest signboard. At least one staff member must be in the office throughout the working day, available to see potential clients. It is usually men, however, who come into the sub-offices regularly, or who take the first step in seeking out assistance. Women find it difficult to come to such a public place, particularly to make an initial request for help.

To overcome this problem, staff often make "cold calls"—unsolicited home visits to women they have heard about or noticed at work, and who they believe might welcome assistance. This method of contact is an important part of the program's aim to reach women entrepreneurs who otherwise would never consider asking for help. This outreach method is sometimes used with men as well. "After all," says the coordinator, "the program is not all that well known, and the *diems* are very large and densely populated." If requests do come directly from women, they are usually made through a third person, either a woman who is already being assisted or a male relative who comes to the sub-office on her behalf.

Once initial contact has been made, and the criteria and conditions carefully explained, the next step is registration, for which the applicant pays LS 2. The fee is considered to be an important statement of the program's philosophy to the prospective client: that this is a business proposition, not charity. The program strongly believes that services that must be paid for (no matter how small the fee) are more valued than those provided free.

Registration is followed by a home visit, during which a staff member establishes the applicant's family circumstances to ensure that she or he meets the program's criteria for assistance. A second visit is then made, this time preferably to the place of business, to conduct a thorough business analysis. Here the client and the staff person discuss the current state of the business, its costs and average income, and its operating methods, so as to discover major problems and identify the most appropriate help that can be given. An important part of this assessment is to judge whether the business is sound enough to support loan repayments after household expenditures have been taken into account.

Applicants sometimes drop out at this stage, perhaps because they are unwilling to disclose what they regard as personal information. Roqhia Hamza Osman, a staff member in Diem Dar el Naeim, recalls how a woman who applied for a loan literally told her to "mind her own business" when asked for details of her income and household expenditure. "Either you give me the money or you don't, but don't interfere," the woman said angrily—and negotiations ended right there. In other cases, staff find that applicants do not meet the program's criteria, that the businesses they are operating or planning are not viable, or that the enterprise is unsuitable for the type of assistance the program can offer.

Once these visits are successfully concluded, and the type of assistance decided upon, a "case book" is prepared, which records all the information collected on the client's background, a detailed analysis of the costings and current profit-and-loss accounts, and the kind of help proposed. The "case" is then discussed with other members of the sub-office staff, and, if they give their approval, the book is sent to the main office for final approval by the program coordinator.

If the case is a difficult one, it is discussed at the weekly staff meetings of group leaders and coordinators held at the main office. Requests for large loans, or for types of assistance which have no precedent, must also be discussed and decided upon at these group meetings. Ultimately, the coordinator has the final say, but almost all decisions are reached through general consensus at group leaders' meetings.

A contract, with a photograph of the client attached, is then signed by EAA, the client, and a third person he or she has brought as a guarantor. The guarantors can be a man or a woman and may simply be a friend or neighbor, someone outside the family who is prepared to sign and assume responsibility for repayment should the client be unable to pay. Experience has shown that women do not have more difficulties than men in finding a guarantor. Micro-loans to groups of three people or more do not need a guarantor. If the loan is for more than LS 1,000, the contract must be signed in front of EAA's legal advisor. Formalities completed, the cash is secured by a staff member from the main office, and he or she then accompanies the client to purchase the equipment or other materials for which the loan has been given. The staff member keeps the receipts and gives the client an invoice for the amount of the loan. "This looks like a tedious process," says a former coordinator, "but at present it seldom takes more than a week to be completed."

During discussions, the staff and the client will have agreed on the time period over which the loan is to be repaid. Throughout the repayment period, a staff member visits the client regularly to monitor the progress of the business and to give advice whenever necessary. The client is expected to bring the loan installments and small regular fees charged by the program to the local sub-office, but this requirement is often waived for women clients: staff generally go to their homes, at suitable after-business hours, so that the women who also have household and childcare responsibilities do not need to make this time-consuming and, for some, unwelcome public visit.

If for some obviously legitimate reason a client finds it difficult to make payments because of illness, family problems, or other unavoidable demands on a client's resources, an extension of the repayment period can be granted, or (in exceptional circumstances) the timetable can be rescheduled so that the repayments are smaller and made over a longer period of time.

Information, Management Services, and Supplies

Business Premises and Market Shelters

Many of the small businesses in the *diems* operate in the open as their owners cannot afford to build or rent premises. In two *diems*, the program has built wooden workshops and communal market shelters which can be rented for a very reasonable fee, on a monthly or even a daily basis (as in the case of women vendors whose businesses are very small and often intermittent). Monthly rents are from LS 1.50 to LS 2.50 for a square meter, while daily charges are LS .30. The program has built, for example, welding workshops, butchers' stalls, radio repair shops, etc., and communal stalls in specially constructed market areas for women retailers of petty goods such as spices and pancakes. More recently, it has completed "women's centers," which are attached to each of the program's sub-offices in the *diems*. These centers can provide rental facilities for skills-training businesses, such as tailoring classes.

Management Consultancy

Advice is offered in areas of business management, such as costing, financial analysis, marketing, etc. The small fees charged for this service depend on the business's income before assistance is given. Rates vary from LS 1.00 to LS 5.00 per month.

Generally, this service goes hand in hand with other types of assistance, but it is always optional; some may not need it because they are already well versed in the running of their business. The consultant may advise the client that he or she would benefit from this service, but clients are not required to accept assistance as a condition for receiving a loan.

Marketing

The program sometimes acts as an agent to secure purchase orders for large quantities of a product which a single business could not possibly fulfill. The order is then divided among many small businesses. For example, large orders have come from Oxfam, United Nations High Commission for Refugees (UNHCR), and UNICEF for women's and children's clothes (divided among the programs' women tailors), aluminum cooking pots, wooden pallets for grain storage, and even painted signboards.

Raw Material Supplies

Although not a very frequent form of assistance, the program has, on occasion, procured bulk quantities of raw materials for businesses when these supplies have suddenly become scarce: flour for women pancake makers, for example, during the 1984–85 drought, or special wood for local bed makers. These raw materials are not imported, but are procured from other parts of the country.

Women's Businesses

Businesses operated by women tend to be small, and almost all production is home-based. Of the forty-seven different types of businesses that have been or are being assisted by the program, women are active in thirteen: tailoring, catering, cake baking, sweet making, ice cream making, hairdressing, laundry, soft-drink selling, henna decoration, spaghetti and macaroni making, *shira* (handicraft) production, needlework, and knitting.

In all, 673 women's businesses, out of a total of 1,678 businesses, were assisted between June 1984 and December 1985. The most common activities were tailoring (122 businesses) and catering (111), which includes not only operating small restaurants but also making and selling *kisra* (local pancakes eaten as bread), tea and coffee, and cooked food sold at vantage points by the roadside (near a busy intersection, for example, or a truck terminal).

Tailoring, which is the most popular activity, is not necessarily the most lucrative. Its great attraction, particularly among more conservative communities, is that the work can be done at home, the most socially acceptable place for women to work, and it can be done in hours snatched between household chores and child care. The largest loans requested by women are usually to buy sewing machines. While no woman tailor has yet defaulted on her repayments, staff say that this does not necessarily mean that women tailors' businesses are thriving: Prompt repayments can often mean that the woman is borrowing money from relatives to repay EAA, rather than meeting the installments from her earnings.

Not only do women tailors compete with men in the same trade, they also are hampered by the fact that it is not as easy for them to operate from public workplaces or to go outside the home to sell their products. Rather, they must either wait for customers (generally their neighbors) to come to them with orders, or depend on a male relative to sell their ready-made garments outside. EAA staff try to help solve these problems by suggesting advertising to attract more customers or alternative market outlets for the male "agents." Too often, however, a woman's tailoring business operates irregularly and marginally and lapses into little more than an income-saving activity by which she can make her family's clothes more cheaply.

Rakia Ebrahim, Tailor

Rakia Ebrahim is a forty-year-old Sudanese woman, who is divorced and who has lived in Diem Korea for fourteen years. Since 1970 she has tried to support her family of six, including her old mother and father, by tailoring, supplemented for the past ten years by her selling cooked food to children on their way to school each morning.

In 1983, a family crisis forced her to sell her sewing machine. She later heard of the EAA program from the Sudan Women's Union and, in November 1984, she received a loan of LS 375 to buy another machine. Originally, she was due to repay this loan in ten monthly installments, but when this proved difficult, the amount of the repayments was reduced and the time period extended for another six months.

Rakia Ebrahim works from her home, has about ten regular customers, and earns a net monthly income of LS 43 for a twenty-hour work week. In itself, this is a tiny weekly income, but not unjust, considering her working hours. If her work time could be increased, so could her income. On the advice of EAA staff, Rakia Ebrahim has recently bought some cloth to make garments which she is hoping to sell through her eldest son, who will hawk them in the local markets.

Some businesses which at first glance may seem to hold little prospect for a steady income can prove to be rewarding. The decorating of brides with henna designs is a rare and valued skill, and once a woman has established her reputation as a talented artist, she can expect quite substantial payments for a single assignment.

Ekhlas Soliman, Henna Decorator

Ekhlas Soliman is a single woman in her early twenties who has lived in Diem Dar el Naeim all her life. She lives with her divorced mother (who sells kisra for a living and also has been an EAA client), her grandmother, and nine younger brothers and sisters, in a small wooden house. In this crowded environment, she practiced the art of henna decorating for three years. In August 1984, she requested a loan of LS 436 to build a small sep-

Decorating a bride's
feet with henna.
(Wendy Wallace)

*arate shelter in the family compound to which her customers could come,
"so that I could work in peace, away from the family." She has already
made sixteen of her twenty monthly installments.*

*Ekhlas Soliman is self-taught. "I wanted to do this work, and I thought
I would be good at it," she says. "Most other decorators get their designs
from books, but I like to make up my own patterns." She has built up a good
reputation and a steady clientele. She receives on average three to four
orders for bridal decorations every month, for each of which she spends
several hours painting elaborate patterns on the bride's hands and feet.
For this her fee is LS 50, but she admits that she tailors the price to what
the customer can afford, and often charges less. She can, however, sometimes recoup on this loss as customers who are better off will quite frequently "top off" the fee to show their appreciation if they are pleased with
her work. She also earns money from customers who want only their hands
decorated for other special occasions, or perhaps "just for beauty." For
this she charges LS 15.*

The Port Sudan Small-Scale Enterprise Program

Apart from her loan repayments, her major expense is for materials, particularly the costly dyes which are imported from Egypt. Her average monthly income has been a quite respectable LS 150, but she is a little pessimistic about the future. Another woman henna decorator has moved into the area and is drawing customers away: last month, only two brides came to her. Ekhlas Soliman understands her marketplace well: "People don't necessarily choose the best decorator. They tend to go to the nearest one."

Perfume making, a local skill, can lead to brisk sales, particularly if a woman can sell her products in a central marketplace. Perhaps the most inhibiting factor for any of these businesses is competition; as Ekhlas Soliman has learned, supply can easily outstrip demand.

While most women would prefer not to work in public, financial pressure often necessitates such activity. Catering, in all its forms, can be relatively lucrative, and many women have taken up this work. The acceptability of this trade depends to a great extent on the social status, ethnic background, and age of the woman, as well as whether she is the head of a household.

Success in catering depends on sound cost analysis and price setting, but the most important factors are location and hours of business. A woman selling cooked food or tea, for example, can develop a good, regular clientele among men workers who eat breakfast or lunch away from home. *Kisra* makers, too, find a ready market because restaurant owners, housewives, and working women often buy their pancakes ready-made. And while there are peak selling hours in the day, the demand for tea and coffee is constant.

Since the profit margins for such catering businesses are small, the amount of income depends on the daily turnover, which can be quite substantial. The working hours needed to make these businesses profitable, however, can be extremely demanding and difficult for a woman with household responsibilities. To catch the lucrative breakfast trade, for example, caterers must have prepared their food or beverages and be at their selling point as early as 5:30 A.M. Often they must return home again to prepare food or drink for their lunchtime customers. In addition, they must buy fresh food every day; therefore, it is not surprising that women with children and other family duties find it difficult to carry out their businesses without interruptions, which mean not only less income, but a loss of regular customers to other caterers.

Food seller, Port Sudan.
(Wendy Wallace)

Aziza Ismael, Cooked Food Seller

Aziza Ismael is a thirty-year-old Eritrean refugee, divorced and the sole breadwinner for herself, her mother, and her three brothers, who are all under 10 years of age. She sells cooked food in a rented, make-shift shelter at "Kilo 8," a large, flat wasteland beyond the diems where the scores of transport trucks that serve the port park while they wait for business. All kinds of allied services have sprung up in this area, such as mechanics, welders, tire repairers, etc., and quite a few are among EAA's clients.

The men employed in transport services generally live in Port Sudan without their families and buy their food ready-cooked. They come from a variety of backgrounds, and each seeks out the kind of food he is used to at home. Aziza Ismael serves Eritrean food and she is well known to her countrymen at Kilo 8. She has been there for more than three years, many mornings by 5:30, to sell them Eritrean pancakes and tea, as well as meat and vegetable stews throughout the day.

She first came to the Sudan in 1975 and moved to Port Sudan three years later. Shortly after her arrival, her husband divorced her, "because my children always died very young." Since then, he has given her no help. To support herself and her family, she began to make cooked food at home to sell at Kilo 8, borrowing the necessary equipment from relatives. Her health was poor in those early years and she could only work intermittently. But gradually her health improved and so did her business— until her relatives took back the equipment they had lent her.

Aziza Ismael learned of the EAA program through a woman friend who was already a client. She applied for a hire-purchase loan to replace her equipment. EAA quickly approved the request. Her case book notes: "She needs to work to support her family. She already knows how to get supplies and knows Kilo 8 very well." There is much competition at Kilo 8, but caterers who build up a regular clientele can do quite well. In October 1985, she was given a loan of LS 300 to buy equipment, to be paid back over fifteen months; and a short-term loan of LS 75 to buy a stock of sugar wholesale, to be repaid over two months.

———————

Although women loan takers are usually illiterate, they have their own ways of keeping track of costs and income, which, while not totally accurate, are reliable enough to use as a base for the initial assessment of a business's viability and potential, which the client and the staff member examine together. A business is judged to be viable if, when all the costs are taken into account, it has the potential to make a genuine profit. Lack of working capital is the most common problem facing women. On average, businesses run by men operate with three times the capital of those run by women. This often means that women cannot buy raw materials in bulk, and therefore more cheaply, thus adding to operating costs and lowering profit margins.

Once a loan is approved, the borrower is assisted in making her calculations more accurate and in working out a detailed cost-and-profit account. It is usually at this stage that the woman is first introduced to the concept of counting her own labor as a cost—that she must pay herself a fixed wage and that this wage must never be regarded as "profit." The concept of "costing" her working time is always difficult for a woman to understand: because so much of her other daily work is unpaid. She therefore tends to consider all income as profit. As a female staff member notes: "We try to help the client understand: *You* are different from *your business*. The wage you pay yourself must come out of *business expenses* because you are *spending your time.*"

For example, in reviewing Aziza Ismael's business procedures, it was found that she was not setting her prices according to her costs, but simply charging the same as caterers nearby. A full analysis was worked out to determine more accurately how much she should charge for different types of dishes, how much she should pay herself as a monthly wage, and what her profit margin might be. These were the calculations:

Monthly Expenses:

Rent	LS 60
Transport (to and from Kilo 8)	LS 8
Water, charcoal, kerosene	LS 15
Loan repayment	LS 29.82
Administrative charge (1%)	LS 2.98
Consultancy fee	LS 2
TOTAL	LS 117.80

Monthly Wage:

This is an additional monthly expense. Aziza Ismael works eight hours a day, six days a week. Labor costs are figured at LS .70, the amount currently judged to be the wage earned for this kind of work by an employee. This cost, therefore, comes to a monthly total of LS 145.60.

Expenditures on Raw Materials:

The costs for vegetables, oil, meat, beans, sugar, tea, etc., were worked out on the average number of meals prepared and sold over a one-month period. Total per month: LS 1,279.50.

Monthly Sales:

Meals of meat (866 @ LS 1.50 each)	LS 1,300
Meals of vegetables (200 @ LS 1.00 each)	LS 200
Tea (1,213 glasses @ LS 0.15 per glass)	LS 182
TOTAL	LS 1,682

TO SUM UP:

Total revenue from sales	LS 1,682.00
All expenses (including wages)	1,542.90
Net profit (estimated)	139.10

Thus, Aziza Ismael's net income, including her wages and estimated profit, was calculated to be approximately LS 284.70 per month. Of this income, the wage is a fixed amount; the profit will obviously change each month, depending on sales. Cash from the profits can be used to reinvest in wholesale purchases, replacement of equipment, etc. With the injection of a little capital (to buy tea wholesale) and with her own equipment, Aziza Ismael has, potentially, a business which can earn enough to support her and her family.

The distinction between wages and profit is vital to understanding what income the business is actually earning. Some women grasp this new concept quite quickly once it is explained to them and then become accustomed to an analytical approach to the business's finances. Others, however, reject outright what seems to them to be an artificial division. "They say, 'No, the business is not separate from me, and whatever I earn is mine to use as I like.' So they end up using working capital for household expenditures and don't realize that this is why their business doesn't work properly."

Since women caterers and vendors, particularly, keep daily accounts, EAA staff assist them with their monthly accounts, recording the costs, income, and profit. Staff generally go to the women's homes to do this, rather than to their places of business, as it is not very practical to conduct what amounts to a training session in accounting while squatting by the roadside, where so many of the women's businesses are located.

Frequently, staff will visit their clients more often than once a month if some aspect of the business requires special attention. "If we notice that the price of a basic commodity has gone up," says one staff member, "we visit the client to see how she is adjusting her business to this. For example, a woman client might have received a loan when meat cost LS 6 a kilo. Now the cost has gone up by about 20 percent. We can advise the client either to put in additional capital, to reduce production, or to increase her prices. In the case of most caterers, we would advise them to increase the cost of a meat dish—though we have to keep an eye open for what others are charging, so that our clients will still be competitive."

Amlasa Mokenen, Kisra Seller
Amlasa Mokenen is a refugee from Eritrea, a 55-year-old woman who has been in Port Sudan for twenty years. During all this time, she has struggled to support a family of eight dependents by making and selling kisra *in Diem Korea. Although she already had quite a brisk business turnover, she never had enough capital to buy her flour in bulk. This not only meant that her basic raw material was unnecessarily expensive, it also resulted in a very low profit margin and added to her transport costs, as she frequently*

had to make special journeys to buy flour. In September 1985, she received a loan of LS 300 to buy 270 kgs. of flour. This loan she repaid in three months, although the installments were high (including administrative charges, LS 105 per month).

Since receiving the loan, she sells approximately 2,600 pieces of kisra a month (at LS .25 each), a considerable increase over previous sales. Her monthly income is now approximately LS 220, even considering that some of the flour bought for the business is occasionally used for home consumption.

The loan has helped her to increase production, and she has a good repayment record. However, the question now is: How will she be able to keep up her high level of production once she has used up the flour bought with the loan? She is being urged to set aside money to buy another bag of wholesale flour and not to use any of the flour to feed her family; but with so many dependents and high household expenses, she may not be able to follow this advice.

———

Regular personal contact between clients and EAA staff builds up a mutual trust and encourages an open, friendly relationship in which advice is readily accepted. The staff member is often treated as a family friend. As the former project coordinator describes it: "The modest but unfailing hospitality of the clients is matched by their relaxed and entertaining reception at the sub-offices." This is another way of saying that the tea flows during visits and there is much joking and laughter in between the serious analysis of business performance and the handing over of monthly installments. It is rewarding for EAA staff to see that, despite the problems these small entrepreneurs face and their often exhausting work loads, they generally possess an enviable zest and an enthusiastic approach towards their businesses.

———

Fatima Osman, Tea Seller
Fatima Osman is 25 years old, divorced, with no children. Although she was born in Port Sudan, her parents were refugees who came from Eritrea in the early 1960s. Her mother is also divorced, and neither her father nor her ex-husband contributes towards the family's upkeep. Fatima Osman has supported herself, her mother, and a younger brother and sister by selling tea in a rented kiosk in Diem el Nour's central market since 1984.

In 1985, she asked EAA for a loan of LS 120 for additional equipment to expand her business (she had heard of the program from a friend). She repaid this loan promptly over five months. She then received a short-term loan to buy a sack of sugar wholesale, which she repaid within a month.

As she is not currently a loan holder, she is considered a "closed" client ("active" clients are those who have not yet repaid all loan installments), but staff members still drop by her kiosk to buy a glass of tea during their busy round of visits to clients in the vicinity. Fatima Osman's stall is always crowded, and it is clearly one of the favorite meeting places for the market's male workers. She sells approximately 300 glasses of tea (at LS .15 each) daily, and works nine hours a day, every day of the week, from 6:00–10:00 A.M., and then again from noon until 5:00 P.M. Her net monthly income is approximately LS 200.

Special Problems of Women's Businesses

The women clients profiled above are fairly typical of business women in the *diems*. Singly and collectively, they demonstrate several of the common problems that prevent these businesses from providing a better income to their operators: lack of adequate capital or equipment; poor management skills; lack of regular business hours; competition; an inability to market products outside the home; and heavy family responsibilities which frequently force women to use business capital to meet immediate needs.

Most staff feel that at least some of these problems could be overcome if women were encouraged to give higher priority to their businesses. "Women often don't succeed in business because, even when they are the main breadwinners, they are not as tough as men in resisting pressures to limit their business production. We should help women find ways of coping with this problem," says the Coordinator. But, as a female staff member notes, "You can't compare women's heavy family responsibilities with those of a single man. Women have to do everything, and sometimes they fail. We try to help women work out a way to divide their time, but many can't make fixed hours if they have children." She also feels strongly that women have a higher commitment to the family, which pushes them into using business capital for daily needs. "It's well known that almost all women's incomes go back into the family, much more than men's. Women don't go to the cinema or buy cigarettes." It is women, not men, she stresses, "who must every day find the food to feed the children."

Saadiya Mahmood Aman, the female group leader of the Diem el Nour sub-office, largely agrees with this view and believes that the program must find new ways of helping women. "We give the same help to women as we give to men. But it's not only capital that women need. They also need training and much advice. We must introduce new kinds of businesses for women. There are so many women who need training in a skill, not only equipment." This is an important point that must be underscored. For example, she is doing all she can to encourage the tailoring teacher who rents a room in the sub-office's women's center to give classes to young women for a small fee. The teacher has received a loan to buy a sewing machine for these classes. She would also like the program to buy the finished products from the trainees for a small sales exhibition in the nearby market in order to encourage them to continue their training and help them get started in business.

In this she is supported by her colleague, Haw Hamid Idris, but other group leaders and the coordinators are very reluctant. They see this as a departure from the program's philosophy of giving help only to businesses which have proven potential. "The others say, 'The project is for self-reliance. If we accept this exhibition idea, then we no longer support self-reliance.' But we say that we would be helping women to become employed and that they would eventually become self-employed."

Project Cost

The total cost of the program, including the revolving fund, from its start in 1980 to the end of 1986, was one million British pounds (sterling) (approximately U.S. $1.2 million). Almost one-third of this sum was spent before the program became operational and any loans had been made (1980–1984).

ANNUAL EXPENDITURES 1980–1986

1980–1983	L 217,625	Preparatory Phase
1984	270,311	
1985	290,900	Operational Phase*
1986	310,862	
TOTAL	1,089,698	

*The program began operation in June 1984.

A large component of the start-up costs comprised staff training and research, primarily due to the experimental nature of the program. However, this is considered to have been a vital component in its successful implementation, and staff training remains a continuous process as more people are recruited to meet the needs of the expanding program.

EAA staff stress that the relatively high cost for the preparatory stage of this project was largely unavoidable and necessary. With hindsight, however, EAA feels that perhaps the research sought more information than was really needed for the program's operation. With the experience and knowledge gained from the planning and preparation of this program, a similar one developed elsewhere would probably need no more than four to six months' research, instead of the 18 months used in Port Sudan. Thus, start-up and preparatory costs would be far less.

The Future

The debate over and the search for better ways to help women and to reach more women clients continues. "Softer" loans for women, or help that is not directly aimed at improving the viability of a business, are not planned. But there is one element of positive discrimination for women entrepreneurs already in the program: men who request loans for catering businesses are refused so as not to increase competition with women in an already crowded field. EAA has also begun to give assistance to retailing activities by women, a departure from their stress on credit for producers who sell their own goods. Thus, assistance has been given to women who sell goods produced at home by other women, and who take a percentage of the sales as their payment.

Home improvement loans are another aspect of the program's services which have proved to be increasingly popular. Some EAA staff believe that this kind of help may serve to improve considerably the quality of women's lives in the *diems*.

Within the program, women and men staff are treated equally and receive the same basic salary, depending on whether they are team leaders, consultants, or assistants. To this salary is added incentive payments based on the number of clients handled by each staff member. In practice, however, there are some differences in the working conditions and pay of women and men. Because women clients frequently must be sought out and often need more sustained advice, since their businesses are more precarious, women staff tend to have a heavier work load than their male counterparts even when they have fewer clients. Moreover, social constraints hamper women staff. While male staff members are given loans to buy motor scooters to make their rounds in the sprawling *diems*, it would be considered "unacceptable" for women to use them. Female staff members must take buses or walk, which again is more time-consuming. As a result, the women's incentive pay, based on numbers of clients, is generally lower than the men's. To redress this unwelcome and unexpected imbalance, which only emerged as the program developed and grew, EAA is gradually phasing out incentive payments.

The long-term future of the program is not yet clear. EAA sees a strong possibility for the development of a local organization within the program and hopes that it will eventually be able to hand over its work to such a non-profit organization. EAA would then remain as a member of the board of trustees. As a first step in that direction, the caseload of team leaders in the sub-offices has been reduced to enable them to take on more of a managerial role in preparation for the gradual shift in responsibility from the head office to the individual teams. But, says the Coordinator, "We have set no time limit; we have made no definite plans, we learn as we go along."

———————————— Lessons ————————————

1. **Reaching out to women where they live and work is a very effective strategy to increase their participation in a loan program.** Unlike so many other loan schemes (not only in Sudan), women can take part in this program without having to gather up their courage to take the daring, often disapproved of, step to go to a public office to ask for a loan. Negotiations take place privately in the women's homes, and even the tiniest loan is given serious consideration by sympathetic program staff, rather than the more usual impersonal "loan committees," which often include representatives from banks and other formal credit institutions that would dismiss such small loans as not worth the bother of administration. While the needs of refugee women are much the same as those of other low-income women (income-earning opportunities that will enable them and their families to survive), they are often more hesitant to believe that they will be included in offers of assistance. Thus, unsolicited introductory visits to women's homes have proved particularly helpful to them.

2. **There is a great advantage in having women work with women.** Both unsolicited and regular home visits are unremarkable and unobjectionable if they are made by women. However, all the staff work with, and are encouraged to seek out, both men and women clients. Although only eight women staff members were originally recruited, more were later employed and given on-the-job training. There are now eleven women and ten men staff members working in the sub-offices, and EAA is intent on keeping this balance.

3. **The type of management training offered must be well-suited to women's needs.** They cannot be expected to find time to attend formal, theoretical group training sessions. Instead, staff visit them at home, at times that suit women who have both business and household work to do every day. The instruction they receive is related specifically to their business, and is given in familiar surroundings by someone a woman has learned to know and trust and who speaks her own language.

4. **A program to assist women entrepreneurs must take into account all the realities of their lives and not expect that they will always be able to meet the same performance standards as male clients, for whom, generally, business is the major focus of their activity.** Women's businesses are under constraints that do not affect businesses operated by men: because few kinds of businesses are socially accepted as "women's work," women struggle against greater competition, and social sanctions often stop them from selling their goods in public places, thus limiting the markets available to them. Women also have less time to devote to their businesses because they also have time-consuming daily household and childcare responsibilities.

5. **The quality and relevance of technical services will be suspect if they are given free of charge, and so will the motives of the service givers.** Serious people, even if their businesses are of the smallest dimension, appreciate and honor straightforward contractual relationships.

6. **Efforts to force or encourage women's individual small businesses to band together as a group are generally counterproductive and impractical.** Collective activities need a clearly defined objective, such as a number of small businesses coming together to purchase supplies at bulk cost. Another successful approach has been for the program itself to secure large contracts for goods, which it then divides amongst various individual clients.

II

ASIA

4
The Muek-Lek Women's Dairy Project in Thailand

Aruna Rao

The Muek-Lek Women's Dairy Project was started in 1985 to encourage the growth of a new agricultural sector, dairy farming, in Thailand. While the major aim of the project was to increase incomes of rural families in the Muek-Lek Land Reform area in Saraburi Province, Central Thailand, it also sought to integrate women into dairying activities, and to offer these women, whether married or single, access to credit.

It is unusual for women to have an opportunity to participate in the formation of a new and highly profitable agricultural industry. The Muek-Lek Dairy Project is unique in that it has channeled government resources and secured commercial bank financing to make women the key participants in a relatively new and growing agricultural sector in Thailand. Primarily the initiative of two prominent Thai women, a banker and the director of a national NGO (non-governmental organization), with the support of an international women's banking organization, the project has had a major impact on increasing women's income, status, and access to government and private-sector resources.

Women in Thailand

Women comprise close to half the population of Thailand, and about 67 percent are active in the labor market. The majority of Thai women live in rural areas and are employed in agriculture, many as unpaid family labor. However, over the last thirty years, the percentage of women in agriculture has declined from 87 to 61 percent, as women have moved into com-

91

merce, manufacturing, and services. In all industries, women are concentrated in the lowest income brackets. Although female literacy is high (84 percent), political participation at the local and national levels is not significant, and women still do not enjoy legal equality with men in a number of spheres.

History of the Dairy Industry

Milk consumption is not a tradition in Thailand. Until thirty years ago, cattle were raised primarily as work animals, and also for beef and manure. The earliest dairying activities were started in the 1950s by Indian settlers around Ayutthaya, the ancient capital of Thailand, located about 80 kilometers north of Bangkok. The fresh milk they produced was sold to consumers in Bangkok. Today, dairying continues to be focused primarily in the Central Zone because of its rich agricultural land and the availability of cattle feed for most of the year.

Following World War II, the Government of Thailand established a milk authority to promote milk production and consumption. However, increasing imports of milk and milk products, which were lower in price and of better quality, undermined local production. Beginning in the early 1960s, the milk-processing industry began to expand when the Danish and German governments assisted in setting up model dairy farms in Muek-Lek. By 1972, there were eight milk-processing factories producing pasteurized and recombined milk. A dairy farming promotion organization was started under government sponsorship to support research on exotic breeds, provide training, and encourage processing and marketing. Most of the support was targeted to large farms in Saraburi province. Between 1976 and 1982, the demand for milk grew by 25 percent per year as incomes (particularly of urban dwellers) improved and more people acquired a taste for milk.

The number of dairy farmers in Thailand has increased from 114 farmers with 3,450 cows in 1962, to 4,000 farmers with about 24,000 cows in 1986. Imported Holstein-Freisian/Sahival cows have become the norm for the industry, due to their high yields and adaptability to conditions in Thailand. Today milk processing remains highly concentrated, with five private-sector processing companies responsible for 90 percent of the country's local dairy production—which still meets only 20 percent of demand. In 1988, annual imports of milk and milk products still amounted to about 2,500 million bhat (U.S. $100 million), thus indicating a significant opportunity for expanding local production.

As a profitable and rapidly growing sector, dairying presented a unique opportunity to increase women's incomes. The efforts of the consortium of banks, government agencies, and NGOs in the Muek-Lek Dairy Project have enabled eighty-two poor families to purchase 500 imported cows, making women significant players in the emerging dairy industry.

Barefoot and sarong-clad, Somchit walks quickly across her small, dry plot of land toward the cattle shed where her seventeen-year-old son is guiding cows into their stalls. It is 4:00 P.M.—afternoon milking time. It takes Somchit twenty minutes to milk one cow; she owns twelve all together. Four years ago, with a 158,000 bhat (U.S. $6,320) loan from the Bangkok Bank, under a program sponsored by the Friends of Women's World Banking in Thailand, in collaboration with a number of government agencies and national nongovernmental organizations, Somchit bought four dairy cows imported from New Zealand. Before she started dairy farming, she planted corn and earned less than 1,000 bhat (U.S. $40) a month. Now she nets over three times that amount.

Muek-Lek: The Setting and the People

Muek-Lek is located in the province of Saraburi, about 250 km. northwest of Bangkok. Thailand's small but growing dairy industry is concentrated in Saraburi province. However, most poor farmers in the region continue to depend on low-return crops, such as maize, for family income. Most families in Muek-Lek were originally squatters who moved into the area to clear government forest land for cultivation. Squatters and landless laborers in Muek-Lek were granted user rights to the land through the government land reform program of 1979. While some families managed to register neighboring plots under names of different family members, thereby retaining relatively large landholdings, the mean size of farms within the land reform area is 30 *rai,* or eight hectares.

Prior to joining the dairy project, 70 percent of all households in Muek-Lek earned less than 10,000 bhat (U.S. $400) per year; 35 percent earned less than 6,000 bhat (U.S. $240) annually—figures that are substantially lower than for other parts of Thailand. The annual expenses of most households exceeded or just equalled income, and many were borrowing from local merchants at an interest rate of 20 percent. This money was advanced against crops during the four-month period between planting and harvesting. Some male farmers were able to take out loans averaging 5,000 bhat (U.S. $200) from the local agricultural cooperative, but this credit was not available to women farmers.

Saraburi has a tropical, savannah climate with three seasons: a rainy season from May to October; a cool season from November to February; and a pre-monsoon hot season from February to April. Temperatures range from a high of 32 degrees celsius in April to 16 in December. Only about

21 percent of the land is irrigated: most of the annual rainfall comes between May and October. The three consecutive years prior to 1985, when the dairy project started in Muek-Lek, were years of drought.

The lowland areas, with poorly drained clay soils, are planted in rice. Maize, sorghum, mung, and soya beans are cultivated in the hilly regions. In the Muek-Lek area, the majority of farmers plant maize as their main crop. Agricultural labor is seasonal and often shared between women and men. In late March and early April, men are responsible for land preparation for the first crop. Tractors are hired for plowing and oxen are used for furrowing. Planting is done in April, mostly by women, and weeding is carried out three or four weeks later by both women and men. Generally, Muek-Lek farmers do not use chemical fertilizers or pesticides. Harvesting, which is done in July, is also a joint female-male activity. Land preparation for a second crop immediately follows harvesting of the first. The second crop generally produces lower yields than the first due to drier weather. Farmers sell their maize directly to local merchants. Despite the ability to plant a second crop, seasonal under-employment is still a problem for both men and women in Muek-Lek.

The Women's Dairy Project

In 1984, the Thai Institute of Science and Technical Research conducted a study as part of a large rural development project covering a number of sites around the country, including Saraburi. The aim was to identify ways to improve the productivity and incomes of local farmers by focusing on cash crops such as cotton and animal feed, or dairying. Dr. Malee Suwana-adth was an advisor to the Institute at the time. She is the Executive Director of the SVITA Foundation, a private, nonprofit organization that promotes small enterprise development in Thailand, particularly among women. Dr. Malee accompanied the research team to Saraburi to explore opportunities for small-scale enterprise development.

The team, accompanied by the Muek-Lek land reform officer, Khun Kamthorn, visited a series of development sites including an ongoing Thai government/Danish dairy project. This project was experiencing a number of difficulties, including low yields from crossbred cows, and lack of local infrastructure, such as all-weather roads to connect farms with the milk-processing plant (located 30 km. away). Over several months the team, along with the land reform officer, examined the feasibility of different income-earning activities, taking into account the farmers' access to land and capital, their technical know-how, and market demand. Demonstration plots of new crop varieties and practices were planted for farmers to observe. When the study was completed, the team discussed their findings

Dairy farmers and their husbands. *(Kim Retka)*

and ideas with local villagers. These villagers then continued to meet as an informal working group to further discuss the various options the team had presented to them. At first the working group included only one woman. Later, with SVITA's encouragement, more and more women joined in the deliberations. Of all the possibilities for augmenting income, the villagers chose to begin dairy farming despite the difficulties faced by other dairy projects in their region. Dairy farming best met their needs because it would provide a steady stream of income throughout the year and help fill their need for employment during slack agricultural periods. They were concerned, however, about the low milk production of local, cross-bred cows.

Soon afterwards, Dr. Malee and an associate returned to carry out a feasibility study to determine the minimum amount of assistance that would be necessary to make dairying profitable for each family. They also visited several small dairy projects sponsored by other NGOs in Thailand. Their findings indicated that profitability would require the purchase of imported cows, which yield higher quantities of milk than local or locally crossbred varieties. But neither SVITA nor the provincial administration could provide the necessary funding, and attempts by the land reform officer to secure loans from the nationalized Bank for Agriculture and Cooperatives and the Bangkok Bank were unsuccessful.

Project Financing

As luck would have it, it was only a short time afterwards that a prominent woman banker, Chinda Charungcharoenvej, Senior Vice-President for the Bangkok Bank, called Dr. Malee to ask if SVITA would be interested in starting a dairy project. Ms. Charungcharoenvej, it turned out, was handling transactions for the Ministry of Agriculture to import dairy cows. Dr. Malee told her about the Muek-Lek project idea and explained the problems of raising investment capital. Putting their heads together, the two women came up with a financing scheme using the services of Women's World Banking, an international organization committed to improving women's access to credit and financial services through loan guarantees to in-country lending institutions which make loans to women. Ms. Charungcharoenvej had been encouraged to develop a program for delivery of credit for women's enterprises in Thailand, and this seemed like the perfect opportunity to get started.

The two women received a commitment of five million bhat (U.S. $200,000) over a three-year period from Women's World Banking. Of this amount, 1.7 million bhat (U.S. $66,667) was immediately deposited with the Bangkok Bank to provide a 50-percent guarantee of the principal needed to start the project. SVITA joined two other Thai NGOs to form an affiliate, Friends of Women's World Banking in Thailand, which deposited 750,000 bhat (U.S. $30,000) in the Bangkok Bank as the local share (25 percent) of the guarantee funds for credit to women's economic enterprises. As a result of these guarantees, the bank bore risk on only 25 percent of the principal investment.

At first, the Bangkok Bank was very reluctant to get involved in this new and seemingly high-risk area, especially since a previous dairy project it had funded had failed. But the Bank was under pressure to meet its legally stipulated mandate of providing a minimum of 11–13 percent of its total lending portfolio as rural credit. And now the Muek-Lek project had three things going for it: (1) with the loan guarantee, the Bank had substantially reduced its risk; (2) its managers were encouraged by the fact that SVITA would be continuously present to organize, supervise, and monitor the dairy loans and other project activities; and (3) a senior bank staff member would be personally associated with the project. So the Bank conducted its own feasibility study and finally agreed to match the Friends of Women's World Banking in Thailand deposit with an equivalent amount of its own and to make loans to those women recommended by the cooperating NGOs at a rate of two bhat for every one bhat deposited, as guarantee, in the bank.

Project Design

To get the project started, the land reform officer and SVITA organized meetings with the villagers to discuss the operational details of starting the dairy project. From the outset, women were expected to play a major role in the project, although all family members would share in the care and milking of the cows. This was a logical decision since women do not migrate for wage work as men do and the activities involved in dairy farming are carried out close to home. Since women already held primary responsibility for family financial management, SVITA stipulated that the principal borrower be the woman, with the male as cosigner, thus reversing the pattern common in Thailand.

Although in most households in Muek-Lek it is the woman's responsibility to manage household finances, women traditionally have not been members of agricultural cooperatives and thus, not eligible to receive such loans. Under land reform, the Muek-Lek farmers, both male and female, do not hold title to their land; thus, they cannot meet the collateral requirements of the larger commercial or nationalized banks. Even if a woman farmer could meet the loan requirements, however, she would be unlikely to be given credit because of the "head of household" criterion which traditionally means that only men are eligible.

The project designers felt strongly that women should be the loan recipients because they would be providing the majority of the labor to the dairy enterprise. In addition, much empirical evidence exists in Thailand to demonstrate that women have better repayment rates than men.

"Women look after money better than men do," says Niphaporn, who bought six dairy cows with her dairy loan. "Men will go out and drink and forget what the loan was for."

By making them the principle borrowers, the project hoped to extend women's financial management skills to activities outside the household and make them feel primarily responsible for repayment of the loan. It also was hoped that this arrangement would give women greater say in family decisions concerning the dairy project. (For additional information on women's experiences with credit, see the Nicaragua and India case studies in volume 1 of SEEDS; and the Port Sudan case in this volume.

As designed, the project comprised six components, divided into two general categories: (1) credit—dairy loans; and (2) risk management—insurance, training, veterinary services, a feed-mill cooperative, and a mechanism for milk collection.

Credit

Credit is often seen as the principle constraint facing many women's enterprises. While access to financing was critical to this project, it represents only one of many constraints which had to be addressed in order to achieve success. SVITA provided the link between the village working group and the bankers in carrying out negotiations on project financing. When the two groups reached an agreement, the land reform officer informed SVITA of their decisions. SVITA was then asked to arrange for the importation of pregnant dairy cows from New Zealand which had been shown to be adaptable to Thai conditions and to yield twice as much milk as local breeds. According to government regulations, a minimum of 500 cows had to be imported in any one consignment, and each cow cost 25,000 bhat (U.S. $1,000). The Bank, in turn, stipulated that a minimum of four cows was necessary per family in order to ensure adequate earnings to repay the loan.

Many families wanted to participate, and eighty-five in the area applied for loans. Of these, some owned considerably more land and were better off financially than others, but, in the end, the Bangkok Bank approved eighty-two of the loan applications. The project required the land-cattle ratio noted in the chart below. The differing loan amounts also included other start-up costs such as the cost of electrical fencing, construction of barns and water wells, milking machines (for some farmers), cattle insurance, and a mandatory two-month quarantine of the cows at the government dairy promotion organization at Muek-Lek.

A woman holding	Could buy	With a loan of
10-20 rai (2.5-5 Ha)*	4 cows	158,000 bhat ($6,320)
21-30 rai (5-8 Ha)	up to 5 cows	193,000 bhat ($7,720)
31-50 rai (8-12 Ha)	up to 6 cows	229,000 bhat ($9,160)

*Eight rai is the average land holding in the land reform area.

The annual interest rate on the loans was 13 percent, one point lower than the commercial rate. Repayment was scheduled over an eight-year period with a one-year grace period. Subsequent monthly payments of principal plus interest were restricted to no more than 30 percent of each family's monthly income. To receive a loan, each borrower had to open an account at the Bangkok Bank. Realizing that it would be impossible for the women to travel 50 km. to the nearest branch of the bank to make their monthly payments, arrangements were made by SVITA to have the pay-

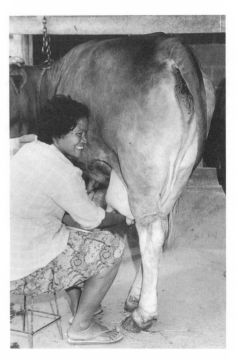

Cows are milked twice daily.
(Kim Retka)

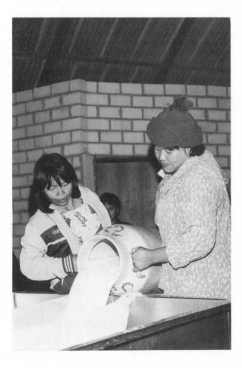

Collecting milk at the processing
plant. *(Kim Retka)*

ments made for them by the Thai/Danish mill-processing plant that would be buying the milk from farmers. The plant keeps a separate account for each farmer, deducting the amount owed the Bank from what is due the farmer for milk purchased at the end of each month.

Risk Management

While dairying offers the opportunity for increased incomes, it carries substantial risks. The success of this project rests on its recognition of the inherent risks and its effective handling of those risks with regard to loan repayment, animal health, women's technical expertise, access to inputs, and access to markets for milk. Had any of these aspects been overlooked, the project might have failed, as had earlier dairy projects in the same province.

Insurance

To protect the investment of the Bangkok Bank and the individual borrowers, Ms. Charungcharoenvej was able to arrange with the Bangkok Insurance Company for cattle insurance that would cover 75 percent of the per-head cost in case of loss. Up until this time, no livestock insurance had been available in Thailand. The insurance premium amounted to 1,100 bhat per head per year. Having the insurance has proved invaluable, especially during the first year of the project when twenty-five cows died of hoof-and-mouth disease resulting from poor livestock management during quarantine. This meant that the affected families could buy another cow.

Training

Training courses in animal husbandry are regularly held by the government-sponsored dairy promotion organization in Muek-Lek. With the assistance of the provincial governor, SVITA persuaded the organization to host a special training course for the farmers participating in the dairy project during a slack agricultural period. One member of each family attended, and 70 percent of the participants were women. All the participants stayed at the training facility for the duration of the course and the provincial administration covered the cost.

Veterinary Services

The provincial veterinary office at Saraburi regularly provides services to farmers free of charge. For the first year of the project, SVITA paid the provincial veterinarians to visit the farms of individual project families on weekends, when they would normally be off work. This enabled the women to learn how to treat many common problems on their own. Now veterinary services are available on demand, within 24 hours of receiving the request, from the provincial office and from the dairy promotion organization.

The one service farmers continue to pay for is artificial insemination, which costs between 150 and 300 bhat (U.S. $6–$12), depending on the breed. While it often requires several attempts before a cow is successfully impregnated, the investment is worthwhile. Farmers can sell a male calf for 200 bhat (U.S. $8) and a female calf for 3,000 bhat (U.S. $120).

The Feed Mill Cooperative

To consistently yield large quantities of milk, the New Zealand cows require enriched feed which was not readily available in Muek-Lek. To produce such feed, the Muek-Lek farmers set up a feed mill with a 200,000-bhat (U.S. $8,000) grant from the provincial government for construction and the purchase of equipment, and a 100,000-bhat (U.S. $4,000) loan from SVITA's Business Development Fund to set up the feedmill operations and for the down payment on a truck.

All the project participants automatically became members of the feedmill cooperative. The farmers elected a committee of ten (made up of members of the original village working group) to oversee general management, quality control, and money collection. From the beginning, the feedmill operations were entirely in the hands of the villagers.

Initially, SVITA provided one of its own staff to help with the accounts. This person was later hired by the feed mill to check the books, first every three months and later at increasing intervals. The cooperative also hired a manager to handle day-to-day operations. During the first year, the cooperative ran into problems: money was being skimmed off and diverted elsewhere. In an effort to revamp, the committee fired the manager and replaced him with a woman who has set the cooperative on a sound footing. The new manager oversees a staff of three: an assistant and two hired hands who grind and mix the feed.

In order to spread the benefits of the dairy project to a wider segment of the local population, the feed mill buys certain feed grains, such as corn, on a preferential basis from local farmers who do not own cattle. Ingredients such as bran and coconut palm powder, which are not produced locally, are purchased nearby.

The dairy farmers buy their feed on credit twice a month. In 1987, after paying back the SVITA loan, the feed mill collected 500 bhat from each member to replenish the revolving loan fund. In its second year of operation, the mill started paying a dividend to its members. Its net profit averages between 10,000 and 15,000 bhat (U.S. $400–600) per year. Thus far, each member family is getting back a dividend of a few hundred bhat each year.

Collecting the Milk

An agreement was made with the Thai/Danish milk processing plant to purchase milk from the Muek-Lek dairy farmers at the standard rate of 6.50 bhat per kilogram. But transporting the milk was a problem for the farmers; some lived 50 km. away from the processing plant and few had access to transportation. Those who owned trucks saw this as an opportunity to make some money and offered to transport the milk at a very high price. Here SVITA, in its role as project advisor, was able to help the farmers weigh the alternatives, including the possibility of using the feedmill truck to transport the milk themselves or taking out a loan to buy a new truck. Seeing that they might end up out of a job, the local truck owners decided to lower their price. Ultimately they were hired by the farmers to transport the milk at a fair price.

Later, SVITA was able to persuade the processing plant to set up a milk collection center in the heart of the Muek-Lek area and to establish twice-daily pickups in their refrigerated trucks. Now the women only have to hire transportation to take their milk to the collection center at a minimal cost of 100 to 300 bhat (U.S. $4–$12) per month, depending on the distance. SVITA also successfully lobbied the Rural Employment Generation Project, a public works scheme, to construct roads linking villages participating in the dairy project with the collection center and the milk-processing plant.

Project Results

> "Dairying provides a steady income that we can depend on," explains Lek. Somchit smiles in agreement. "We are no longer worried about being constantly in debt," she says. As a result of the project, women's workloads have increased by an average of two hours per day. Previously there were seasonal highs and lows, but now the work is spread out more evenly throughout the year. "But working hard is good," says Lek. "We have an increased income and we are proud."

Improved Income

Prior to joining the dairy project, many families in Muek-Lek were unable to escape a yearly cycle of debt. For families that became part of the dairy project, things have changed. The figures below indicate that Muek-Lek dairy farmers have doubled or tripled their farm income over a two- to three-year period.

Activity	Income	Expenses	Net Income
Corn Farming	Bt. 30,720	Bt. 20,224*	Bt. 10,498
	($1229)	($809)	($420)
Dairy Farming	Bt. 95,730	Bt. 58,651**	Bt. 37,079
2nd Year	($3830)	($2346)	($1484)
Dairy Farming	Bt. 122,205	Bt. 73,213**	Bt. 48,992
3rd Year	($4888)	($2928)	($1960)

*Includes cost of seeds, plough and thresher rental
**Includes bank repayment (30% of monthly income), cost of veterinary services, feed, and transportation

In addition, many families continue to grow corn for the local market, even though women's participation in field agriculture has, in many cases, declined as a result of their involvement in dairying. Additional income is sometimes earned by family members who work as casual laborers, both skilled and unskilled. Sawon's husband, for example, occasionally finds work as a carpenter, earning 80 bhat ($3.20) per day; Lamoon makes 100 bhat ($4.00) every day, in addition to her dairy income, by selling home-made noodles in the village market.

How are families spending their extra income? For one thing, they are eating better. The variety of foods consumed has increased and the quality has improved. Instead of eating only preserved fish, for example, families can now afford fresh fish. And instead of eating only two meals a day, they can now eat three. Most families with school-aged children also report spending more on their education. With her extra income, Chin sends her oldest son to school in Bangkok. Similarly, Noo is now able to send both her children to a government school in Saraburi.

Almost all the families in the dairy project have invested in more cattle. In the three years since the project started, the number of dairy cows has doubled. Some families also have used their dairy income to improve their farms, such as planting better-quality grass in fields that otherwise would be left fallow. Many have made improvements on their houses; for example, some have replaced bamboo walls with stronger wooden board and a few have even constructed concrete houses. Finally, several of the women have managed to pay off their entire loan.

Increased Skills

Niphaporn is a confident and articulate young mother of two. Her husband, who suffers from a severe nervous disorder, is confined to bed. Their children, a girl aged four and a boy aged two, live with her mother in Bangkok.

Niphaporn sees them once a month when her mother comes to the village with medicines for her husband. Niphaporn's day starts at 4:00 A.M. when she turns on the electric power generator and rounds up the cows. In the cool season, the animals are washed with warm water prior to milking. In her experience, "If a cow has just given birth, it gives 22 kg. of milk a day; but if it has been eight months or more since it has calved, it gives less than half that amount." By 7:00 A.M. the cows (she now owns 16) have been machine-milked and are back out to pasture. Then, with the help of a hired hand, she cleans out their stalls. During the rainy season, after breakfast, she cuts the enriched grasses which she grows for feed. In the afternoon, the whole milking process is repeated. Today Niphaporn is earning more than 3000 bhat per month, after expenses, from dairying.

Women dairy farmers have expanded their traditional financial management responsibilities to include the family dairy enterprises in which they have a primary entrepreneurial stake. The women are also more involved in day-to-day operations and care of the animals than any other family member. It is usually the women who milk the cows, mix the feed, and call the veterinarian. Most of the women learned these skills through the government training course in animal husbandry. In addition, since the project began, the women have gained confidence in dealing effectively with government officials.

As yet, however, the women dairy farmers do not actively participate in the running of the feedmill cooperative. "As long as it's running all right, the women tend to let it be," says Dr. Malee of SVITA. "For example, they don't ask questions about how the money collected is used. But that may change over time," she adds.

Strengths and Weaknesses of the Muek-Lek Experience

The role of outside catalysts in a project can be both a strength and a weakness. The sophisticated framework for providing credit and minimizing risk which permitted the successful establishment of the Muek-Lek Dairy Project is largely attributable to the crucial roles played by SVITA, the local land reform officer, and the Bangkok Bank. Their involvement was responsible for the sound planning that has characterized every phase of project implementation. The personal contacts and drive of Dr. Malee, Ms. Charungcharoenvej, and Khun Kamthorn were crucial in putting all the pieces together into a workable whole.

However, outside support must be used carefully so as not to undermine people's ability and willingness to learn how to control and manage income-earning activities on their own. Given the risk factors involved in dairying, the project sought to ensure that the financing, training, and technical and marketing aspects of the project would not have to be the direct responsibility of the participants. Rather, the intermediary agencies brought existing services within reach of the women farmers and, as much as possible, integrated project mechanisms into existing institutions so that they became a part of the standard operating procedures of these organizations. For example, loan repayment is directly handled by the processing plant which purchases the milk. This was designed to relieve the individual farmers of this responsibility.

When SVITA withdrew from the project in 1987, the Saraburi provincial administration took over its role as project facilitator. The day-to-day business of dairy farming and feedmill management was in the hands of the farm families. When senior government officials had to be contacted or outsiders tried to interfere with project operations, the farmers were able to call upon the land reform officer for help. While this project approach is not an example of the totally "participatory" approach evident in other case studies, it was successful in linking women with systems that could respond to their needs—credit, technical services, training and marketing—without exposing them to the very real threat of failure. As a result, poor women achieved access to governmental support systems originally designed to serve the needs of large farmers. It has also provided a basis from which women can develop the skills needed to exert greater control over project management, now that they have experienced financial success and are firmly established as dairy farmers.

———————————— Lessons ————————————

The Muek-Lek project is exemplary in that it captured a growing industry early to the benefit of women, before control by large-scale interests had become entrenched. The project placed ownership of significant productive resources, in this case dairy cows, squarely in the hands of women. Overall, it offered poor rural women an unusual opportunity to learn new skills in a highly lucrative, relatively young, and growing sector of the mainstream agricultural economy.

1. **Women can successfully become lead beneficiaries in a new industry when the venture is supported by proper research and planning, and provided with sufficient technical and financial support from the government and the financial community.** Dairying in Thailand is a nontraditional activity for women, as well as men. The decision to make women the primary recipients of loans for the dairy project has ensured their opportunity for leadership in this new field. This is particularly significant because in Thailand, as in most developing countries,

key productive resources such as credit are generally unavailable to poor rural women.

2. **The flexible division of labor between men and women in rural Thailand, and the relatively high level of underemployment common during the slack agricultural seasons, made it possible for the women to take on the added responsibility of dairy farming.** Because family members were willing to shift work burdens and there was seasonal unemployment in the area, it was possible to introduce and carry out project activities. The men's willingness to take up more of the field agricultural activities, as the women became more involved in dairying, made it possible to handle the increase in farming chores.

3. **The minimum land requirement for keeping dairy cattle, 10 rai or 1.6 hectares, could be met by most families within the Muek-Lek land reform area.** This ensured access to the project by the majority of the poorest women. In other parts of the world, many families own or control far less land.

4. **A balance must be struck between potentially high risks and potentially high returns on investment.** Prior to beginning dairy farming, the annual income of approximately 70 percent of Muek-Lek households was 10,000 bhat. The four-cow minimum required by the project meant that participating families must take out a loan of at least 158,000 bhat—an indebtedness fifteen times higher than their pre-project annual income. Fortunately, the success of the project resulted in a three-fold increase in incomes by the third year. Still, the level of indebtedness is a risk which warrants serious attention.

5. **The risks of a high-yield/high-loss venture must be minimized through a systematic effort to build capacity and skills of participants and provide for insurance to compensate for potential losses.** Incorporating appropriate training for farmers, access to veterinary care, and project-controlled access to high-quality feed helped the project reduce the risk incurred through the importation of high-yielding breeds which are generally more susceptible to local diseases. By providing the farmers training in animal husbandry and by ensuring on-going provision of veterinary care, the project was able to avoid significant loss of livestock. It also was able to institute the first insurance coverage for livestock ever to be underwritten in Thailand. In addition, establishment of the feedmill cooperative, which is owned by the farmers, ensures a continuous supply of high-quality feed.

6. Establishing clear linkages to marketing channels was another key element in the success of the project. Prior to implementing the project, market links were firmly established with the milk processing plant, thus ensuring a steady flow of income to participants. Quick and effective response to transportation problems, experienced early in the project, strengthened these linkages and, given the perishable nature of the product, prevented any loss being incurred by the farmers. Many income-generating projects for women in the Third World flounder for lack of an assured market for the products they produce.

The author wishes to thank Dr. Malee Suwana-adth and Khun Chinda Charungcharoenvej for providing valuable information and for freely sharing their comments and insights. Also, the author gratefully acknowledges the assistance of Robert Retka, who served as translator during field interviews.

Appendix

Women in Dairying: The India Experience
Kalima Rose

Unlike the experience in Thailand, dairying is a traditional occupation in rural India, performed largely by women in some 75 million households who daily feed, water, bathe, and milk the family cattle. Dairying also provides wage and in-kind income for poor women who care for the cattle of large dairy producers; and, for landless and marginal families, income derived from the sale of milk helps bridge gaps between seasonal agricultural labor.

In 1969, the National Dairy Development Board (NDDB) of India initiated a massive program called "Operation Flood" designed to expand marketing opportunities for the rural poor while, at the same time, creating a larger source of milk for urban areas through the establishment of village milk cooperatives. Built into the program was an extensive network to transport milk from village to processing centers to market, thus shifting much subsistence milk production to commercial production while, at the same time, ensuring fair rates for producers. The program worked on a model of one to four cows per household and was considered "low-risk," since rural families already owned cattle and knew how to care for them. Yet, while it is women who actually care for the cattle, the program initially targeted men to join the village cooperatives and to occupy all the management positions from local to district to state level. The men, therefore, also collected the payments and managed the co-ops.

Women's entry into the NDDB movement began in 1978 when the Self-

Employed Women's Association (SEWA) of Ahmedabad, in Gujarat State (also home of the NDDB), lobbied the Dairy Board to extend training to village women in the areas of animal husbandry, dairying, and cooperatives. The aim was to enable women to assume decision-making roles in the dairy movement while, at the same time, gaining some control over income earned. As a union of women who work in the informal sector in both rural and urban areas, SEWA was able to link assetless women with the nationalized banks to get loans to buy cattle, while the NDDB developed training materials for illiterate women and helped organize women's cooperatives. Although for the first four years they met resistance from vested interests and from men who were reluctant to allow women to control resources, the women's cooperatives eventually became stabilized, giving women their first economic and decision-making roles in the dairy sector.

In 1983, the Dairy Federation of the state of Andhra Pradesh and The Ford Foundation created a state-wide program targeting formation of women's cooperatives. Women extension staff were trained to organize the all-women co-ops, which now number 225 and include 16,000 women. Beginning in 1986, similar initiatives were begun on a large scale in Bihar, one of India's poorest states, where existing cooperatives had been plagued by corruption. There are now 125 co-ops in the state with 6,000 women members.

By 1990, some 25,000 women had been organized as members of over 500 all-women cooperatives in India. Experience shows that women's cooperatives tend to be more stable than those controlled by men and they produce more milk than men's co-ops under similar conditions.

The most important elements for success of the cooperatives have been well-developed networks for delivery of training and support services. Some cooperatives have tapped the nationalized banks for loans and subsidies under the Integrated Rural Development Programme, while others have had greater success by creating their own revolving loan funds, which are not subject to the delays, security demands, and inflexible payment schedules imposed by banks.

Due to women's previous exclusion not only from business and financial control, but also from access to basic literacy and numeracy skills needed to manage accounts, management by women has been an enormous challenge in rural areas and has required extensive training. Management and administration of women's dairy cooperatives is done completely by women, except in Andhra Pradesh, where 80 percent of the co-op secretaries are men.

In recent years, the NDDB has begun to solicit the active participation of women in the dairy movement and has appointed two women to each of its five-person teams of extension workers. However, NDDB is not promoting formation of all-women's cooperatives but rather participation of women in mixed co-ops. Many women-in-development activists still feel that all-women cooperatives are a better strategy: mixed co-ops currently have only 10 percent women members, and, as women are generally conditioned to defer to men in public, mixed societies are less conducive to women taking control.

Some observers believe that the NDDB may come around to promotion of all-women cooperatives, but whether they do or not, all cooperatives still face the issue of self-sustainability. Outside donors to the state federations continue to support the costs of organizing women's cooperatives and the salaries of women extension workers. Once a cooperative is established and registered (two to three years), it becomes self-supporting, but women extension workers still continue to provide valuable support. However, even if the state programs were not to continue covering the cost of female extension workers in the future, the existing co-ops should be able to continue on their own.

While the examples noted above are all progressive steps that have been taken, more still needs to be done to acknowledge and promote women's roles in the Indian dairy industry.

5

Wasteland Development and the Empowerment of Women: The SARTHI Experience

Madhu Sarin

For large segments of India's rural population, rain-fed subsistence farming on small landholdings continues to be their economic mainstay. However, even in years of good rainfall, agricultural production does not meet all the needs of the household, since most families have little or no access to cash income. Agricultural production, therefore, has to be supplemented by collecting vegetative produce (referred to hereafter as "biomass"), such as firewood, fodder, small timber, and medicinal roots and plants, from the surrounding natural environment.

Under the traditional gender division of labor, the gathering of biomass is generally women's work. Women thus have a much greater stake in the distribution and management of local natural resources, as they suffer the most from land degradation and deforestation. However, simply involving women in raising and planting trees, shrubs, and grasses is not an adequate response, because the broader spectrum of gender relations denies women any ownership or control over land resources or the produce from the land. Unless development projects empower *women to gain greater control over the use and management of local resources, women are unlikely to benefit from land rehabilitation efforts in any lasting way.*

This chapter describes an innovative approach to rehabilitation of wastelands developed by SARTHI (Social Action for Rural and Tribal Inhabitants of India), a nongovernmental organization based in the Panchmahals District of Gujarat State in Western India. By assisting rural women to organize themselves around the rehabilitation of patches of degraded common land, SARTHI has been able not only to help them meet their needs for biomass in a more efficient and ecolog-

110

ically sound manner, but also to empower them to start asserting themselves in dealing with a broader range of problems.

———

India's Wastelands

Of India's roughly 300 million hectares of land, some 40 million hectares are not arable. Of the remaining 260 million hectares, about two-thirds are privately owned. The other third consists of what is referred to as "common" land and is under the control of government departments or local institutions. Between 30 and 50 percent of both the private and common land is estimated to be ecologically degraded to varying degrees. In India, this land is generally referred to as "wasteland"; that is, land that is not producing its potential of biomass due to ecological degradation, over-exploitation, or the absence of a clear management system.

It is primarily on nonprivate or "common" wastelands that the resource-poor rural population of India depends for gathering biomass. Because of growing concern over the rapid degradation of the country's land resources, the government has initiated a large program for wasteland development.

The Panchmahals District

The forests of the Panchmahals have been famous throughout Indian history. It was here that the Sultans of Ahmedabad and the Mughal emperors came on elephant hunting expeditions. Unfortunately, little of this forest land has survived under the combined pressures of illicit cutting of timber and commercial exploitation both by the princely rulers and, following independence, by the state government. Clearance for agriculture and uncontrolled grazing of domestic animals have also depleted forest land. Excessive grazing is particularly harmful as it destroys natural regeneration. Furthermore, each drought year brings a fresh onslaught as a desperate local population searches for fodder, firewood, and a source of income due to the failure of local rain-fed agriculture.

The most recent droughts occurred from 1985 to 1987, bringing acute misery to people in the region. Besides total crop failures, there was a scarcity of fodder needed to feed livestock, resulting in a heavy loss of cattle. In an area where seasonal migration for wage work is already common (as rain-fed agriculture yields only one crop per year), even larger numbers of people were forced to migrate to other areas in search of work.

Panchmahals is one of the most industrially backward districts in the

Indian state of Gujarat, with 89 percent of workers still engaged in agriculture and allied activities, most making a living as small and marginal farmers. Ninety percent of the district's cultivated land is rain-fed, which leaves the area vulnerable to crop failures. Compared to Gujarat as a whole, Panchmahals has a higher population density, a far lower literacy rate (particularly among women), less urbanization, and a much higher population of *Adivasis* or tribal people.

Adivasis *are considered to be the indigenous inhabitants of India and nationally constitute about 7 percent of the population. In Santrampur Taluka (an administrative subunit of Panchmahals District), where SARTHI is working, 66 percent of the population is Adivasi, as compared to only 14 percent for the state of Gujarat as a whole.*

The Adivasis are essentially forest dwellers living primarily in the forest belt of central and eastern India. Among them there are a large number of different tribes, each with its distinct culture, identity, and language. Although they live in areas rich in natural resources, "development" has generally passed them by.

The British introduced several measures to protect the cultural identity and economic interests of the Adivasis, and, following independence, the government of India similarly used various legislative and administrative measures to protect their interests. A "schedule" or list of recognized tribes entitles those belonging to any of the "scheduled tribes" to a range of benefits and facilities, including reservation of a certain percentage of government jobs and seats in institutions of higher education, special loan and subsidy programs, and so on. In areas where over 50 percent of the population belongs to scheduled tribes, special tribal area development plans are being implemented. Legislation prevents the purchase of an Adivasi's land by non-Adivasis.

Despite all these measures, however, the marginalization of these Adivasi tribes has increased rather than decreased. Large development projects, such as dams and power and steel plants, have displaced more Adivasis from their traditional habitats than other segments of the population. Destruction of forests through commercial exploitation and other development projects have largely destroyed the Adivasi's traditional economy—which is based on gathering and hunting in the forests—without providing them with secure, alternative livelihoods.

Wasteland Management

Throughout India, a significant proportion of land is under the control of the government. For example, approximately 22 percent of the entire country's common land is controlled by state forest departments. In the area of Panchmahals where SARTHI is working, the state forest department controls 16 percent and the state revenue department another 9 percent. This land is referred to as "revenue wasteland." In addition, roughly 4 percent of the country's total land is controlled by village *panchayats* (the smallest unit of local government, covering one or more villages). This land is meant to be used primarily for common grazing. Of approximately 50,000 hectares of grazing land available in the district, at least 10,000 hectares have been encroached upon by private individuals. The rest of the land is in a degraded and unproductive state due to the absence of any regulatory or management system.

As landholdings in the area are very small, people have always relied on supplementing agricultural production by collecting biomass from the surrounding common lands to meet many of their subsistence needs. The decline in the amount of common land available, along with the continuing degradation of what remains, has made this a difficult task. As collecting subsistence biomass is traditionally women's work, the resulting hardship has fallen on women's shoulders.

Women's Status and Their Relationship with Natural Resources

The status of women in Panchmahals, as in many parts of India, is low, while their workload is heavy. In addition to performing housework, many women work as laborers for daily wages either in the fields of large landholders or on public works projects. Women of landowning families also perform substantial agricultural tasks. While men do the plowing and marketing of produce, women shoulder major responsibilities for hoeing, weeding, irrigating, harvesting, and processing. In addition, "women's work" includes collecting cooking fuel, fetching water, and caring for livestock. This binds them to the natural resource base much more than men. It is women who have to pay the price for environmental degradation by having to walk longer distances in their daily search for fuel, fodder, and water. As several women of the area have noted, "Men just expect to be served cooked food. They aren't bothered about where the firewood comes from. That is *our* problem!"

Due to the declining forest cover, the forest department has started enforcing restrictions on the collection of nontimber forest produce by local villagers. For instance, collecting green wood as firewood is forbidden. However, as adequate quantities of the permitted dead and dry fallen wood are no longer available, women are forced to cut green branches. If forest guards catch women cutting or carrying green wood, they either snatch the women's sickles and axes, confiscate their headload of wood, extract a bribe, or physically or orally abuse them. As forest guards are all men, the fear which most haunts the women is that of physical molestation or abuse.

Desertion, domestic violence, and alcoholism (despite prohibition in Gujarat) among men, as well as husbands taking second wives to beget sons, are common problems faced by women in the area. On top of that, during drought years women often have to shoulder the burden of all the agricultural work if men migrate in search of wage employment. Some women also have to migrate with men to look for work in more prosperous areas.

Further, as is true elsewhere in India, women in Panchmahals own little land or property. Decision-making concerning land use is, therefore, almost always the exclusive preserve of men. This makes rehabilitation of degraded lands by women a particularly difficult task.

Evolution of SARTHI's Women's Program

SARTHI started working in the Santrampur area twelve years ago as a branch of the Social Work and Research Centre (SWRC), an NGO based at Tilonia in the state of Rajasthan. About six years ago, it became an independent entity and adopted its current name. SARTHI's mandate is to promote integrated rural development in underdeveloped areas by improving the quality of support provided by local NGOs. Its initial work consisted of conventional development projects such as installing hand pumps, deepening wells, and starting income-generating programs. Experience over the years has caused SARTHI to shift its focus to leadership development and promotion of organized action by groups of underprivileged sectors of the community, particularly women.

SARTHI's women's program evolved through initiatives undertaken with three cadres of female village workers: cook stove builders (*chula mistris*), women health workers, and paravets (veterinary technicians).

When SARTHI began an improved cook stove program in 1983, it was the first time the organization had worked exclusively with women. Selected village women were trained as stove builders to erect improved stoves in and near their villages. By 1987, a village-based cadre of thirty stove builders and four supervisors had been developed. The four supervisors became SARTHI's first full-time local female staff. As each stove builder was in touch with at least thirty to fifty other women, SARTHI found itself in contact with a large network of local women. Through regular monthly meetings of the stove builders and their supervisors, the organization developed a better understanding of the problems faced by women in the area.

Women's groups first developed around the installation of improved cook stoves. *(Madhu Sarin)*

In July 1988, SARTHI conducted a training program for *dais* (midwives, both traditional and new) in response to women's demand for access to improved health services. These Women Health Workers (WHWs) became the second cadre of trained village women. The WHWs' role is to monitor women's health problems in their villages and assist those they cannot help to get aid from government services in their area.

In May 1990, again in response to a need articulated by local women, ten village women were trained to work as paravets. This meant that yet another cadre of skilled local women was created. Within a span of barely two months after their training, the women paravets had managed to get almost 3,000 cattle vaccinated against foot-and-mouth disease.

Each of these programs provided opportunities to bring women together in a forum outside the traditional family and allowed SARTHI to learn firsthand about women's problems and concerns. These programs also clearly demonstrated the women's capacity to organize and bring about change.

Taking It One Step at a Time

With the third successive monsoon failure in 1987, the hardship of the local people became acute. Agonizing tales of cattle dying, women's unending search for fuel, fodder, food, and water, and outbreaks of various illnesses and diseases started pouring in. For the first time, SARTHI began to give serious thought to developing a more holistic approach to meeting women's needs.

In April 1987, a group of village women and SARTHI female staff were sent to PEDO,[1] a sister NGO in Rajasthan, to attend a large women's *mela* (literally a fair, but the word can refer to any large gathering of people for a specific purpose). The objective of the *mela* was to provide local women with an opportunity to discuss and share their problems and learn from the struggles of their sisters from other areas.

The women came back enthusiastic and excited about the possibilities of organized action. As a follow-up, in November 1987, the four women supervisors attended a training program for women staff at PEDO. Besides sharing their experiences as women, the participants discussed the possibilities of women taking collective action to solve some of their problems. For the first time, the women participated in an analysis of the environmental crisis—its causes and what women could do to reverse the trend.

The objective was to get the women to reflect on and examine the nature of environmental changes that had taken place in their area in recent years, including the causes of these changes and their impact on their daily lives. This proved to be an eye-opening exercise. The women had never looked at the totality of the problem in such a way before. For the first time, they consciously understood the significance of the trees and forests to their survival. Whether it was a decrease in soil productivity; reduced and uncertain rainfall; declining water tables; drying up of perennial water sources; scarcity of fuel, fodder, and nutritious foods; or increased health problems, they could trace the causes of all of these problems back to the destruction of the forests.

Afterward, small groups of women carried out a planning exercise. They were asked to estimate the number of trees and shrubs that each member of the group required to meet her subsistence needs for firewood, fodder, construction material, and so on, and to list the local tree species suitable to meet each need. The process generated tremendous interest and excitement among the women, as it provided them with a concrete basis for discussing action strategies with other women.

For example, the women calculated that if cows or buffalos had to be supported entirely on tree leaf fodder, ninety large trees would be required to feed one animal each year. For a goat or sheep, fifty trees would be needed. A list of twenty-one local species suitable for fodder was generated. Similar calculations were made for the timber required to build a two-room house. The estimate was five to six large trees or 150 smaller ones. In addition, they estimated that 100 bamboo stalks would be needed to support a tiled roof and 200 to 300 kilograms (about 440 to 660 pounds) of wood would be needed for baking the tiles. The women were quite amazed at the number of trees needed to meet even their most basic needs.

Up until then, SARTHI did not have a specific program for involving women in wasteland development, but after the experience at PEDO, the women staff started discussing natural resource management issues with village women during their field visits. These experiences were then further reinforced by a ten-day training program on environmental reconstruction held at PEDO in January 1988. Eight SARTHI staff members (four of them women) participated. This event represented a qualitative shift in SARTHI's method of formulating program priorities. Instead of imposing their own predefined objectives, for the first time the staff members attempted to respond to women's priorities as articulated by women themselves.

The development of the women's wasteland groups has to be seen against the above background. At least some members of the stronger groups have participated in one or more of the camps, training sessions, or visits organized by SARTHI. These experiences have been instrumental in helping women overcome their shyness or reservations about getting involved.

SARTHI's Initial Work on Private Wastelands

SARTHI's initial attempts to rehabilitate degraded lands began during the drought years of 1985 to 1987. Large numbers of cattle were dying due to the scarcity of fodder, and the remaining forests were being chopped down for firewood to earn income necessary for survival. Generating short-term wage employment by motivating landowners to plant fuel and fodder trees, therefore, seemed an appropriate intervention, as the immediate need for wages could be combined with a longer-term goal of increasing the productivity of degraded private lands.

With this objective in mind, SARTHI asked its field staff to identify interested small and marginal farmers who owned wastelands in their respective areas. There was no specific focus on involving women, although the female staff were asked to encourage women's participation. At this point, no local groups of either men or women had been formed and SARTHI staff were expected to rely on their contacts with local villagers that had been established through the organization's other ongoing projects.

After the planting season, review workshops were held with the staff in August and November 1988. They indicated that several sociopolitical problems had been encountered while implementing the new program. These included:

Two of SARTHI's women staff members explain the problems of a wastelands plantation to their colleagues. *(Madhu Sarin)*

- Although landowners agreed to participate in the program, when earthwork started, many of them preferred to work on government drought relief programs instead of on their own lands. This was because SARTHI paid lower wages than the government programs and also because SARTHI insisted that the work be done according to specifications. As a consequence, SARTHI's field staff had to hire outside labor to work the landowners' land!
- Initially the landowners had specified a wide range of species they wanted to plant, but at the actual time of planting most demanded only eucalyptus, even though it is believed to deplete the soil and subsoil water. One man even threatened to sue SARTHI for damaging his land unless eucalyptus was planted. (Eucalyptus is a fast-growing tree used extensively in India for construction and for making paper. Until recently, it provided a good cash return, although prices have since crashed due to overproduction.)
- Many landowners were hostile to the project due to a rumor that SARTHI would eventually take away both the land and the trees.
- Once the planting season was over, few landowners took an interest in protecting the plantings or completing the boundary trenches.

It was clear that these landowners did not share SARTHI's interest in helping them develop their wastelands as a long-term asset. They seemed to equate this work with other government drought relief projects whose only interest is in earning wages.

It was during these review workshops that staff learned of the work on four hectares of common land by one women's group in Muvasa, a village located about 10 kilometers from SARTHI's headquarters. This wasteland project had been started by SARTHI staff shortly after their return from the PEDO training program. Although some conflict with residents of an adjoining village who used to graze their cattle on that land was mentioned, the staff members faced fewer of the type of problems experienced with the landowners.

The Shift to Working with Women's Groups

It was the response of the Muvasa women's plantation group to a crisis in February 1989 that ended SARTHI's ambivalence about working with groups to develop common lands. Indeed, from that time on, all the field staff started organizing women's wasteland groups.

The incident that inspired this change was the following. The Muvasa group had harvested its first crop of grass from its four-hectare plantation using voluntary labor. As the group had not yet decided what to do with the grass, it had all been left on the plantation itself.

One evening, while passing by, three drunken men from the adjoining village threw an unextinguished cigarette stub on the grass. All the grass went up in flames and the fire damaged many of the young plants carefully nurtured by the women.

Initially, the mishap sent a wave of despondency among the women's group and SARTHI. The plantation was the best out of the previous year's effort. But the women quickly gathered their wits and called a meeting to discuss what to do. Were they going to permit the three men to get away with such an act of irresponsibility? Did their labor have no value? If they did not punish the men, their future efforts could be similarly nullified. The group members and SARTHI staff discussed the incident with village leaders and a cross-section of the population. They found that the majority were in favor of the culprits being punished. The women decided to demand compensation from the three men. The value of the damage was discussed, and it was decided that the men should be made to pay 1,400 rupees (U.S. $78 at the 1989 rate of exchange).

The men were summoned and told the group's verdict. Seeing the group's firmness and sensing that the sympathy of the entire village was behind them, the men paid the Rs. 1,400.

When the Muvasa field center staff narrated this incident during SARTHI's monthly staff meeting, the rest of the staff felt envious and

Wasteland Development and the Empowerment of Women _____ 119 inspired. The response of the women's group was worlds apart from the bickering, irresponsibility, and manipulations of the private landowners. From then on, all the field staff strove to replicate the Muvasa group in their own areas.

Formation of the Muvasa Women's Group

It is useful to look at the process involved in the formation of the first group in Muvasa in order to understand the dynamics in operation in this and subsequent women's groups.

In early 1988, SARTHI had initiated private wasteland development with a few landowners in Muvasa. As many of these landowners did not work on their own land, SARTHI had to hire other laborers for this task. Most of these laborers were Adivasi women from the most disadvantaged families in the village. (In India, it is very common for tribal women to work as manual laborers.)

As they went about their work, the women talked about their own hardships. They regretted their inability to participate in the program because their own landholdings were too small. Champa Ben and Vikram Bhai, SARTHI's field staff in Muvasa, took a lead from this and started exploring the possibility of the women's developing a piece of common land as a group. The women showed immense interest, and SARTHI was willing to pay for the land preparation and planting work. (Most Indian villages have at least some common grazing land to which all households have access. The management of this land is the responsibility of the panchayat. Many villages also have some revenue wastelands, i.e., land belonging to the revenue department, falling within the physical boundary of their panchayat. This is also effectively perceived of as common land, even though the revenue department has the power to transfer it to individuals or groups.)

Impromptu meetings on the work sites resulted in some ground rules being worked out for the group. All those who became members would have to perform land preparation and planting work themselves. The group would accept collective responsibility for protecting the plantation. Each member would have a right to an equal share of the produce. All decisions related to the plantation would have to be made collectively. Only women would be eligible for group membership, as it is they who suffer most from fuel and fodder scarcity. All interested women in the village, including higher caste (*Patel*) women, would be invited to join. However, as the economically better off Patels do not allow their women to go out to work and because Patel women already have too much work to do on their families' larger landholdings, their membership was in effect ruled out.

With the group beginning to come together, the panchayat was ap-

Women working together to solve one of their major problems created, for the first time, a legitimate space—outside the family—for women to get together. *(Madhu Sarin)*

proached. The panchayat gave a "no objection certificate," allowing the women to plant four hectares of common land, with a commitment to renew the lease after ten years, and making no claim to any share of the produce from the land.

Some of the more active women then went from house to house asking other non-Patel women whether they were interested in joining the group. A total of twenty-nine women became members. They were all from the poorest families in the village, with some owning less than one acre of land. They were of different ages and all were married.

Dealing with Men's Suspicions

Even before the group started its work on the land, village men started questioning why the organization was working only with women. The husbands of some members felt that housework was suffering and that the time spent in meetings was wasted. At the family level, each woman had to use a combination of assertiveness and diplomacy. The women started getting up earlier to finish their housework before going to work on the land or to attend meetings.

SARTHI's staff dealt with the men's suspicions by calling a meeting of the whole village to explain why they were working with a women's group.

Women's increasing hardship due to scarcity of fuel and fodder and their having a greater stake in dealing with the problem were discussed. Although this and other discussions helped reduce suspicions, many men continued spreading rumors that SARTHI would abduct the women, take away their jewelry, etc. Some men would stealthily listen in on the group's discussions.

Slowly, however, as the group worked steadily and the women's self-confidence increased, the rumors and suspicions died down. SARTHI also helped by securing the participation of some local men in its other projects so that the men got better acquainted with the organization.

Appropriating a Legitimate Social Space for Women

Obtaining social consent for the women to organize themselves to deal with one of their major problems created, for the first time, a legitimate space for women to get together regularly. For the first time, too, a group of village women obtained the right to manage a small part of village common land resources in accordance with *their* needs and priorities. Although none of the women individually owns any part of the land, they have gained acceptance of their right to manage it collectively. This in itself is a major breakthrough.

SARTHI's staff took care to ensure that representatives from each group participated in all negotiations with the male-dominated panchayat and the revenue official (who maintains a record of land rights) to obtain the necessary documents for getting the land leased to the group. In the process, for the first time, the women got firsthand experience dealing with land-related matters. They began to see that their belief that only men have the competence to deal with such matters is a myth.

SARTHI's staff also ensured that the women themselves made all management decisions related to the plantation, to suit *their* situations and circumstances. For example, instead of the women being asked to work fixed hours, a system of flexible work hours was established. An account of the work done by each member was kept by the group, and payment was made on the basis of output. This enabled the women to combine wage work on their plantation with their household work. Slowly, the women gained self-confidence so that now they are able to demand that their husbands also help with household chores while they go to work, attend meetings, or participate in training camps.

Overview of SARTHI's Experience with Women's Groups

At present, SARTHI is working with about seventeen women's wasteland groups, spread across all five of its field centers. In all cases, the land is

either *panchayat gauchor* (community grazing) land or revenue wasteland. Initiation of women's groups in other villages has taken different
routes than in Muvasa. In some cases, SARTHI's field staff have first
scouted around to find the necessary wasteland and have then tried to
motivate local women to develop it as a group. In other cases, seeing the
work of the Muvasa group, some male village leaders have approached
SARTHI asking for a similar women's group to be formed in their village,
offering the necessary wasteland.

As may be expected, the experiences of the individual groups have varied. While some are developing well, others are still weak, and some have
fallen apart during the early stages of their formation. A complex range of
factors influences each group's development. These include:

• Power dynamics within the village and competing interests for use of
  common land;
• Women's status and the extent of their exposure to the outside world;
• Men's attitude towards women taking such initiatives;
• The skill, experience, and leadership qualities of the field staff, particu-
  larly the women staff; and
• The extent of firewood and fodder scarcity in the area.

The most effective strategy for strengthening weaker groups has proved to
be facilitating interaction between them and older, stronger groups.

Sharing Experiences with Other Groups

Each of the stronger groups has had to deal with a range of problems, but
their determination and assertive methods for handling these obstacles
have helped them consolidate and build group credibility. The need to take
such action in the early stages of group formation has, in effect, minimized
subsequent problems for these groups.

In addition to taking members of newly formed groups to visit older
groups, SARTHI recently organized a two-day workshop in which representatives of several groups shared their experiences and problems. One of
the major difficulties faced by many of the new groups is the attempt by
manipulative village leaders to use the women to further their own interests. This was clearly the experience reported by the Paderi group during
the recent workshop.

The Paderi women's group was formed in 1990, and SARTHI helped it
plant a variety of species on a piece of degraded wasteland. In the beginning,
the group seemed to be working well and appeared united. During group
meetings, village men maintained a safe distance from the venue of the
meeting lest the women ask the men to serve water to the women, reversing

the traditional roles! However, over time, group unity began to break down, and the plantation was no longer being protected from grazing animals.

The four members of the group attending the workshop claimed that one drunken man had refused to respect the boundaries of the plantation and had threatened violence against anyone attempting to stop him. The women had come to the workshop to demand, on behalf of the group, that SARTHI pay for a full-time watchman to protect their plantation. Despite being told that, as a matter of principle, SARTHI does not pay for watchmen—because protection can effectively be done only by the groups themselves—the women remained adamant about their demand.

Informal discussions with the local field staff subsequently revealed that the husbands of two of the group members were currently running for election as the village *sarpanch* (head of the elected panchayat). Both were trying to use their wives to extract a benefit from SARTHI that would strengthen their own position within the village. The women had fallen prey to this manipulation, with the result that the group had split into two opposing factions.

Representatives of other groups present were asked whether they had faced similar problems and how they would deal with the situation the Paderi group was facing.

Karsan Ben of the Wankdi group said that some months ago, four or five goats belonging to their village *sarpanch* were caught grazing inside the group's plantation. Eighteen women got together, caught the animals immediately, and had them locked up in the cattle pond (yard) maintained by the *panchayat*. Interestingly, this area is looked after by the *sarpanch* himself. He was not allowed to release his own goats until he had paid a fine of Rs.700 to the group! With not even the *sarpanch* having been spared by the women, others got the message loud and clear. There were no further incidents of grazing in their plantation.

Earlier, when the Wankdi group had begun planting on its land, the members had decided to allow male family members to work on the plantation. However, the men's performance proved unsatisfactory. For example, it was found that while carrying plants uphill from the nursery, the men had been dropping some on the way to reduce their load. This resulted in fewer plants being planted than were taken from the nursery. The group therefore forbade the men, including members' husbands, from working on their plantation in the future!

Similarly, the group has learned to be firm about not permitting any men to sit in and listen while they are having their meetings. As women in the area practice *purdah* (covering their heads and faces) in the presence of older male relatives, they cannot talk openly in front of men and this defeats the purpose of the women meeting separately. The extent to which the women have succeeded in making group meetings a "women-only" space is evident from a remark overheard from some village men. They were telling each other to stay away from the women's meeting lest the women start demanding the right to attend exclusive men's meetings!

During the workshop, Kapuri Ben of the Wandariya group narrated her group's experience in the early days. After completing work on their land, the women had planted *lpomea* (a nonbrowsable shrub) as live fencing all around it. One man living near the plantation uprooted the lpomea fencing because he wanted to continue grazing his cattle on the land. With SARTHI's help, the group registered a complaint with the police and the man had to pay a hefty fine. He never tried letting his cattle into the plantation again. However, to compensate him for the loss of the grazing facility and to avoid alienating him from supporting their objectives, the group engaged him as their watchman.

Kapuri Ben asserted that there was no problem with any men trying to beat any of their group's members physically. If anyone tried any such thing, the women would beat the men back!

Nani Ben of the Muvasa group said that if the Paderi group were united, no drunkard would dare threaten group members or graze his cattle on their plantation. She narrated a recent situation faced by her group. As the group's plantation is located some distance from where the women live, one man living near the land had been letting his cattle into their plantation at night. He was even cutting their grass on the sly. The women decided to catch the man red-handed.

One day, fifteen group members hid themselves inside the plantation. When the man sneaked in with his cattle, all the women jumped up and confronted him. The man started verbally abusing the women, saying that they could not stop him. At this point, Kanta Ben, one of the group members, grabbed him by the neck of his shirt and demanded that he apologize for being abusive. Frightened out of his wits, the man repented. Since then, he has never interfered with the plantation.

Members of the Gara group asked what was the use of forming a group if so many women were still going to allow one drunkard to intimidate them. The only solution lay in collective action.

The Paderi women got the clear message that the solution to their problem did not lie in pestering SARTHI to pay for a watchman to protect their plantation. They promised to go back and try to pull their group together so that they could protect their plantation themselves.

Returns from the Groups' Plantations

The older groups have started getting some returns in the form of biomass (fodder grass, seeds, some legumes, and small amounts of firewood) from their plantations and are in the process of refining their harvesting and distribution systems. The Muvasa group has harvested grass three times. The first crop got burned, but during the second year, the women took half the grass they cut for their own use and sold the other half. During the third year, the women divided up the crop equally among themselves to feed their cattle.

The Wandariya and Wandki groups have not been able to harvest much grass yet, as their land is rather stony. However, the Wandariya group has already produced some tree leaf fodder and firewood from their efforts at regenerating existing trees by cutting the multiple shoots from existing root stock to allow only one healthy shoot to grow. The cuttings are used as firewood.

The Gara group is planning to allow its members to cut green grass this year, as it is a more nutritious fodder. Each member will be asked to pay a small amount for the grass in order to build up the group's common fund.

By planting seeds of an improved fodder grass variety, the poor-quality local grass is slowly being replaced by a much more nutritious grass on all the plantations. The groups have also started collecting grass seeds to supply to SARTHI for use in new plantations.

Additional Benefits

Besides providing a source of biomass under the women's own control, participation in group activities is leading to other improvements in the women's lives. For example, follow-up visits by WHWs revealed acute nutritional deficiencies (particularly of vitamin A, which leads to night blindness in children and pregnant women) among villagers. Discussions about dietary patterns and nutritional beliefs and practices revealed that the limited variety of foods being eaten resulted in insufficient consumption of healthy foods such as milk, milk products, leafy vegetables, fruits, and, to some extent, legumes. Milk products and fruits are not readily available in the area, and, during the dry summer months, neither are green leafy vegetables. Even when such foods are available, women often lack the time to prepare them, due to their excessive work burdens.

These discussions, in turn, led to the integration of nutritionally important trees in SARTHI's wasteland program, including *aonla* (phyllanthus emblica), a local species whose fruit is one of the richest known natural sources of vitamin C, and *sengwa* (moringa oleifera), the leaves of which are rich in vitamins A and C. (These leaves can be lightly cooked and served as spinach during the summer months when no other leafy vegetables are available.)

During 1989, a resource team began collecting folk knowledge about local trees and shrubs to aid in the selection of species for the wasteland program. It became evident from the *dais* that there was a rich local tradition of using medicinal herbs and plants for women's health problems. Since the local forests yield many medicinal herbs and plants, integration of species of medicinal value became a new facet of the wasteland program.

As a result of the women's wasteland groups, between 1989 and 1990 women of different villages formed about twenty women's savings groups. These groups emerged out of the strongly felt need of the women to create their own source of credit for emergency loans, thus removing the need to rely upon exploitative local money lenders.

Intergroup meetings have become the forum for all three cadres of SARTHI's trained women field staff to interact with village women and to increase their awareness and knowledge about various problems. In addition, several awareness-generating and leadership development camps[2] have been organized for selected village women at SARTHI's headquarters, and camps on clean drinking water and the environment have been held in several villages. Many women have been sent to *melas,* workshops, and camps organized by other organizations on themes relevant to women's lives. Visits between members of different local groups have also been organized.

Each opportunity for a village woman to step outside the village and interact with large numbers of other women is in itself a very empowering experience. Traditionally, women have few opportunities to interact with women outside their family and community networks. Even within the community, the only times women get together are for events such as marriage, death, or religious ceremonies, where they are expected to perform their traditional roles. Through the SARTHI program, women are able to share experiences with women from diverse castes and communities. Besides acquiring new knowledge, they are able to shed some of their traditional *sharam,*[3] shyness, and inhibitions.

Today, SARTHI's women's activities are becoming the organization's major program. Due to women's positive response to each awareness-raising effort, SARTHI has essentially switched from individual beneficiary-oriented projects to programs geared toward organizing and mobilizing women and youth, as well as men. Because the internal hierarchy of families and communities can severely restrict empowerment, most frequently by gender or age, use of the group dynamic can be an effective means to break down such barriers to participation by women and other nondominant groups.

Members of the Wandariya group in front of their plantation. *(Madhu Sarin)*

Future Directions

Although all the groups will soon start harvesting some biomass from their plantations, a major problem they face is that, in most cases, their plantation areas are too small to meet all their needs, and additional village common lands are simply not available nearby. If the women's groups were to try to enclose more of the limited amount of available grazing land, they would face the danger of getting into conflict with families dependent on use of those lands to graze their cattle.

However, having entered the field of natural resource management, the women are now looking at how other public lands in the area are managed. The largest category of public land with tremendous potential for increased productivity is forest land now held by the state forest department. Fortunately, the Gujarat forest department realizes that it cannot improve management of its forest lands without the cooperation of villagers living in the vicinity. The department is, therefore, in the process of introducing a joint approach to management of forest land, and SARTHI has begun exploring the possibility of the women's groups participating in this program.

The task of legally securing the women's groups' tenurial rights to the common lands remains to be completed. All the groups have obtained "no objection certificates" (NOCs) and supportive resolutions from their panchayats to work the land and enjoy its produce for a number of years. But the legal validity of these NOCs and resolutions remains ambiguous. One concern is whether a newly elected panchayat can overrule or withdraw an NOC given by the previous government.

Such legal ambiguities can be compensated for to a considerable extent by the empowerment of the women; the newly elected panchayat would not have the courage to withdraw the land for fear of the repercussions. However, this can only be done by broadening the base of support for the women's groups among different sections of the community and by strengthening the women's political voice within local institutions. Most of the groups have achieved remarkable success thus far in demanding supportive action from panchayat members during every crisis or conflict, on the grounds that it is the panchayat's responsibility to see that the terms of their NOCs are honored.

The potential of recurring conflicts over scarce common land resources from competing interest groups will remain high. The women's resolve to assert their rights will be put to the test repeatedly over time. For example, the Muvasa group is now having to fight yet another major battle. Apparently six families from an adjoining village recently chopped down and stole most of the trees from their plantation. The group registered a complaint with the police and demanded action from the panchayats of both villages against the culprits. For the first time, the panchayats of two villages have been involved, resulting in inter-village tensions. SARTHI helped the women organize a rally that took the group's case to adjoining villages to broaden their base of support. However, information about the final outcome of the Muvasa group's latest struggle is not yet available. But given the determination they have displayed thus far, they are sure to fight on—and a long fight it is sure to be!

————————————— Lessons —————————————

As primary gatherers and users of biomass, women are in the best position to implement wasteland development activities, as they possess both the knowledge and the motivation to carry out such programs successfully. However, as women in a male-dominated society, they require assistance in overcoming a range of obstacles that have traditionally hindered them from working together, taking action, and asserting their influence within the community. SARTHI's experience of organizing women around the development of wastelands yields important lessons in terms of both the management of natural resources and the empowerment of women.

1. Bringing women together in groups provides them with the power they need to break the confines of the family and community norms.

Women's collective needs cannot be met unless the gender division of labor at home and in the wider society is challenged. Women's participation in the wasteland groups has allowed them to challenge the hierarchy of the family, as evidenced by some husbands taking on household chores to enable their wives to attend group meetings or to participate in training camps. Women's new self-esteem is also visible as wives begin to drop some of their traditional subservience to husbands on the strength of having to honor decisions taken by their group. Finally, individual group members have been able to bring an end to physical abuse and violence in their homes due to the support of their group.

2. **Among the strengths of the women's wasteland groups are the standards of democratic participation and fairness with which they operate.** Decisions about hours, output, and quality of work are all made democratically, and all participants share equitably in both the labor and the resulting product. This model contrasts markedly with patterns found in male-dominated social, political, and governmental institutions that increasingly serve the needs of special interests, as was exemplified by the behavior of the private landowners with whom SARTHI originally worked.

3. **By defining conditions of eligibility to join the first women's wasteland group at the outset, the Muvasa group created realistic expectations about members' rights and responsibilities.** As an explicit condition of participation, all members had to work on the land themselves in order to be entitled to an equal share of the produce. This strategy naturally excluded higher-caste women from membership based on their work status rather than because they were not asked. At the same time, the process ensured that there would be coherence among the group in that all the members shared a similar background.

4. **Trained field staff are needed to facilitate creation of a women's space within the community.** This is a minimum condition necessary to organize women, particularly where there are no traditional opportunities for them to get together outside the confines of the family. Lack of public and social space for women is an obstacle to their asserting their rights. When such a space is created, it provides women with a new resource and implicit acknowledgment of their rights by the community.

5. **Women's sense of collective power is enhanced by creating opportunities for women to move about not only outside their homes, but beyond their communities as well.** Not only is geographic mobility symbolic, but it also provides practical opportunities for women of different backgrounds to receive training, learn new skills, and gain an

understanding of the structure and functioning of government institutions. Attendance at "outside" meetings can foster women's self-confidence to speak out in larger gatherings and to assume leadership roles.

6. **Sensitizing field staff to gender issues and encouraging them to explore locally appropriate strategies for empowering women can be a more effective approach to the development of successful projects than simply imposing a predetermined program.** Thus, the organic process by which the women's wasteland groups have developed has now become a model for the broader range of SARTHI's development work.

7. **The women's wasteland groups were able to validate and "mainstream" their gains by insisting that their respective panchayats uphold their land rights when challenged from both within and outside of their communities.** By holding the panchayats accountable for enforcing NOCs (no objection certificates) given by them, the women established their equal standing as citizens of the community. Had they selected a less public strategy, they might have marginalized their standing. This action is also likely to result in the women using their right to vote in panchayat and state elections in the future to promote their interests, thereby increasing women's participation in political processes and institutions.

8. **The women's groups evolved both by rewarding productivity and by challenging directly and immediately all efforts to trivialize or exploit their work.** They successfully demanded recompense for damage to their plantations and punished or directly confronted all attempts to intrude upon or distract time and resources from their work. The immediacy and intensity of their responses undoubtedly were important to their being taken seriously by both other women and men in their communities.

9. **The short-term and practical gains the women have made can be complemented by changes planned strategically across generations.** On the short-term level, the wasteland projects offer an opportunity for adult women to gain collective tenurial rights over at least community-held land resources. This can be viewed as a first step in the assertion of women's rights to own private land in their own name—something that is highly uncommon in India. Some group members have already articulated the hope that their daughters will at least have an equal opportunity to share in their parents' property. Only through such strategic thinking will gender relations begin to change in the long term.

Dedication

The author would like to dedicate this essay to the memory of Champa Ben, a resident of Godhar Village, where SARTHI's headquarters are located. Starting as a shy and apprehensive local woman who had to be coaxed into traveling to the mela *at PEDO, just three hours away, to attend the stove building training program in 1984, Champa Ben blossomed into a wonderful and sensitive activist and trainer. She, together with her male colleague Vikram Bhai, was instrumental in getting the first women's wasteland development group formed in Muvasa. Sadly, Champa Ben died of cervical cancer at the age of 30 in December 1989. Even through her death, however, she made local women aware of the importance of timely medical examinations to reduce the incidence of female deaths due to such diseases. The author would also like to express her gratitude to:*

- *The members of all the women's groups for giving so much of their time and for sharing the exciting process of change they are experiencing;*
- *The director and all the field staff of SARTHI for sharing their insights and knowledge; and*
- *Her dear friends and colleagues, Renu Khanna and Chandrika Sharma, with whom she has worked and learned together since they began their explorations into changing rural women's roles in the management of local resources.*

Notes

1. PEDO also started as a branch of SWRC and has a mandate similar to SARTHI's. It is located only three hours away by road. Due to the personal rapport between the directors of the two NGOs and their overlapping program goals, each group frequently participates in activities organized by the other.

2. Camps are normally one- to five-day events during which a selected group or village is provided with information on one or more selected topics. *Melas* are similar to camps but tend to be larger. Both *melas* and camps may be residential, requiring participants to stay away from home. Participants' travel and other costs are normally paid for by government or NGO sources.

3. There is no adequate translation for the Indian term *sharam,* which includes an acute sense of shame and embarrassment over having to act or behave outside one's traditional role. It is this sense of *sharam,* more than anything else, that keeps Indian women so strongly bound to tradition.

References

Listed below are a few publications that deal with issues related to the environment and women's empowerment. Please contact publishers directly to determine availability, costs, and applicable shipping charges.

Asia & Pacific Women's Resource and Action Series: Environment, (APDC, P.O. Box 12224, 50770 Kuala Lumpur, Malaysia, 1992)

Cold Hearths and Barren Slopes, the Wood Fuel Crisis in the Third World, by Bina Agarwal (ZED Books, 57 Caledonian Road, London N1 9BU, England, 1988)

"Community Management of Waste Recycling: The SIRDO," by Marianne Schmink, available in English & Spanish (SEEDS, P.O. Box 3923, Grand Central Station, New York, NY 10163, USA, 1984); Also available in *Seeds: Supporting Women's Work in the Third World* (The Feminist Press, 311 East 94 St., New York, NY 10128, 1989)

"Forest Conservation in Nepal: Encouraging Women's Participation," by Augusta Molnar, available in English, Spanish and French (SEEDS 1987) Also available in *Seeds: Supporting Women's Work in the Third World* (The Feminist Press, 1989)

"Gender Planning in the Third World: Meeting Practical and Strategic Gender Needs," by Caroline O. N. Moser (*World Development*, vol. 17, no. 11, 1989)

Women and the Environment: A Reader, Sally Sontheimer, ed. (Monthly Review Press, 122 West 27th. St., New York, NY 10001, USA, 1991)

The Bankurra Story: Rural Women Organise for Change and Technical Cooperation report, by Nalini Singh (ILO, World Employment Branch, New Delhi, India, 1988)

"Women, Environment and Development," *The Tribune*, Newsletter 47, September 1991 (IWTC, 777 United Nations Plaza, New York, NY 10017, USA)

III

NORTH AMERICA

6
Self-Employment as a Means to Women's Economic Self-Sufficiency: The WomenVenture Business Development Program

Katharine McKee, Sara Gould, and Ann Leonard

While the "feminization of poverty" has been widely recognized as a global phenomenon in recent years, this term originated in the United States; for even though the U.S. remains one of the world's wealthiest nations, the number of its women and women-headed households living in poverty is growing, mainly in the inner cities where fewer unskilled jobs remain. In rural communities, many factories have closed, family farming is declining, and few other nonfarm options are available. Today, American women face many of the same obstacles that limit women's economic participation in other parts of the world.

Women at Work

The official rate of women's participation in the U.S. labor force has risen dramatically during this century, from 18 percent in 1900 to 57 percent in 1988.[1] However, jobs in manufacturing, which traditionally provided the best-paying employment options for low-income, unskilled women, have decreased dramatically, as many companies have moved their assembly lines to developing countries to take advantage of lower wages and less government regulation. Still other industries have relocated from urban settings to suburban areas, where most low-income workers cannot afford to live.

Most of the new jobs that have opened up for women since 1980 are in service industries, such as retail sales and fast-food vending, which pay at

137

or slightly above the legal minimum wage. Therefore, it is not surprising that, despite the increased level of female economic participation, women in the United States still earn, on average, only two-thirds the income of men.

In addition, by 1982, 54 percent of all working women were mothers with children under 18 years of age.[2] For many years, the standard explanation for why women were paid less than men was that they tended to leave the labor force to have children, thus losing seniority and experience. However, recent studies suggest that when women find employment that offers a salary and opportunities similar to those offered to men, women are no more likely to quit work than their male counterparts.

Women in Poverty

In 1987, 12 percent of all American families were living below what the government considers "the poverty line";[3] but 34 percent of households headed by women were poor.[4] In fact, the average "married couple" family (most with both husband and wife earning) had a median income more than twice as high as the average female-headed household. Of the women who headed 87 percent of all single-parent households by 1985, more than one-third were poor.[5] For women belonging to certain minority racial groups, the situation was worse: While 16 percent of all women in the U.S. were poor in 1985, 13 percent of white women, 35 percent of African-American women, and 31 percent of Hispanic-American women were living in poverty.[6]

In addition to disparities in pay, one of the major causes of women's poverty is their disproportionate level of responsibility for children and other dependents. In fact, statistics show that when couples divorce, the woman's standard of living (and that of her children) often deteriorates drastically. Even in those cases where the courts mandate monthly child support payments to the parent retaining custody of minor children (generally the woman) from the other wage-earning parent, as many as 40 percent of women awarded child support never receive any payments, while an even larger number receive only partial or sporadic payments. Still others have no legal recourse to child support at all.

Lack of child-care options is also a major constraint faced by working mothers. (Child-care issues are discussed at length in Chapter 7.) Poor-quality child-care facilities and the breakdown of extended family networks make this issue a constant concern. In addition, because many poor women are single mothers or divorced, they often face a sense of isolation; they do not have a support network to help them deal with the frequent crises they face or to give them a boost in their quest to better their lives.

A number of programs funded by federal, state, and local governments exist to assist families living in poverty. These include unemployment insurance, social security benefits for children, food stamps, health services, and monthly stipends to help with rent and other expenses. These public transfers of income and services are often referred to as "welfare" or "public assistance." For many poor women, these economic transfers fill the gaps left by unstable employment and often serve as the major source of support for their family. Yet, in recent years, the actual value of these economic transfers has been steadily decreasing due to inflation and cuts in government programs, while the costs of housing and health care continue to spiral upward. In addition, programs such as unemployment insurance and social security tend to favor men, since these programs are based on the amount of wages earned, and men not only earn higher salaries but also tend to be employed for longer consecutive periods of time.

While welfare programs may prevent starvation, they do not necessarily alleviate hunger, as money often runs out well before the arrival of next month's welfare check. And programs such as Aid to Families with Dependent Children (AFDC), the largest source of public assistance in the U.S., themselves present obstacles that prevent women from bettering their lives. Regulations governing eligibility—to receive not only income but also access to health care and other services—severely limit the assets a family can possess without losing all welfare benefits. The assumption is that people will leave welfare for full-time wage employment and will not need further assistance. There is no provision in the system for a gradual or partial transition off of public assistance through part-time employment or self-employment.

The regulations themselves, therefore, drastically reduce the ability of poor women to make the difficult climb out of poverty to self-sufficiency. While for most families reliance on welfare is a temporary measure, for a small segment of America's poor, the current welfare regulations have contributed to a growing cycle of poverty in which second and even third generations of women are raising families on public assistance.

Self-Employment and Low-Income Women

In the early 1980s, it became evident that new solutions were required to meet the needs of the increasing number of people, particularly women and children, living in poverty in the United States. One option that generated a great deal of interest was self-employment, particularly microenterprise development. Small businesses have always been an important source of employment. Between 1980 and 1986 (a period of economic recession), the number of women-owned small sole proprietorships in the U.S. skyrocketed, increasing by 62.5 percent to a total of 4.1 million businesses.[7]

Experience over the last decade has shown that for *some* poor women, self-employment can offer the means to become self-supporting and to gain increased self-esteem, provided they are offered assistance that includes development of business skills, access to credit, and other support services. However, it is important to keep in mind that small business development remains largely a high-risk, labor-intensive activity that often, at least initially, must be combined with a low-wage job in order for a family to make ends meet; it should, therefore, be viewed as an option suitable for some people, but not as a substitute for the development of wage employment for the majority of low-income people.

In the United States today, there are a growing number of programs that have been developed to assist low-income women become self-employed. One of the pioneering efforts, which has served as a model for many other programs throughout the United States and beyond, was the Women's Economic Development Corporation (WEDCO) in St. Paul, Minnesota, the first microenterprise development program to provide services directly to low-income women. Over the years, as it sought to respond to the broader employment needs of women, WEDCO expanded its services. In 1989, WEDCO merged with an employment counseling program, and subsequently the organization changed its name to "WomenVenture" (WV) to reflect its expanded range of services. Today, the "WEDCO" component of WomenVenture is referred to as its "business development program."

This chapter focuses on the evolution of WomenVenture's business development program (the name WEDCO is sometimes used in the text where historically appropriate). This model, which has provided a way of helping women start businesses and become self-sufficient without incurring overwhelming risks, continues to be an example of interest to other organizations seeking to help women become self-employed.

———

Wanda is a single parent with a three-year-old child. She was referred to WEDCO/WV by a local bank after she had accused the bank of sex discrimination when they denied her request for a loan to buy a truck. Wanda wanted to start a business to haul trash and rubbish from construction sites. She had walked into the business loan department of the bank with a toddler and no business plan. When Wanda came to WEDCO/WV, she was given assistance in developing a business plan and cash-flow projections.

Armed with these documents and new knowledge, Wanda was able to lease
two trucks and establish herself as a minority contractor[8] for the city. In
addition, she has started a small tool rental business out of her house.

───────

WomenVenture's business development program was created to help
women like Wanda. Since 1984, more than 1,000 women have been
helped to start their own businesses, receiving loans in support of these
microenterprises amounting to over three-quarters of a million dollars. An
even greater number of women have been assisted in deciding *not* to go
into business for themselves, but rather to gain needed education, skills,
and paid employment. WomenVenture is well aware that starting a very
small business that can generate enough income to support a woman and
her household is not easy for anyone. For women who are poor, the barriers are even greater. From the very beginning, it was recognized that if the
WEDCO program was to reach and serve women like Wanda, it would
have to be very different from traditional small business assistance programs in the United States.

The Beginning

In 1982, the United States was in the midst of a recession whose effects
were beginning to be felt in the State of Minnesota.[9] Jobs were becoming
scarce, particularly in the industrial sector. In addition, for many women,
available employment options did not meet their needs, not only for
income, but for flexibility in meeting family-care responsibilities and to
have some control over their lives.

Thus, in the fall of that year, two women concerned about the growing
feminization of poverty in their home state decided to take a fresh look at
ways to promote economic self-sufficiency for women. Working together,
Kathryn S. Keeley, then Executive Director of Chrysalis, a women's counseling center in Minneapolis, and her colleague, Arvonne Fraser, of the
Hubert Humphrey Institute at the University of Minnesota, were able to
raise sufficient funds from local foundations to support a planning process
to examine the causes of women's poverty and to suggest program and
policy initiatives to increase women's incomes and improve the quality of
their lives.

The planning began late in the fall of 1982; by March 1983, a new area
of economic opportunity for women had been identified: self-employment
and small business development. To develop a program to help women
take advantage of these new opportunities, an advisory group was formed
made up of at least sixty women and men in the Minneapolis–St. Paul

Founding members of the WEDCO/WV business development program (clockwise from upper left: Kathy Keeley, Sue Henderson, Pat Sandin, Rommel White, Paula Manillo). *(WEDCO/WV)*

area. They participated in several task forces that explored the following areas: the language of economic development and entrepreneurship and ways to make it less intimidating to women, particularly low-income women; the kinds of day care, housing, income maintenance, and other services women would need to make the transition to self-employment; and the types of training and financial assistance required to meet the needs of low-income women. In addition, Chrysalis carried out a survey of 300 predominantly low-income women interested in microenterprise development. They identified lack of financing—particularly small loans (amounts from $500 to $10,000)—as a primary need.

It was at about this time that Barbara Allivato, then Vice-President for Urban Development at the Minneapolis-based First Bank System, happened to see Kathy Keeley on television describing the preliminary findings of the planning process. Keeley's enthusiasm and credibility sparked Allivato's imagination. She recognized that women business owners represented a unique opportunity for her bank.

At this point, events began to move quickly. In September 1983, the advisory group in the Twin Cities recommended the formation of a new organization, the Women's Economic Development Corporation (WEDCO). Kathy Keeley was named Executive Director. WEDCO opened its doors to clients in January 1984. Initial financial support came from three private foundations, but soon expanded to include corporate support and eventually funding from the State of Minnesota.

With the resource base taking shape, Kathy Keeley began to build a staff. In addition to Keeley, initial staff included an administrative assistant and a second professional person, who began the intake and assessment work with WEDCO's first clients. Within three months, the need for additional expertise in both marketing and finance was clear, but resources could fund only one position. Keeley devised a creative solution; she created two part-time jobs and filled the positions with women who were business owners themselves and wanted to remain engaged in their own enterprises.

The new organization set out to achieve three main goals:

- To increase the economic self-sufficiency of women through self-employment;
- To improve women's access to financial resources; and
- To act as a catalyst in linking women with emerging business opportunities.

As the staff began working with clients, these goals took shape and gained greater clarity. Because the term "economic self-sufficiency" is a vague one, staff engaged in discussions about what they meant when they used it. They reached general agreement that economic self-sufficiency for a woman meant that she was able to earn enough income to support herself and her family. In fact, WomenVenture chooses to emphasize the word "self-employment" rather than "business" in their initial discussions with clients because they have found that while most potential women entrepreneurs can see themselves as becoming "self-employed," initially they cannot visualize themselves as owning and operating a business—the concept implies something too big.

From the onset, it was realized that one of the most important services WEDCO could provide was to help women gain access to financial resources. This meant opening two different doors: (1) pursuing creative partnerships with conventional lenders who could assist some women; and (2) establishing an in-house loan fund to provide first-time credit for women considered "bad risks" by banks.

Finally, staff decided that the most effective way to link women with emerging business opportunities was to make those opportunities visible. This involved highlighting recent advances made by women and bringing them to life by featuring the experiences of real women as role models, as well as bringing greater visibility to women operating nontraditional businesses.

The Business Development Program

Beverly is a Native American[10] *woman about fifty years old. She came to WEDCO/WV after a bank in St. Paul turned down her request for a loan to start her own pest control business to support herself, her husband, and two children. Beverly needed to borrow $3,500 to buy equipment and to obtain the necessary insurance and licenses. The bank denied her request due to a lack of collateral: she owns no property because lands belonging to Native Americans are communal and are held in trust by the U.S. Bureau of Indian Affairs. With help from WEDCO/WV, Beverly completed a two-page business plan and set out to visit Native American reservations in Minnesota, North Dakota, South Dakota, and Nebraska to bid on pest control accounts for tribal buildings, schools, and Native American health service offices. When she returned, she had $22,000 in signed contracts— more than enough collateral to secure a WEDCO/WV loan. In addition, she was able to register as a minority contractor to get work with public housing projects and other public sector businesses. The business is now providing Beverly and her family with steady employment and a good income.*

———

WomenVenture's clients face all the problems typical of most start-up enterprises—limited business and management experience, lack of adequate financing, need to build a customer base from scratch. As women, however, they confront additional obstacles: barriers of isolation, lack of self-confidence, heavy family responsibilities, lack of formal business training, very limited money of their own to invest in their enterprise, and, all too often, sex discrimination by bankers, customers, and suppliers. Furthermore, many women do not get much encouragement from their family, husbands, or partners in trying to achieve self-sufficiency through creating their own businesses.

To tackle all these barriers to self-employment, a very comprehensive assistance program was designed. The components include:

• Training in business planning and management;
• One-on-one consulting tailored to each client and her business idea;
• Exercises to build self-esteem and personal effectiveness; and
• Financial packaging and loans.

Thus, WomenVenture provides encouragement and social support for clients' income-earning efforts, as well as business skills and services.

The program also offers follow-up assistance to help clients with the production, marketing, cash flow, and personal problems that arise once they have launched their self-employment enterprises. Another important role that WomenVenture plays is to provide a place where clients can come to discuss the challenges they face with business professionals and other clients.

How the Process Works: Self-Screening and a Step-by-Step Approach

To better understand the business development process, we will follow a typical client through the initial phases of the program. Erica is a single parent with two children. Before coming to WomenVenture, she had worked at a variety of low-paying jobs (factory assembly line, hospital aide, clerical work). For several years, she had been making jewelry at home for her family and friends; people frequently suggested that she ought to go into business. Thus, when Erica came to WomenVenture, she already had an idea of what she wanted to do.

Erica heard about WomenVenture through friends and went to one of the regular orientation sessions ("Considering a Business") to learn more about the rigors of starting a business. About twelve women were there (approximately 500 attend these sessions each year). Some already had small businesses or part-time, home-based self-employment activities. Many, like Erica, had a specific business idea and had come to see whether WomenVenture could help them turn their dream into reality.

At the orientation sessions, staff give potential clients an overview of the risks and opportunities, successes and failures, frustrations and rewards of self-employment. Again and again they emphasize that owning and operating a business is not for everyone and requires many skills, as well as long hours of planning and hard work. On average, less than half of the women who attend an orientation session continue in the program. But Erica was determined. She signed up for the next step in the process, an individual interview with a staff person, referred to as a "business consultant." Typically, WomenVenture consultants have themselves started and run at least one small business or self-employment venture. Many continue to do so while serving on the staff.

At a potential client's first interview, she presents her business idea, plan, or problem to the WomenVenture consultant. As she describes her plans, the consultant takes notes and asks many questions. She then goes over a detailed outline describing the different services and assistance that WomenVenture can provide if the applicant chooses to become a client. The consultant explains that in addition to providing training, technical assistance, and advice to the client as she prepares her business plan, WomenVenture can also help her obtain the financing needed to start up her venture, either from a bank or from its own loan fund.

The consultant also explains that the client she will need to agree to carry out a series of specific tasks—referred to as "homework"—that make up the business planning process, if she wants to move on to the next stage and continue receiving advice and services. If she agrees, she and the consultant will decide how much she will have to pay for each service. WomenVenture offers its services on a sliding-fee basis, depending on the woman's income; fees range from as low as $20 up to $60 per consultation.

WomenVenture's leadership believes that they must be "businesslike" with their clients, just as their program trains clients to be businesslike with customers and suppliers. Paying a fee for classes and consultations will encourage women like Erica to think hard about whether they find the services valuable and whether they are prepared to move on to the next stage.

At this point, many clients are uncertain about whether they want to proceed, and about half drop out; but Erica is ready to begin. She signs an agreement setting out the roles and responsibilities that she and WomenVenture will each assume. The next step for her is to attend a training session or workshop that will get her started on the step-by-step business planning process. After that, she will meet with her consultant as she completes each section of "homework."

A basic principle of the WomenVenture business development model is that the business planning process is broken down into many different steps so that clients will not feel overwhelmed and will be able to acquire skills and knowledge at their own pace. The building blocks of the training and assistance program are a series of worksheets covering the different components of starting a business: deciding which product to make or which service to provide; determining who will buy from you and how much they will be willing to pay; analyzing your competitors; figuring out what equipment and supplies you will need to purchase or lease, and where to get them on the most favorable terms; preparing your home for the business or identifying a suitable location; and so on.

Each client must complete one worksheet before moving on to the next. She may decide not to continue at any point. WomenVenture believes that the business development process should be self-paced, with the client deciding how quickly to plan, start up, and expand her business.

Classroom training and individual meetings with consultants help clients complete each step. Typically, a client will attend six to ten consultations or classes over a two- to eight-month period to complete her business plan. At times, WomenVenture has also developed work groups to give clients a chance to work closely with other women on learning specific skills and solving problems. Work groups in marketing, selling, record keeping, pricing, dealing with personal problems, or financing, for example, provide clients with in-depth training and opportunities to fine-tune their business ideas while getting feedback and support from other women.

A very important component of the WomenVenture planning process is identifying the client's income needs and the business's financing needs. Consultants help each client figure out a two-year budget that covers her basic needs and those of her family, including expenses such as child care that are often overlooked by traditional business planners. With staff help, each client also estimates the expenses, revenues, and net profits that her venture can expect to accrue during its first two years of operation. Then comes the moment of truth—will the business or self-employment activity produce enough money for the client to be able to support herself and her family? If not, it is back to the drawing board. Approximately one-half of clients have to restructure their plans at this point. The consultants try to help them figure out how to reduce expenses and increase revenues so that their business idea can be viable.

Joanne wanted to start a seamstress business that would be located in a fabric store chain. WEDCO/WV assisted her to develop a business plan and identify her market. She then requested a very large loan from WEDCO/WV, which was denied because the debt service required would overextend the business. It was suggested that she rethink her plan—starting somewhat smaller and planning to grow more slowly, without assuming a large debt. In the end, Joanne was able to start her business with $4,000 in capital; she now feels that this was the most helpful rejection she ever received from a funding source.

Sometimes at this point, despite all the work put into her self-employment plan, a client is forced to conclude that her business idea will not work. WomenVenture staff feel strongly that one of their most important roles is to help women decide *not* to become self-employed, if this would worsen their economic and/or personal situation. In fact, WEDCO founder Kathy Keeley strongly emphasizes that self-employment is not for everyone. "Self-employment is," she stresses, "only one means to women's self-sufficiency."

Getting Financing—The "Stepping Process"

If the client's plan appears viable, the step-by-step planning process helps her to assemble the information she needs to apply for a loan from a bank or

Two successful clients of the business development program. *(Donna Weispfenning)*

from WomenVenture. Not all clients need to borrow money to start or expand their businesses. Some are able to pull together money from savings or from family and friends, but since many participants are low-income women with little savings, financial packaging is an essential part of the

WomenVenture model. After Erica completed all the sections of her business plan, the consultant helped her to prepare a written loan application.

Bank Financing

Whenever possible, WomenVenture encourages clients to apply for a bank loan, since a long-term goal is to make traditional financial institutions more responsive to the credit needs of women's businesses. After Barbara Allivato learned about the program and got involved, WEDCO developed a particularly close working relationship with First Bank. In the program's first four years, with funds provided by First Bank and others, 120 loans and guarantees were made to WEDCO clients, ranging from $50 to $125,000, for business start-ups and expansions.

Yet building partnerships with banks has not been easy. Most bankers continue to view WomenVenture's clients as high-risk borrowers, because most have no previous business experience and few personal or business assets. In addition, bankers usually are not familiar with the types of self-employment activities the women want to carry out. With each new loan officer, another education process is required to explain the program's goals and methods and present its strong track record.

Perhaps the most important constraint is that it is not profitable for a bank to make such small loans because the transaction costs are almost the same as they are for large loans; indeed, because more individual borrowers are involved, small loans are more expensive to administer. Very few commercial banks will even consider making a business loan under $10,000; some will not accept applications under $50,000. At First Bank, the WomenVenture-referred loans were all granted from the bank's personal loan division rather than its business loan division. While this permitted the bank to make smaller and more flexible loans, it also made it more difficult for clients to benefit from an experienced business lender's advice and to build up a track record as a business borrower.

WomenVenture Financing

Because most of its clients' needs cannot be met through partnerships with banks, it was recognized from the outset that it would be necessary for WomenVenture to capitalize its own loan fund by raising money from foundations and corporations. Several different approaches to lending have been tried to date. Originally, two funds were created: one to guarantee bank loans and another to make direct loans and investments. When this division, however, did not prove workable, the money was combined into one fund. As of the end of 1991, The Seed Capital Fund had $307,000 in assets and made loans ranging from $30 to $28,000. WomenVenture is currently initiating a new lending program with funding provided by the U.S. Small Business Administration (SBA). These SBA funds will be used to finance nontraditional enterprises of low-income women and men, up to a maximum of $25,000. Clients make applications to the loan funds the same way they apply to a bank.

The lending program embodies several WomenVenture principles. First, it is designed to be a "stepping process" for clients. Stepping loans start out small—just enough to allow the entrepreneur to test her business idea, make repayment, and build up her business without incurring unreasonable debt. For example, a client is often given a very small loan that is just enough to allow her to purchase some inventory, print some brochures or business cards, etc. WomenVenture then asks the woman to go out and try to sell her service or product, committing itself to finance 50 percent of any sales or services she generates, thus ensuring that she can deliver her orders.

This process provides the woman with an incentive to try her business idea, while at the same time minimizing risk to the loan fund, as repayment is tied directly to sales. Once the woman demonstrates that she can get clients and deliver her orders, she becomes eligible for progressively larger loans. In this way, her business can grow gradually as she is learning and practicing new management and marketing skills. At the same time, she is building a track record as a borrower. As soon as possible, she is encouraged to "graduate" to a bank loan, so that WomenVenture's limited loan funds can be made available to other clients.

A second guiding principle is that financing should be flexible, tailored to the specific financing needs of the client's particular business or self-employment activity. Each client is responsible for negotiating the duration, interest rate, pace of repayment (tailored to her business's cash flow), and other terms of her loan with the loan committee. Interest rates are at or near market rates, as WomenVenture does not believe in subsidizing women's businesses. They treat their borrowers as business owners, just as a bank would, so that the women understand that this is not a giveaway program but serious business in a real-world context.

Third, every client must pledge some type of collateral for her loan, even if it consists of property a bank would not typically accept as security: flowers, cleaning supplies, pianos—even very old cars. Also accepted are signed sales contracts to deliver goods or services to customers, or other "intangibles." WomenVenture then files liens (charges upon real or personal property for the satisfaction of a debt) with the State of Minnesota on the collateral, so that their clients see that this is legally a business loan. This is a very important step in the process, not only because insistence on collateral helps to ensure that the clients feel a strong commitment to repay and that they understand the risks involved in self-employment, but because it helps clients build credit histories that they can later present to banks.

———

Leslie had experience working as a florist but had failed at starting her own floral business. Upon analysis of her situation, WEDCO/WV agreed to provide her with a $500 loan to buy roses to sell for Valentine's Day (a U.S. holiday when flowers and candy are frequently given as gifts). She rented a store front for $200 for one month and bartered with the local newspaper for an ad in exchange for roses for their office. She bought ladders and buckets in which to display the flowers and hand painted a sign that offered a "love bunch" for $8.99. Within five days, she was able to earn $3,000 from the sale of the roses. She then repaid her loan and used the remaining funds to provide the capital she needed to start her business.

Three years later, WEDCO/WV made Leslie a second loan of $500 for Mother's Day and again set a five-day term of repayment. She was able to generate enough cash to pay that loan in time and to buy her first cooler to keep her flowers in. Leslie went on to borrow $70,000 through a city program to purchase her own building and now operates from two locations. Today, Leslie's business has sales of over $500,000 annually. She owns three stores and two buildings and currently employs fifteen other people. Not only is she supporting herself and her own family, but she is helping other women to do the same. She also served for a time as the president of the local merchants' association.

———

Of course, not all of WomenVenture's loans are so successful. During the first four years of the WEDCO program, when the loan fund was most active, the default rate ran at less than 20 percent. Clients whose loans appear to be "in trouble" are given special assistance in order to help stabilize their businesses, solve problems, and pay off their loans.

But overall, WomenVenture's loan record looks good. Over the years, with about $900,000 in loans to clients, their loss rate has averaged approximately 4 percent of outstanding principal in any given year. This compares favorably with other community development loan funds in the United States.

Self-Employment Isn't for Everyone

WomenVenture works on the principle of self-screening. Its staff do not believe that they can determine which business ideas will succeed and fail;

rather, they help each individual client judge her venture's feasibility for herself and then decide whether she has the skills, abilities, and determination to develop, market, and finance a business. Women are allowed to "self-select"—to identify which business idea is right for them and to continually test their own readiness to operate a microenterprise successfully. By the end of this self-selection process, clients will have demonstrated to themselves, their families, and WomenVenture that their proposed business is viable and that they are committed to carrying it out.

Many women screen themselves out after completing just part of the process. Upon further examination, a client may decide that her proposed business does not suit her needs after all, either because it cannot generate enough earnings or because it does not fit her current personal goals and circumstances; perhaps she cannot commit enough time and energy to make it work at this point in her life. She may decide to put off self-employment until family and day-care responsibilities change. A number of women return to WomenVenture at a later date when they feel more secure about making a commitment.

Building a Broader Base of Support for Working Women

In the early WEDCO years, about five women per day would inquire about the business development program. Out of any five, approximately two would actually try to start their own businesses. The other three usually needed assistance in securing employment and skills training, education, and support services to meet their economic needs.

To better assist these women, in 1989 WEDCO merged with CHART, a career and employment counseling program, to create WomenVenture, an organization offering more comprehensive self-sufficiency services beyond business development. WomenVenture (WV) seeks to secure a stronger economic future for women through focusing on three areas: employment and career development, business development, and financial responsibility.

In addition to the business development program, WomenVenture has developed a Career Resource Center to meet the needs of the large number of women for whom self-employment is not the best option. To keep costs in line, this service was recently restructured as a self-help, self-paced program designed to give women access to a "tool box" of information and support systems as they make the transition to better jobs or new careers. A major component is The Exchange, a program that capitalizes on WV's extensive network of business professionals who consult with clients on a volunteer basis. Also included in the program are a job listing book, job search workshops, a reference library, and support group activities. The idea is to provide clients with an accessible, affordable, and responsive mechanism to meet their particular needs.

WomenVenture's services are available to any woman, regardless of income. (Men sometimes inquire about WV programs, but only a few actually become clients.) Most WomenVenture clients are low- to middle-income women, and a significant proportion are single mothers; many clients are women who, following a divorce, suddenly found that their standard of living had plummeted and were faced with being the primary or sole support of their family.

For most clients, the regular WomenVenture programs can meet their business and employment needs. But many women living below the poverty line face additional obstacles, especially women who are AFDC recipients. To help these women on the road to self-sufficiency, special programs are necessary.

The SETO Program

In 1986, efforts began to design a program to provide business development services to women receiving public assistance. The Self-Employment Training Opportunities (SETO) program is modeled on Women-Venture's regular business development program, but places greater emphasis on building women's self-confidence and teaching problem-solving and business-related skills. The training period for SETO clients is also longer, since most participants have little or no previous business experience and often limited formal education.

In addition to lacking money, education, experience, and self-esteem, SETO clients face another major obstacle: they are receiving public assistance. AFDC provides poor families not only with cash income but also with other benefits, such as food stamps and access to health care. However, the eligibility requirements for recipients of AFDC severely restrict the amount of income or assets a family can accumulate and still receive benefits, thus actually discouraging people from trying to become self-sufficient.

Families on AFDC as a unit are not allowed to accrue more than $1,200 in personal belongings, income, savings, or assets (except for the value of an automobile); nor are they allowed to separate business assets and income from their personal finances. At first, WomenVenture tried to work around these restrictions by various means, such as leasing equipment to clients and paying vendors directly on behalf of SETO clients, but none of these strategies proved to be satisfactory. They therefore sought changes in the restrictive government regulations.

In 1988, WomenVenture became part of a national demonstration program initiated by the Corporation for Enterprise Development, a nonprofit advocacy organization with headquarters in Washington, D.C. This demonstration program, operated on a trial basis in five U.S. states, allowed AFDC recipients twelve-month waivers from AFDC eligibility requirements while they attempted to make a gradual transition from public assistance to self-sufficiency. This meant that SETO participants had one year in which to build up equity in their businesses without suddenly losing all their AFDC health, food, and income benefits.

Patricia Tototzintle, who managed the SETO program, describes the typical SETO client as follows:

> In general, SETO clients are single moms struggling to raise their children. Their monthly AFDC check does not cover all of their regular monthly expenses. The majority of our clients have no savings to fall back on, no real assets or property, no friends or close relatives able to provide financial support to a new business, and they are not considered good credit risks. As low-income single parents, they are faced with daily barriers relating to housing, food, clothing, transportation, child care, and education. Low self-esteem is common among our clients as they enter the program.

From March 1988 through November 1991, 398 women attended SETO orientation sessions. Of these women, 229 enrolled in the training program and 188 completed the course. Sixty-eight new businesses have been launched, twenty-three of them with SETO loans. (SETO has its own financing program, making stepping loans from $500 to $5,000.) Fourteen of these businesses also include a partner or other employees. Seventeen of these new business owners have already made the transition off AFDC and are now able to support themselves and their families without the help of welfare benefits. Another nineteen clients completed the training and then, using their new skills and self-confidence, were able to find regular employment; they are currently off AFDC as well. Thirty-one SETO clients chose to enroll in other education or training programs in order to pursue their employment goals.

———

Kim is 25 years old and has a seven-year-old child. She has been on AFDC for the last six years and wants to start a snow-plowing business. She wanted to borrow $6,000 to purchase a truck and plow. She planned to mow lawns in the spring and summer and to work part-time as a waitress to provide year-round employment. WEDCO/WV assisted Kim in completing her business plan and cash flow projections. It soon became clear that the snow-plowing business could not generate enough income to support her and her daughter. The lawn-mowing business actually looked much more attractive when the financial projections had been completed. There-

fore, Kim decided to postpone the snow-plowing business and not go into debt or jeopardize her welfare benefits. Between mowing lawns and working part-time as a waitress during the spring and summer, Kim can save enough money to make a down payment on a truck and plow by next winter. She expects to be off welfare before the year ends.

———

The problems faced by SETO clients are similar to those of other WomenVenture clients, but usually they are intensified. Child care is an ongoing concern to most, as is transportation. In addition, many women face opposition from family members, particularly spouses or partners, who often attempt to undermine their determination to support themselves.

———

A SETO client had completed her cash flow projections and was in the final stages of planning her business. Her husband was unemployed. She came to WomenVenture for her scheduled appointment wearing sunglasses to camouflage her black eyes and bruises. She said she had been sitting at her kitchen table working on her business plan when her husband, who had been drinking, flew into a rage, picked her up, and slammed her down onto the floor. She said he had never done anything like this before. It was suggested that her decision to go into business might have something to do with his action. The client called a few days later to say that she and her partner had talked things out and everything seemed to be back to normal. However, the night before her next WV appointment, he again flew into a rage and physically abused her. Thereafter, she decided not to mark her future appointments on her calendar, and the beatings stopped.

———

A client's partner had been a drug addict for sixteen years. He had harassed her every time she tried to work or go to school and did the same after she completed her SETO training. She filed a restraining order to protect herself and her children, but he continued to threaten her until he finally moved out of the state. That ordeal over, she learned that her 15-year-old daughter was pregnant.

———

Because SETO clients do have special needs, new approaches have been developed. A Research and Development (R&D) track has been

Many WomenVenture clients are mothers with young children to support. *(Laura Crosby)*

established for those who need more time and/or experience in developing their business ideas. R&D clients work together in small groups where they receive ongoing support and critiques of their ideas as they move along. They also have access to smaller "circle loans" of from $10 to $100 (called circle loans because loans are given to group members on a rotating basis). These loans allow clients to develop and test various prototypes before actually developing their business plan.

In 1990, a Business Law Clinic was formed, with the assistance of a local college. Law students, supervised by practicing attorneys working on a pro bono basis, provide free legal assistance to SETO clients that they could never afford on their own.

WomenVenture also offers SETO clients monthly support group meetings, help in handling social service–related problems, and follow-up assistance once their business is under way. The new staff position of "circuit rider" has recently been created to aid SETO clients at their place of work.

―――――――

Stacey Millet joined WomenVenture in 1989, just after the merger of WEDCO and CHART. She has a background in both journalism and business, having oper-

ated her own microenterprise as well as having worked in the corporate world. Initially, Stacey was involved in marketing the career services programs and developing some of WV's educational materials. However, in October 1991, she took on the new assignment of "circuit rider," to provide on-site assistance to SETO clients. Once their business is in operation, many of these women experience a sense of isolation, as they rarely have family members or friends who understand and can assist them in meeting their business needs. Stacey views one of her major roles as making the women aware that there is someone on call who understands and can help.

Accomplishments to Date

In 1984, when WEDCO began, its founders thought that it might help about twenty-five new businesses get started. But since 1984, Women-Venture has assisted over 1,000 new businesses get under way in Minnesota and has provided training and consultation services to an average of 900 women per year. As of April 1990, over $886,000 had been loaned to eighty-one women in the form of ninety-two direct loans and fifteen guarantees to banks. Thirty-eight of these loans have been repaid in full; thirteen have been written off.

While WomenVenture clients have started businesses in all industry sectors, they are concentrated in what are called "service" industries. A breakdown is illustrated here:

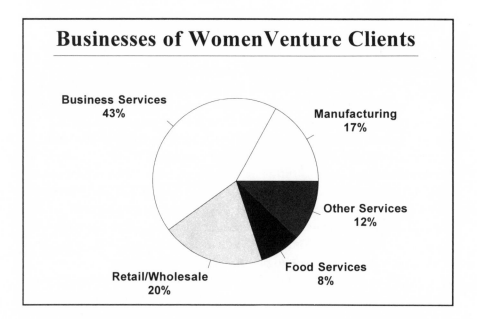

Businesses of WomenVenture Clients

Business Services 43%

Manufacturing 17%

Other Services 12%

Food Services 8%

Retail/Wholesale 20%

In addition to food services and retail sales, WomenVenture businesses include a medical transcription business, wholesale book distribution, temporary day-care employment service, picture framing, tailoring, graphic arts, a florist business, monogramming, and silkscreening.

A 1987 evaluation of the business development program included interviews with current and former clients. Respondents reported positive changes in terms of greater self-confidence, sharper focus on and better planning for life goals, taking charge of one's life, and personal organization, which they attributed to their association with the program. Two-thirds of clients surveyed who now defined themselves as "moderately successful," and one-quarter who now considered themselves "extremely successful," gave substantial credit to WEDCO for their improved situations. Clients defined personal success in various terms, including achieving balance and satisfaction in life, having financial stability and security, having satisfying and fulfilling work, setting and reaching goals, having a successful business, having a positive sense of self-worth, reaching one's potential, and having healthy and supportive relationships.

Aside from the direct financing involved, the services valued most by clients were training, completing a business plan, loan packaging, and doing financial projections.

Broader Impacts and Future Challenges

> We believe that the program is about changing people's lives, removing barriers, and giving them new economic tools. Long-term, we believe that we are developing people who see themselves as having marketable skills, life choices, and economic opportunities. —Kathy Keeley

A difficulty that will be faced by most successful programs is when the time comes to expand their services in order to meet greater demand and/or to respond to the more diverse needs of their clients. While the merger with CHART, which resulted in the establishment of WomenVenture, seemed like a sensible approach to broadening WEDCO's ability to help women seeking self-sufficiency, the merging of two organizations with different operating styles, unique staffing dynamics, and somewhat diverse clienteles, was not easy. New ways of managing programs, working with staff and clients, raising funds, and the like, were required. One reason the new name WomenVenture was adopted was to help create a sense of unity between the two programs.

In addition, the success of the WEDCO model brought an ever-increasing amount of publicity and requests for information from individuals and organizations throughout the United States and beyond. While this attention created important opportunities to have a broader impact on the field of microenterprise development, it also placed additional stress on a small staff trying to run a service program with limited resources.

Another common transition organizations must face is when the founding members move on, as has happened with most of the core staff who established the business development program at WomenVenture. Keeley herself stepped down as president in early 1992, to work directly with the Corporation for Enterprise Development in Washington, D.C., seeking to design new welfare policies that invest in the economic development of low-income people. She was succeeded by Kay Gudmestad, who came to the Twin Cities with a background in management of nonprofit organizations serving the needs of women and girls and in small business management. In her view:

> The time has come for WomenVenture to undertake a comprehensive organizational development process that will complete the transition phase initiated by the merger and enable the organization to achieve a new level of quality in service delivery. Through the evaluation of impact of existing services and assessment of needs in this community, WomenVenture will position itself to build its leadership role in this community and continue to contribute to national thinking in small business development for women.

WomenVenture continues to evolve as it keeps pace with the times and with the needs of its clients. The organization has streamlined its operations, paring its operating budget down to $930,000 for 1992 (from a high of $1.4 million) and reducing the staff from 33 to 18. One of the goals is to make greater use of volunteers—linking clients to the appropriate professionals—rather than have staff do all the work.

WomenVenture has also created several new approaches to help low-income women achieve self-sufficiency:

- Project Blueprint addresses the issue of occupational segregation by recruiting and training women for well-paying jobs in the male-dominated construction trades. It combines traditional career-training skills with manual and physical training, job placement, and personal effectiveness skills.
- Passport is a pilot program operating in two low-income communities in Minneapolis and one in St. Paul. It is designed to help community residents find permanent jobs or become self-employed, and to establish community businesses.

What about the issue of self-sufficiency? Fees from clients currently cover less than 5 percent of WomenVenture's operating budget, which is not surprising, given that in 1991, 58 percent of its clients had annual incomes of $15,000 or less. WomenVenture, therefore, tries to seek as broad a funding base as possible, receiving support from a range of sources including foundations, corporations, individuals, state and federal governments, and contractual work.

WomenVenture continues to be a strong advocate for women's economic development, not only locally, but also at the state and national levels. The organization has made good use of attention from the media, including being featured on *60 Minutes,* currently rated as the most popular TV news program in the United States.

It was largely through WomenVenture's lobbying efforts that the demonstration program offering waivers to AFDC recipients was created; and WomenVenture continues to lobby for extension and expansion of such programs nationwide. The "WEDCO" business development model has also served as the inspiration for numerous women's economic development projects in other parts of the United States (some of these are profiled in the appendix). Visitors from over forty states and from foreign countries have come to the Twin Cities to study the business development model. WomenVenture has also produced a variety of manuals that both individuals and organizations can use in helping women establish and successfully operate small businesses.

———————————————— Lessons ————————————————

1. **Programs to assist low-income women to become self-employed must provide their clients with three unique types of services.** First, they must provide them with information, technical assistance, and access to credit—the tools they need to successfully start and grow their businesses. Second, they must also provide women with special training and experiences that will help them build up their self-confidence and increase their sense of self-esteem so that they can overcome the numerous hurdles they will face, both personally and professionally, and be able to compete successfully in the marketplace. Third, they must help their clients address and overcome the gender-related obstacles that, as women, they will encounter in the business world.

2. **Self-pacing and self-selection help women gain skills and confidence at the same time.** At WomenVenture, women are free to move ahead at their own pace and can exit (and re-enter) the program at any point without feeling that they have failed. The "stepping" principle has been used both to divide the program's content into manageable elements and to provide financing in increments that prevent fledgling entrepreneurs from overextending themselves.

3. **The best way to build client self-reliance is through participation in and exposure to good business practices.** WomenVenture insists that clients develop a business plan (that includes the business's target market, funding requirements, performance expectations, and at least a two-year projected cash flow) before they apply for credit. Even if Women-Venture provides the financing, clients are charged market rates of interest and are required to put up some collateral in order to receive loans. This puts the transaction on a firm business footing and prepares the client to operate as a business.

4. **To assist clients effectively, programs themselves must practice what they preach; they too must operate in a businesslike manner.** Staff need to have a working knowledge of how to run a business, particularly how to project cash flow and assess working capital needs. Programs must also be realistic about what is possible within the current marketplace and keep attuned to its fluctuations.

5. **To successfully help low-income women achieve self-employment, programs must become agents of change.** From the start, WEDCO/WomenVenture took an activist role within the community and, gradually, at both the state and national levels, in order to change policies that limit women's ability to become self-supporting. As part of this effort, WomenVenture has made very effective use of the media. This has helped them to increase public support for their program and recruit new clients, as well as to influence public policy.

Notes

1. U.S. Department of Labor, Bureau of Labor Statistics, *Handbook of Labor Statistics* (Washington, D.C.: Government Printing Office, 1983), and U.S. Bureau of the Census, *Statistical Abstract of the United States 1990* (Washington, D.C.: U.S. Government Printing Office, 1990).

2. Allyson S. Grossman, "More Than Half of All Children Have Working Mothers," *Monthly Labor Review* 105 (Feb 1982), as cited in Bianchi and Sprain, *American Women in Transition* (New York: Russell Sage Foundation, 1986).

3. The "poverty line" is an index level, determined by the United States Government, that reflects the consumption needs of families depending on their size. In 1990, a family of three living on an income of U.S. $10,419 or less was considered to be living in poverty. The poverty line is defined by a comparison of total annual household income, before taxes, with the cost of basic commodities and services (for example, food and rent). Each year the rate is adjusted for inflation.

4. *Statistical Abstract of the United States 1990.*

5. Rebecca M. Blank, "Women's Paid Work, Household Income, and House

hold Well-Being," in Sara E. Rix, ed., *The American Woman 1988–89* (New York: W.W. Norton & Company, 1989).

6. U.S. Bureau of the Census, "Poverty in the U.S.: 1985," in *Current Population Reports,* Series P–60, No. 158 (Washington, D.C.: Government Printing Office, 1987).

7. *The State of Small Business: A Report of the President* (Washington, D.C.: U.S. Government Printing Office, 1989).

8. In the U.S., federal, and some state and local governments, support development of minority-owned businesses (e.g., African-American, Hispanic-American, Native American) by giving them preference when bidding on various government contracts and services.

9. Minnesota is a large state located in the north central portion of the United States. The state capital, St. Paul, is located directly across the river from its "twin" city, Minneapolis. The urban population of the Twin Cities combined is approximately 2.5 million people.

10. "Native American" refers to the descendants of the native people populating North America before the arrival of European settlers. Many Native Americans live on tribal lands, called reservations, held in trust by the U.S. Bureau of Indian Affairs.

Appendix

Programs

The following is a sampling of microenterprise development programs in the United States selected to show the wide range of constituencies and geographic locations being serviced by such programs. A more comprehensive listing of U.S. programs can be found in the *1994 Directory of Microenterprise Programs* listed under publications.

Women's Self-Employment Project (WSEP)
166 West Washington, Suite 730
Chicago, Illinois 60613
(312) 606–8255

WSEP provides credit, technical assistance, and training through an individual lending program, a group lending program (the Full Circle Fund) and an Entrepreneurial Training Program. WSEP's services are targeted to low and moderate income women in the Chicago area. Its goal is to assist these women to achieve self-sufficiency through self-employment.

Coalition for Women's Economic
Development (CWED)
315 West 9th Street, Suite 705
Los Angeles, CA 90015
(213) 489–4995

CWED provides credit and technical assistance services to low-income women in the Los Angeles area through a micro-business workshop, a solidarity circle program, and a revolving loan fund. The solidarity circle program is modelled after Acción International's model which forms groups of borrowers in order to provide peer support and exchange and to encourage loan repayment.

Good Faith Fund
400 Main Street, Suite 118
Pine Bluff, Arkansas 71601
(510) 535–6233
The mission of the Good Faith Fund is to widen the profile of future entrepreneurs to include women, minorities, and dislocated workers through the delivery of credit and credit services and to raise the income levels of low-income and self-employed people. The Good Faith Fund was one of the first programs developed in the U.S. to test the Grameen Bank's (Bangladesh) group-lending model. Created in 1988, the Good Faith Fund currently offers group and individual loans to entrepreneurs in rural, sparsely populated counties within the state of Arkansas.

Maine Displaced Homemakers Program
Stoddard House
University of Maine
Augusta, Maine 04330
(207) 621–3432
The program's primary goal is to help prepare disadvantaged women to participate fully in the state's changing economy through innovative pre-employment and self-employment training and support services.

The Lakota Fund
P.O. Box 340
Kyle, South Dakota 57752
(605) 455–2500
Located on the Pine Ridge Indian Reservation, the Lakota Fund's mission is to support the development of private Lakota-owned and -operated businesses on the reservation by providing financial and technical assistance and by fostering personal development. Its circle banking project uses a group lending methodology inspired in part by the Grameen Bank.

Center for Community Self-Help
413 East Chapel Hill Street
Durham, North Carolina 27701
(919) 683–3615
Affiliated with the Self-Help Credit Union, this program is a partner with local organizations in the North Carolina Urban Microenterprise Program. The Center also provides small- to medium-sized loans and technical assistance to businesses and projects that address the economic needs of rural, minority, female, and low-income people in the state.

Eastside Community Investments (ECI)
3228 East 10th Street
Indianapolis, Indiana 46201
(317) 633–7303

ECI's goal is to create jobs and to improve the quality of housing in a disadvantaged section of Indianapolis. It has pioneered an innovative self-employment program for day care providers and also is a participant in the demonstration program to provide self-employment services to women on AFDC.

Women's Initiative for Self-Employment (WISE)
P.O. Box 192145
San Francisco, California 94119
(415) 512–9471

WISE links lower-income women with skills, information, and financing to help them support small and microenterprise business development. It also works to remove institutional barriers that prevent women's equal participation in the economy.

Other Organizations that Provide Information on Self-Employment and Microenterprise Development in the United States

Association for Enterprise Opportunity
320 No. Michigan Avenue
Suite 804
Chicago, Illinois 60611
(312) 357–0177

The Corporation for Enterprise Development
777 North Capital Street, N.W.
Suite 801
Washington, D.C. 20002
(202) 408–9788

The Self-Employment Learning Project
1333 New Hampshire Avenue, N.W.
Suite 1070
Washington, D.C. 20036
(202) 736–5807

Women's Economic Development Program
The Ms. Foundation
141 Fifth Avenue, 6th. Floor
New York, New York 10010
(212) 353–8580

Publications

Please contact publishers directly to ascertain availability, cost of publications, and/or shipping charges.

The Business of Service Business, The Business of Small Business, The Business of a Professional Practice, and *Loan Fund Manual* (WomenVenture, 23-24 University Avenue, Suite 200, St. Paul, Minnesota 55114, USA. Telephone: (612) 646–3808; FAX: (612) 641–7223)

The Business of Self-Sufficiency: Microcredit in the United States, by Valjean McLenighan and Jean Pogge, 1991. (Woodstock Institute, 407 South Dearborn, Chicago, Illinois 60605, USA. Telephone: (312) 427–8070)

Enterprising Women: Local Initiatives for Job Creation, 1989. (OECD Publications Service, 2, rue André-Pascal, 75775 PARIS CEDEX 16, France)

1994 Directory of Microenterprise Programs, Margaret Clark, Tracy Huston, and Barbara Meister, eds., 1994 (Self-Employment Learning Project, The Aspen Institute, 1333 New Hampshire Avenue, N.W., Suite 1070, Washington, D.C. 20036, USA. Telephone: (202) 446–6410; FAX: (202) 467–0790)

Hopeful Change: The Potential of Micro-Enterprise Programs as Community Revitalization Intervention, by Jacqueline Novogratz, 1992. (The Rockefeller Foundation, 1133 Avenue of the Americas, New York, New York 10036, USA. Telephone: (212) 869–8500)

Opening the Marketplace to Small Enterprise: Where Magic Ends and Development Begins by Ton de Wilde, Stijntje Schreurs with Arleen Richman, 1991. (Kumarian Press, 630 Oakwood Ave., Suite 119, West Hartford, Connecticut 06110–1529, USA. Telephone: (203) 953–0214; FAX: (203) 953–8579)

Widening the Window of Opportunity: Strategies for the Evolution of Microenterprise Loan Funds prepared by Shorebank Advisory Services, Inc., 1992. (The Charles Stewart Mott Foundation, Mott Foundation Building, Flint, Michigan 48502–1851, USA. Telephone: (313) 238–5651)

Women's Ventures; Assistance to the Informal Sector in Latin America by Marguerite Berger and Mayra Buvinic, 1989. (Kumarian Press, West Hartford, Connecticut [see address above])

IV

INTERNATIONAL

7

Child Care: Meeting the Needs of Working Mothers and Their Children

By Ann Leonard and Cassie Landers
with Caroline Arnold (Nepal), Jorge Mejia (Ecuador),
and Aster Haregot (Ethiopia)

*During the past decade, program initiatives in the areas of "women in develop-
ment" and "early childhood development" have each received attention, but generally each subject area has its own proponents and practitioners, as well as its
own agenda for action. Rarely is it acknowledged that the major constituency for
all of these efforts is one and the same: women with young (infant and preschool)
children. Today most women within both the developing and developed worlds
must work to ensure the survival, let alone the well-being, of their families. One of
the most gnawing questions all working mothers face is "Who will care for the
children?" And beyond the issue of who will provide care for children is the question of the quality of care the children will receive, an issue that affects their
health, their socialization skills, and their intellectual development.*

*In this chapter, developed in cooperation with the Consultative Group on Early
Childhood Care and Development, with support from UNICEF, we seek to bring
together the critical elements of women's work and child care, reviewing the
issues from three different perspectives: child care as a means of enabling women
to work, as a source of employment for women, and as a way of meeting the developmental needs of young children. We will examine three different UNICEF-supported approaches to child care on three different continents—Asia (Nepal),
Africa (Ethiopia), and South America (Ecuador)—that have been developed with
the needs of working women in mind and, in two instances, alongside program
components that support women's economic activities. These examples not only
offer positive solutions for women who work, but also provide opportunities for*

many women to receive training and to develop management and leadership skills, as well as gain employment as child-care providers.

Overview

Women's Work and Child Care

They already grow most of the developing world's food, market most of its crops, fetch most of its water, collect most of its fuel, feed most of its animals, weed most of its fields.

And when their work outside the home is done, they light the Third World's fires, cook its meals, clean its compounds, wash its clothes, shop for its needs, and look after its old and its ill.

And they bear and care for its children.[1]

The vast majority of mothers in the world today are working and earning. Where they work may range from the family compound, to nearby fields, to local markets, to industrial parks, to corporate headquarters; but in both developing and developed countries women are economically active, providing support for themselves, their children, and their families. In 1985, the official rate of female labor force participation was 32 percent. In India, for example, women were contributing, exclusive of services as housewives, 36 percent of the nation's net domestic product. In fact, since 1950 the growth of women's participation has surpassed that of men by two to one.[2]

In the Third World, while women have always carried a heavy burden of work in suport of the family, the effects of industrialization, urbanization, migration, and the severe global economic recession of the 1980s have forced more and more women to seek paid employment, generally in addition to their unpaid but vital household production responsibilities. An even greater number of women, however, earn income in the informal sector, where work is typically low-paying and insecure.[3] In addition, the same factors noted above, combined with changing social patterns, have resulted in many more women becoming the primary source of economic support for their families: In Ghana it is reported that over 29 percent of households are headed by women,[4] and in some societies the number can reach as high as 50 percent of all households with children. As Marianne Schmink notes in her introduction to the report, *Women, Low-income Households and Urban Services in Latin America,* "Many women in working-class households are in sole support or important contributors to household income," and "For mothers, access to some form of day care is probably the single most important factor determining participation in income-earning activities."[5]

Working Mothers

Not only are more mothers working but, in both the modern and traditional sectors, more mothers with very young children now find it necessary to venture further from home in order to provide a livelihood for the family. While it is difficult to find statistical breakdowns of the number of working mothers in most parts of the world, especially where large numbers of women are employed in the informal sector, in the United States today nearly 57 percent of women with children under the age of six are employed, and the trend appears to be growing.[6] The number of women returning to the job market in the U.S. within one year of giving birth, for instance, rose from 31 percent in 1976 to 50.8 percent in 1987.[7] Results of the Infant Feeding Study show that in Bangkok, Thailand, approximately one-third of mothers surveyed were working within the first year following childbirth; 20 percent employed away from home by the time the child was two months old; and 31 percent by the time the child reached 12 months. In Nairobi, Kenya, 25 percent of mothers surveyed were working by the time their child reached six months, and 29 percent were employed when the child was nine to ten months of age.[8]

For all of these working mothers, the critical question is who is going to care for their children while they are working, because, in virtually all parts of the world, providing suitable child-care arrangements is the responsibility of the woman. As Dwyer and Bruce point out, "Becoming a parent has a significant effect on women's time use and very little on men's."[9] Balancing the need to work against the safety and welfare of her children is an ever-increasing source of anxiety for working women, one that is alleviated only when adequate child care is available.

Availability of Child Care

One problem is that, in too many cases, adequate child care is not available, and when suitable arrangements do not exist, women face not only limitation of employment options and confinement to low-income occupations (where there is generally greater flexibility), but frequent high levels of stress, anxiety, and fear. In a study of the need for and availability of child care in Mexico City, Kathryn Tolbert found that the economic crisis of 1982 had forced many married women back into the job market. Most were coping with their child-care needs by taking children with them to work; leaving children with relatives, neighbors, or older siblings; and, for short periods of time, leaving them alone (sometimes tied to their beds to keep them safe).[10]

Economic necessity, migration, and changing social patterns are also making extended families a much less reliable source of child care. As Tolbert discovered in Mexico City, "Grandmothers, important in myth and reality in the Third World for caring for children, are present in only 15 percent of the homes, while other extended family members are present in 10.8 percent of homes."[11] Research has shown that reliance on family and neighbor networks in urban settings is often a reciprocal arrangement which does not allow for full-time or regularly scheduled employment.

Another serious deficiency of the extended family model is where older siblings—usually girls—are removed from school to care for younger children. Not only may the care they provide be of dubious quality, but the girls themselves are being deprived of educational opportunities.

Obviously, there is a need for another caregiving alternative: delegation of responsibility to a formally or informally organized system of child care. Such programs come in forms ranging from highly organized preschool facilities to informal home day care arrangements where caregivers look after a group of neighborhood children. Child-care programs may also be located within cooperatives and factories, or provided by communities, with varying degrees of participation by and cost to working mothers.

While recent initiatives in child care have increased the number of children enrolled, unfortunately there are not nearly enough of them. In addition, many of these new programs have been almost totally child development–oriented and have not been designed with any thought of meeting the needs of working mothers. Hundreds of small-scale demonstration projects, as well as several large-scale initiatives in early childhood education designed to foster children's abilities, are in operation. For example, through an Integrated Child Development Services project, India now provides non-formal preschool programs for more than 25 percent of all children between the ages of three to six and is expanding its reach to include the needs of very young children, as well as pregnant and lactating mothers. In Peru, more than one-fourth of all children between the ages of three and five are targeted for preschool and integrated child development programs, while in Sri Lanka, this expansion is seen in efforts to cover all five-year-old children by extending the age of entry into primary school downward and transforming the first year of schooling into a kindergarten.[12]

However, the reach of such programs is generally limited due to inadequate human and financial resources and/or lack of government commitment. In addition, many of these programs have serious drawbacks for working mothers: care is often offered only for children age three and above, and, typically, programs operate for three to four hours a day and only during the week. And when care for infants is available, there often is no provision for mothers to continue breastfeeding. The failure of such programs to consider the logistical and economic constraints faced by working mothers drastically reduces the number of children they can benefit. Another problem of many comprehensive child development programs is that while their overall goal is to address the health, nutrition, and development needs of young children, in reality many are able to provide only minimal, "custodial," care.

Yet, some child-care programs tailored specifically to meet the needs of working women do exist, and some effective strategies have been identified. In addition to those cited in this chapter, India's "mobile crèches" are day-care facilities located at construction sites that provide services to women construction workers with small children. In rural areas, some agricultural cooperatives have developed systems of day care where women take care of children on a rotational basis during peak planting and harvesting seasons.

The classic factory day-care facility, fostered by the International Labour Organization in the early decades of this century, still offers worksite care for young children of factory workers in some locations. However, the success of such initiatives has been limited at best, given that employers often choose to replace women workers with men rather than assume the costs of day care. Also, women workers frequently are unwilling to submit their children to the hardships and indignities of traveling with them on overcrowded public transportation to and from work sites every day. Taking children far from home, even for good-quality day care, raises many concerns for low-income mothers. As Anderson and Panzio found in Lima, Peru, "The lack of guarantees of a minimal level of safety was evident as well in the women's fears about sending small children away from home for whatever purpose." Women are reluctant to take children on city buses not only because accidents are common, but because "women traveling with sacks of merchandise, their market baskets, and small children are powerless to defend themselves" both against thieves and against sexual harassment.[13]

Transportation is, in fact, a critical issue for many working mothers because not only do they work long hours and for meager pay, but they often live far from work sites. Most of the urban poor are congregated in marginal settlements located on the periphery of large cities. Transportation may take "one-fifth to almost one-third of a minimum daily wage and may take between three and five hours a day." This means that "work days for women who must travel from one part of the city to another are often as long as 13 or 14 hours when transportation time is included."[14] For a rural woman, the distance between the village and her fields may be great, and she must also put in long hours traveling, usually by foot, to seek water, fuel, and fodder.

Programs that offer child care for a limited time each day may address health and nutritional needs and provide educational stimulation for children, but they offer little beyond added frustration for most working mothers. In the case studies that follow, we see how the problem of working women and child care is being addressed through direct participation of local communities in three different regions of the world. In two of the cases, Nepal and Ecuador, new "home care" approaches for addressing child-care needs are operating alongside more traditional, center-based approaches. It is clear that the home care approaches, and the community-supported and -operated model in Ethiopia, are more successfully meeting women's needs not only by providing quality care during realistic working hours, but by helping to empower women to better help themselves, their children, and their community. As Tolbert notes about similar approaches in Mexico, they "are the seeds of social change for women through a process of dignifying their need or desire to work, legitimizing the community's concern for its children, and by bringing together women with similar needs to form, often for the first time in their adult lives, meaningful associations with a group of women from outside their family."[15]

Child-Care Providers

In addition to offering convenient, quality, affordable child care to women who work, these cases demonstrate that community-based child care can also provide employment opportunities for local women. Working as a child-care provider is not only a source of remuneration for many low-income women, but an opportunity to receive training, develop management skills, and increase their status within the community. On the other hand, once trained, child-care providers may still earn less than other comparably skilled workers: When working women as a whole continue to earn on average two-thirds of the income earned by working men, it is not surprising that the wages paid to those entrusted with the care of their children are at the bottom of the salary scale. For example, in Ecuador, trained preschool teachers earn approximately 40 percent of the salary of primary school teachers, and in the U.S., a 1989 survey revealed that child-care providers were earning on average 30 percent of the salary paid to the average elementary school teacher.[16] The result can be frequent turnover of day-care personnel as the newly "trained" providers move on to more lucrative employment.

Whether or not women with children, particularly young children, should work may still be a fashionable topic of debate, but the fact is that they do work and must earn in even greater numbers. What is needed now is to recognize this reality and develop more and better options for providing child-care solutions suitable for working mothers, while at the same time providing children with a safe and supportive environment that meets their developmental needs. It is hoped that the following examples offer some indication of what is possible, as well as point to what still remains to be done.

Nepal: Project Entry Point

Background

Nepal is a country of great diversity. Wedged between India and China, the land descends from the world-famous peaks of the Himalayas, through the hills, to the flat sub-tropical plains known as the *terai*. Ninety-four percent of Nepal's population live in rural areas; around half in villages inaccessible by road. The country's great variety of terrain is matched by its great diversity of ethnic groups and cultural practices.

The population of Nepal is close to eighteen million, including eight million children under the age of fifteen. Large families, averaging six children or more, are the norm. The significance and resilience of the family constitutes a point of convergence across the different ethnic groups. However, in all cases, pressure is now being felt by these large extended families as land holdings, which have been divided and redivided for generations, become too small to support so many people.

Population and ecological pressures are making life ever more precarious. Nepal is currently ranked as one of the world's poorest countries. (According to the World Development Report of 1985, only three other countries had a lower GNP per capital.) Any improvement in the Nepalese economy has been largely offset by population growth (2.66 percent and increasing). Despite investments in agricultural development, most of Nepal's rural population is undergoing a process of impoverishment resulting in increasing nutritional stress—with women and children most at risk.

Women's Lives and Women's Work

Throughout Nepal the vast majority of people are subsistence-level farmers. The family farm produces almost 80 percent of the average annual household income. In the division of labor, the major workload falls upon the woman and it is simply assumed she will fulfill multiple roles. According to comparative time allocation studies, a Nepalese woman must spend almost eleven hours a day just to maintain the family's subsistence level. Men, by comparison, are involved in the family farm enterprise for approximately six hours daily.

According to the Status of Women Reports compiled by Tribhuban University in 1981, there is a general pattern of female predominance in agricultural decisions (and also household matters). Ninety-six percent of women described as "economically active" are engaged in agriculture as low levels of education continue to negatively affect employment of women in the formal sector. In addition to their contribution to the family farm and household maintenance, women also undertake "informal" economic activities, such as small trade, marketing, various crafts, and shopkeeping, to supplement the household income. However, the time rural women in Nepal can spend on activities with potentially higher economic return is limited by their extremely heavy burden of providing food, water, and fuel for the family and caring for children.

As mothers, women play a critical role in their children's development, but they are often limited in their ability to nurture and stimulate their offspring because of social conditions that deprive them of access to food, services, resources, and information. Equally important, they simply have very little time available to spend with their children. Each year it is necessary to go further up in the hills to collect fodder and fuel, taking more and more of their time.

In Nepal, almost 40 percent of children drop out of school during the first year, and of those who remain, 25 percent have to repeat grade one. This is indicative of the difficulty many children have in coping with the school environment. Access of girls and women to educational opportunities is particularly limited, and today 82 percent of Nepalese women are illiterate. This has had a negative impact on their access to knowledge and their participation in the development process. Early on, girls are expected to participate in household labor, particularly in child care, thus reducing the likelihood that they will attend school. Combined with a general lack of confidence in the education system, this has meant that only 30 percent of school-age girls currently are enrolled in primary school; in some districts enrollment of girls is as low as 13 percent, and even when enrolled, their attendance is about 50 percent lower than that of boys.

Child Care and Development

The vast majority of births in Nepal take place in the family home assisted by a traditional birth attendant. The first few months of a child's life are often spent with the mother. Until children are six months old, they are often carried or kept in a basket. Infants usually receive a great deal of affection. Grandparents spend hours playing with them and they are constantly surrounded by other family members. They receive a lot of physi-

Children on an outing in Nepal. *(UNICEF: M. Kawanaka)*

cal contact, which is important, as the quality of early social interaction is central to all children's development.

By the time a child is able to crawl, she/he is increasingly likely to be left in the care of other family members while the mother attends to farm work. As the young infant begins to explore, she/he is exposed to a highly contaminated environment. Thus, from early on, the child's development is subject to frequent set-backs as disease undermines an already precarious nutritional status.

Many Nepalese children suffer from gross deprivation of their most basic needs and one out of six dies before reaching its fifth birthday. Such high infant and child mortality rates (113 & 165, respectively) not only underscore the vicious circle of poverty, but also point to increased risks of damage for the survivors: According to the National Nutrition Survey's weight for-age data, two-thirds of Nepalese children under the age of six are malnourished and an additional 5 percent are very severely affected.

By the time children can walk, they are considered old enough to be left in the care of an older sibling. Girls of five, or even younger, are entrusted with the responsibility of looking after children of one or two. From this time on, the child's information concerning the world comes mostly from other children, rarely in the form of direct instruction but rather by means of imitation. Parents, however, are held responsible for the child's cleanliness, eating habits, and moral qualities.

Identifying the Need

In Nepal, child-development programs must have a strong orientation towards health, nutrition, sanitation, and parental education, because the majority of children who do survive will, for the most part, continue to live in the same potentially debilitating conditions of poverty that put their lives at risk and now threaten their development. There is also an important place for a psycho-social component—often interwoven within other activities—as the developmental perspective complements the emphasis on survival by addressing the question of how these children will live the rest of their lives.

Planning child development programs in Nepal must also take account of the increasing stress women are under just to meet the family's subsistence needs. The demands that accompany their dual roles as nurturer and worker can become overwhelming. The challenge, therefore, is to develop effective programs **which simultaneously address both women's and children's intersecting needs.** Women's lack of access to education and information, as well as the pressures on their time, must be taken into account. Fathers, and the community as a whole, also need to be involved. Education and information should not be directed only at mothers.

In Nepal, expertise in the field of early child development is extremely limited as education below primary school falls outside the formal education system. The Nepal Children's Organization operates centers that provide pre-school education and day care for about 4,000 children; however, these centers are situated in district headquarters and serve the needs of government officials and town residents. While many private preschools can be found in Kathmandu, Nepal's capital, in rural areas there is an almost total lack of any sort of child-care facilities.

Taking Action

The early childhood program described here has been developed as an integral part of the UNICEF-supported Production Credit for Rural Women (PCRW) project. Administered by the Women's Development Section (WDS) of the Ministry of *Panchayat* (the unit of local government in Nepal) and Local Development, the PCRW project provides support for a range of interlinked credit and community development activities carried out by village women. Overall the PCRW project reflects UNICEF's basic services strategy: The child is set within the context of his or her community and the emphasis is on working towards social and environmental changes within the community that will benefit the community at large and thereby enhance children's overall health and development.

The PCRW project works through field staff to assist low-income rural women to take advantage of credit schemes available through national banking institutions for agricultural production, cottage industries, and services. As these are the types of activities women are already doing, they are considered the most suitable income-generation activities. The PCRW's community development component offers groups of women the opportunity to participate in the definition of local problems and the search for solutions. The activities undertaken vary from site to site according to perceived needs and available resources.

Besides having their own intrinsic merits, PCRW's economic and community development components strengthen each other because a woman's ability to take full advantage of economic opportunities often depends on the availability of services provided through community development efforts. And, as the focus of community development efforts has been on women's needs, the emphasis has been on projects that reduce the time it takes women to complete their daily chores—for example, providing water near the village or a mill for processing oil and grains, as well as establishing child-care facilities.

In the original project design, child-care arrangements were envisaged as one small component of PCRW's community development approach, as the main concern was to free up women's time so that they would be better able to engage in income-generation activities. But more and more frequently field workers identified child care as a priority until it became a vital facet of PCRW's complex of interrelated activities.

Experience has shown that while child development efforts that are part of broader community development efforts are better able to benefit from multi-sectoral support and to garner cooperation from the community, the task of actually involving parents and establishing genuinely community-based participatory programs is long and complex. Further, the ability of communities, themselves often on the edge of the cash economy, to take over the running costs of the child-care centers has also been problematic.

PRCW planners realized that in Nepal, center-based child-care arrangements alone were not the answer. Working with UNICEF, they developed several low-cost strategies firmly based in the community and able to reach greater numbers of children:

- Home-based programs to be run by mothers themselves on a rotational basis for children up to three years of age;
- Community-based child-care centers for children three to six years of age;
- Parent education classes, based at child-care and community centers, covering subjects from prenatal care to concerns of school-age children;
- A child-to-child program that would strengthen older children's abilities to promote the health, welfare, and development of younger children.

While all four strategies have been implemented to some degree, it is the home-based programs that have clearly been the most effective at meeting women's immediate needs for child care, providing a safe and nurturing environment for young children, and offering local women a chance to learn new skills and develop self-confidence.

The Home-Based "Entry Point" Program

Referred to in Nepali as *praveshdwar,* which translates as the "entry point," or first door into a big, important place, this is by far the most innovative component of the Nepal project. Because of her central role in the family, the "entry point" program concentrates on the mother and begins in the village home.

Mothers who want to participate form themselves into a group (usually six). As with other PCRW activities, the group is the focal point for action. Before training is provided, the community must have arranged for a site for the program that includes a latrine and a kitchen. In some places the community has given a room to the program; in others, particularly in the terai, where cold is not a problem, they have constructed a small shelter. But in most instances, the mothers run the program on a rotational basis in their own homes (although often, if one of the mothers has a room that is not much used, she will offer this to the program) for children one to three years old. The members meet weekly to ensure that the program is running smoothly, and each group establishes a schedule according to its own needs.

A basic kit of materials, in a tin trunk, is supplied to each group. The kit contains cooking utensils, plates, cups, a bucket, a jug, personal hygiene materials, a rug, two dolls, three puppets, a ball, and a drum. Besides the basic kit, a play material kit is also supplied, containing materials that help introduce specific concepts such as shapes, colors, body parts, and domestic animals. Nine different kits are presently available; neighboring groups periodically exchange kits, in this way exposing the children to a wide variety of toys and play materials. Various bamboo toys, made by the fathers, are also used.

As almost all the mothers are illiterate, a pictorial chart is used to indicate the daily schedule of activities. Children engage in individual play activities that teach a variety of different skills and concepts, and they play simple, creative, non-competitive games. A strong emphasis is placed on personal hygiene and use of the latrine. Each day the mothers contribute food to provide a nutritious meal.

Sri Maya is an "entry point" mother living in the middle hills of Nepal. This morning she is arranging a set of bamboo toys made by the village fathers as she waits for the children to arrive. Suddenly she hears laughing and chattering outside. The other children have started to arrive with their mothers and are wondering what game they will play today. Sri Maya gestures a formal namaste *(the traditional greeting in Nepal) and then, one by one, takes the five children from their mother's arms and gives them a hug.*

She discusses the weather for a moment with the women—they may be a little late coming to collect the children today. It looks as if the rains may be coming soon and the planting needs to be finished. This is no problem— one of the joys of running the group themselves is the flexibility it provides.

After helping the children get washed up, Sri Maya takes them outside where they play a new game in which they dance around while Sri Maya plays a madal *(drum). When she stops they have to pick up as many corn-cobs as they can and place them in a big cane hoop. It takes them quite a while to get the idea and Sri Maya's four-year-old son has to help the two-year-olds.*

One of the most notable things is the way Sri Maya is interacting constantly with either the whole group or an individual child. Even while preparing their lunch she is talking with them—discussing the pegboard one has just completed; commiserating with the child who has a sick dolly; suggesting where someone else might look for the ball. And so the day progresses through games and stories and songs—Sri Maya always available to lead the exploration, join in the laughter, and wipe away the occasional tear and spill.

Benefits from the "entry point" program, however, are not limited only to the children participating. The quality of interaction between mothers and all their children changes due to increased knowledge and confidence in their new role. Mothers also find that, although they are spending one day per week looking after a group of children, they actually have more time to engage in other activities, including income generation.

———

I used to think this program would interfere with my work but Naresh doesn't seem to get sick like he used to—I used to always be having to spend time at home because I was too concerned to leave him, he got so ill. Before, even when he was well, I used to worry about getting back to the house in the middle of the day to make sure everything was OK—and my fields are so far away it took me one and a half hours. . . . And Sumita is so happy because she has been able to go to school instead of caring for him all day.

———

Moreover, by working cooperatively over an extended period of time, the mothers learn basic management skills and increase their sense of group responsibility. The skills and confidence they gain are then carried over into other community development and income-generation projects. And this is a two-way process: income-generation groups often end up starting a home-based child care program. As of May 1989, there were fifty-four groups in operation in eleven districts of Nepal and proposals had been received from fifty already established credit groups who were busy making preparations to start child-care programs as soon as they could be scheduled for training.

Training, Supervision, and Evaluation

Expertise in the field of early childhood development is, as previously mentioned, limited in Nepal. Therefore, at the beginning of 1986, UNICEF supported the establishment of Seto Gurans National Child Development Services. Seto Gurans has now assumed the lead role in meeting the training needs of the PCRW early child development program.

Training for the home-based program takes place on-site and lasts for four days. The training approach was originally developed in a small village through discussions and activities of WDS field staff and groups of village women. Since then it has continually been modified in response to field needs. Components include, in addition to general child development themes, a focus on health, habits of hygiene (especially important where 95 percent of the population do not have access to a latrine), and nutrition. In the nutrition component, mothers learn basic elements of both nutrition

Children in "entry point" homes get individual attention. *(UNICEF: M. Kawanaka)*

and growth monitoring. Nutritious meals are prepared using only locally grown food.

While the mothers attend their training course, the fathers are shown how to make the toys which will be used in the program. These toys are constructed out of bamboo, a material that is readily available throughout the country. The women are then trained in how to use these toys to play a variety of games that will be used to present different skills and concepts to the children. The training emphasizes the importance of the mothers' roles as "teachers," and aims to build up the women's confidence in their ability to manage and run the program. While practical arrangements are discussed during the training, the day-to-day decisions involved in running the program will be made by the women themselves.

Virtually all of the mothers in the "entry point" program are illiterate, so a good deal of time is spent on how to use the picture inventory in the basic kit and the daily schedule. In the beginning, the mothers are often shy and reticent, but it never takes long before everyone is laughing and joining in the games.

Throughout the training, the mothers are involved in making up words to songs and deciding how they want to organize their daily schedule. They are surprised that their opinions are not only invited, but used. That it really is their program is very evident to anyone observing one of these training sessions. It is almost possible to feel the group grow in strength and dignity while, at the same time, they are falling over themselves laughing as they try out some of the games.

The early child-care and development program in Nepal also includes child-care centers serving groups of 25–35 children, three to six years old. Currently there are approximately sixty child-care centers serving some 1,800 children scattered through thirty-two of Nepal's seventy-five districts. Operated under the guidance of a community child-care management committee, each center is run by two women selected from the community, a teacher, and an assistant (known as a *sevika*). They are trained during a one-month course at Seto Gurans. While the women are supposed to leave their children at home, in reality there are always at least five or six infants who are still breastfeeding or children who are unwell and can't be left at home present during these sessions. In cases where a woman is living alone and has no one to look after her children, she will bring them along. In marked contrast to almost all other training programs in Nepal (even those that are supposedly serving the needs of women and children), Seto Gurans believes it is important that women who need to bring their children still be accommodated in the training program. This has always been done successfully, although it sometimes puts an extra burden on the training staff. Still they have no doubts that it is a correct policy decision.

Staff of the Women in Development Section, which administers the PCRW project, are divided into two major groups: (1) field staff (WDOs and WDAs) who facilitate the design and implementation of economic activities and community development projects; and (2) central staff who provide the technical, logistic, and administrative support required for field work. Training for both central and field staff is an important part of capacity building. As with other PCRW activities, the group is the key. Before any training is provided, a great deal of time is invested in the group formation process. The field workers (Women and Development Officers, or WDOs, and Women and Development Assistants, WDAs) have the vital role of initially mobilizing groups within villages. One of the great strengths of PCRW's field staff training is the attention given to respecting, building rapport with, and motivating village women. This has become the indispensable base for all PCRW village-level training. Once a program is established, field staff continue to support, supervise, and provide further training, factors that are, perhaps, the most important contributions to the long-term success of the program.

Program Strengths

The early childhood program has a number of notable strengths, all of which are closely interlinked. These strengths pivot around the way program goals and activities have both evolved as family and community-based approaches and have been designed to meet the needs of working mothers. This is particularly true of the entry point program. Activities are not rigid, externally imposed prescripts, but rather exhibit a built-in flexibility that allows families and communities to take the lead role in deciding how they want things to run. The planning process starts with village women and is responsive to their perceived needs. Planning, management, supervision, and support are all highly decentralized.

A second strength is that the multi-faceted child development efforts have been integrated within broader community development and economic activities. This too has had a positive impact on community participation. Moreover, the complex relationship among women's work, credit opportunities, and early child care and development programs has been recognized.

Recognition of the crucial importance of the group process has been another strength. Forming groups around common purposes, such as obtaining credit or starting a home-based program, is critical to building women's confidence in their own abilities to improve their lives. The mutual support the women thereby provide to each other has many implications for improving their children's well-being as well. It is this principle of building on the strengths of women, families, and communities, rather than using a "deficit model," which is so important.

This recognition of strengths is also central to the development of a training program that emphasizes respect for what people already know and do, and confidence building. In addition, training curriculum and program materials are all highly relevant, attractive, practical, and well matched to the educational levels of the trainees. Recognition of the interactive effect among health, nutrition, and stimulation is implicit in the design of the curriculum; and this integrated approach is evident throughout all aspects of the early child care and development program.

Collaboration among a number of different agencies at different levels has contributed to the success of the early child education program. Collaboration between WDS and UNICEF, and Seto Gurans, has been important at all levels. UNICEF has provided both financial and practical assistance and has played an important role in supporting conceptualization and development of alternative, complementary approaches.

Seto Gurans has provided vital technical assistance and support for development of training, materials development, and supervision systems. At the district level, links with the government health services and with the community health component of PCRW have been emphasized.

Problems Encountered

In Nepal, dispersed populations, difficult terrain, and lack of motorable roads place severe constraints on efforts to reach out to the children of Nepal and reinforce the need for strengthening the decentralized supervision system. Another major constraint is the continued dependency of the program on external funding. While the vital importance of achieving self-sufficiency has been recognized for some time, progress has been slow. This is a lesson that should be kept in mind by other agencies embarking on similar efforts.

Effects on Women, Children, and Community

Informal and anecdotal evidence suggests that the program is having a significant positive impact. The ability of early child care and education programs to free up mothers' time is an obvious and important benefit to women. The Chief of the Nutrition and Child Care section of WDS says that the comment, "We are mentally free now," is one she hears time and again when visiting the entry point groups and day-care centers.

Within the home-based program, it is also clear that the mothers' active involvement in running the program has been just as important to their self-development as other PCRW activities. As their confidence increases in their new roles as "teachers," some begin to assume leadership roles in the community, and the management and organization skills they learn are useful in other activities.

One also sees the contrast between the children attending a home-based program or a child-care center and children from a neighboring village where no early childhood activities are operating. This contrast is evident in terms of the children's general appearance, their health and nutritional status, and, equally important, their responsiveness, interactions, and interest in exploring their surroundings. As one supervisor said, "There is a difference. The spark is strong. There is hope and happiness"; or as a three-year-old in a home-based program put it, "It's fun. My mother knows how to play all these games."

The supervisor goes on to note that "the impact of the program on children's health, nutrition, and school performance is striking." Recent

Play activities at an "entry point" home. *(UNICEF: M. Kawanaka)*

reports from WDOs in Kotari, Sivangunj, and Tharpu districts report that all their child-care center children are going on to the elementary school, and these are children from villages where previously fewer than a third of all children ever attended school. In addition, as Mikana K.C., one of the most experienced supervisors, points out, "children who have participated in an entry point program or a child-care center don't drop out or have to repeat classes like the other children do."

―――――

"Childhood is the initial stage of life as the foundation is the first design of a house. The house can be strongly built only if the foundation is laid strongly. Similarly, if the child is to prosper and be strong, we must make the early childhood days good. Because life is so hard for almost everyone here, it is hard to think enough of children's health and better future, but our early childhood programs have created new avenues. Sometimes it is hard to provide even two meals a day, but we believe we can make our children's future brighter, as someone reaching their destination with a torch in the dark. . . . I think we will reach our goal taking our own steps. . . ."
Radha, a mother from Utter Pari, Surkhet, Nepal

―――――

Looking to the Future

In looking toward expansion of the early child development program, attention needs to be given to issues of program replicability and sustainability. The integrated nature of the program, its "process" rather than "product" approach, makes replication more complicated than for projects focused solely on one problem.

Low-cost programs facilitate expansion. However, whether or not low-cost programs can be developed that function effectively on a large scale is still an open question and careful cost analyses are needed. The idea that community participation does not cost anything must be abandoned. Where mothers and community members are the basic service deliverers, their training needs are considerable, and training must be a continuing affair that is combined with intensive and capable supervision. The supervisors themselves also need good professional support.

For example, within the PCRW's early childhood education component, it costs approximately $120 to get one home-based group established, equipped, and trained. After this, no external support is needed for the day-to-day operation of the program. While this is an impressively low figure, it must be remembered that the program is still small-scale and relatively new. The costs of follow-up training and support still need to be determined.

Income generation has been stressed as a primary means of achieving self-sufficiency and is a logical point of contact between PCRW's programming for women and for child development. Fruit tree growing and pig breeding are examples of activities that have been initiated in support of the child-care center program in all sites. But while the child-care centers may continue to be major focal points of the early childhood program, one of their most important functions eventually may be to serve as training and coordination resources for a variety of complementary early child care and education activities.

Ecuador: Community-Based Child-Care Programs in the Suburbios of Guayaquil

Background

Located on the shores of the Guayas River, which flows into the Pacific Ocean, the city of Guayaquil is Ecuador's second largest city and most important port. During the last several decades, Guayaquil has grown from 260,000 inhabitants in 1950 to 2,750,976 in 1989 (as estimated by the National Institute of Statistics and Censuses), as an oil boom, beginning in 1972, brought an expansion of modern industry and increased public expenditures in urban areas. Large-scale migration to Guayaquil has resulted in the growth of marginal slums and squatter settlements. Known locally as suburbios, these areas are characterized by extremely poor living conditions exacerbated by insufficient employment and income opportunities, substandard housing, and inadequate access to the social infrastructure.

Identifying the Need

In all the suburbios, women have been forced to make a more significant contribution to family income in recent years, working both at home and outside, as the cost of living has continued to rise. Nearly a third of working women perform income-earning activities at home, and 18.7 percent earn income outside their homes. Over half of this latter group work as domestic servants. More than 16 percent of all households in the suburbios are headed by women.

Children in the suburbios frequently suffer from poor health, as hygiene and sanitation in the outlying areas of Guayaquil are very inadequate and malnutrition is common. A study of local child-care practices, undertaken in 1988, found that when women with young children must go out to work, they often resort to locking their children up in the house while they are away, or older daughters end up minding younger children, thus missing school.

Taking Action

As existing child-care facilities in the marginal areas of Guayaquil were few, and those available were beyond the means of most residents, UNICEF and the Government of Ecuador incorporated day care as an integral part of the Project of Basic Urban Services of Guayaquil, begun in 1979 to promote integrated development within the city's marginal areas. The project included four basic components: Preschool Child Care, Primary Health Care, Social Communication and Recreation, and Women's Promotion and Organization. The Program of Preschool Child Care began in 1979. The Program of Women's Promotion and Organization finally got under way in 1983, under the joint aegis of two institutions: the National Office of Women and the National Institute of Children and Families (known as INNFA, from the Spanish acronym).

The four programs were geared toward improving living conditions for inhabitants of selected marginal urban sectors of Guayaquil through provision of services and efficient, low-cost opportunities that incorporate community participation into the design, implementation, and evaluation phases of the projects. They are of particular interest because their aim is to address problems affecting residents of the marginal areas of the city through a variety of different but interrelated activities. For example, the need of women in the suburbios to earn income was addressed directly through the Women's Promotion and Organization Program, which focused on income-generating activities, and less directly through the Preschool Child Care Program, which not only provided a source of good-quality, reliable child care that enabled women to work, but also provided employment as care-givers to two specific groups of women: home care mothers and high school and college-age promoters. Likewise, the Primary Health Program provided services to children involved in the preschool program.

Setting Up the Child-Care Program

Like the Nepal program, the Program of Integrated Care for Preschoolers in Guayaquil provides two models applicable to an urban setting: the Community Home, and the Community Center models. The Community Home for Children (HCI) model provides care for children of working mothers in homes within the community. However, in this case, it is in the home of a female neighbor who has been trained to work full-time as a child-care provider. She is helped by an assistant also trained by the program. Generally fifteen children, ranging in age from three months to six years, stay at the HCIs between eight and nine hours a day, five days a week.

The Community Center for Children (CCI) model offers care for a maximum of 100 children at a site provided by the community (a community center, church, or sports club). Children from three to six years of age attend these centers five days a week, from three to four hours a day, during either the morning or afternoon session. They are cared for by young people selected by the community and trained by the program, known as community promoters.

Both community promoters and care-giving mothers are selected by the community. In the case of care-giving mothers, they must have experience raising children, their house must be adequate to provide good quality care to additional children, and they must know how to read and write. In the case of community promoters, they must be secondary school or university students and reside within the community. Their duties are considered half-time employment. Supervisors are university-level professionals with experience in child-care programs. The basic selection criteria for families participating in the program is that they are low-income, the mother is working or looking for work, the family has no other appropriate member who can take care of the children, and the family promises to comply with program requirements.

The Women's Promotion Program

The Women's Promotion Program seeks to assist women to improve their lives through provision of information, consciousness raising, training, expansion of productive roles, and relief of domestic burdens. It encourages women to come together to solve problems and to design, execute, and evaluate social programs.

In addition to organizing women within the community, the women's program has developed a Basic Staples Marketing Network made up of "honest" storekeepers, selected by the community, who promise to sell basic staples (such as rice, sugar, eggs, etc.) at fair prices in exchange for access to training and credit programs operated by INNFA. The women's program has also managed to establish, in cooperation with commercial banks, a loan program for micro-entrepreneurs, as well as offering training in a variety of areas, including nontraditional subjects for women such as auto mechanics and appliance repair. While the program gives priority to women, it does not necessarily exclude men. A woman belonging to one of the program's neighborhood organizations may also be a care-giving mother or promoter within the preschool program or may have worked as a community health promoter.

How the Preschool Programs Operate

Both the Community Homes and the Children's Centers are nonconventional and non-institutional. They focus on the use of community resources—that is, human resources (mothers, young people, leaders), physical facilities (community locales, buildings) and economic resources (contributions from the child's family)—that are mobilized to provide better care for children.

In the home care program, mothers bring their children to the designated neighboring home at 7:00 A.M., where they are greeted by the care-giving mother. During the day the children participate in a variety of recreation and stimulation activities, such as painting, paper-cutting, pasting, singing, dancing, etc. They also are given three meals during the day.

———

Doña Emperatriz de Lara started working as a day-care mother nine years ago and has been taking care of children in her home, uninterruptedly, ever since. Everyone who lives in the area knows her and her husband, a mild-mannered tailor, and their three student daughters. Her house, which is always open to visitors, is very clean and always being remodeled and enlarged. Although the maximum number of children per household as defined by the program is fifteen, she is always taking care of seventeen or sometimes even eighteen because her neighbors ask her to do so, and it is hard for her to turn them down. "This child came here three months ago skinny as a rail," says Doña Emperatriz, "and look at how plump and healthy he is now."

At the child-care centers, children stay either from 8:00 A.M. to noon or from 2:00 to 6:00 in the afternoon. Most of this time is spent in stimulation and recreational activities. The children are given a snack midway through their stay. They are usually divided by age groups; each promoter assumes responsibility for no more than twenty-five children.

Anita started working as a promoter in a child-care center seven years ago; she had just finished high school. She was particularly dynamic in working with children, never running out of energy. Little by little, Anita started helping her colleagues, showing them how to fill out the children's attendance cards, how to organize and lead meetings with the children's parents, and what exercises and songs the children liked most. So, after awhile, she was appointed as a supervisor and formally hired by the Ministry of Social Welfare to provide technical support to the other children's promoters. She probably is more widely accepted than other supervisors who do not come from the community; the children's parents know her well and feel confident about asking her advice.

Education of Mothers, Family, and Community

An important activity carried out by the program, but one of the most difficult to accomplish, is educating the mothers who bring their children to the homes and centers for care. (Mothers and daughters are included in training events; fathers and brothers are invited but usually do not attend.) For one thing, there is the disparity in the mothers' educational level; second, many of them work downtown (especially as household servants) and put in long days which do not allow them very much time for meetings; the lack of available time is an even more serious problem for mothers who are the head of the household and carry enormous responsibilities on their shoulders. Therefore, parent education basically is achieved in two ways: during the daily interaction that occurs when mothers leave off and pick up their children and through meetings with the parents' committee in the Community Home every two weeks.

Factors Contributing to the Success of the Program

The Preschool Child Care Program effectively meets what the community feels is an urgent need. Working mothers view the Community Homes as a feasible and positive child-care solution well adapted to their needs. Parents view the Community Centers as an opportunity for their children to develop, to make friends, and, above all, to get ready for school.

The cost for these services to parents represents a small percentage of their income and is quite low in comparison with similar, privately-run services. However, the program does require that parents participate actively in the operation of these services by attending periodic meetings to discuss the economic problems, logistical aspects, food supply, etc. A very positive result of this greater involvement is that parents gradually acquire a greater awareness about the development of their own children.

Problems Encountered

While the program has been successful in mobilizing the community to support the integral care of children, a number of bureaucratic and political problems have been encountered. Government procedures for hiring personnel, for example, or for distributing funds to the communities are slow and complicated. And when a decision is made to transfer a certain amount of decision-making capacity and resources to community organizations, the necessary steps are not always taken to prepare the community, either in terms of training or in setting up control mechanisms.

On the local front, community leaders involved in hiring local promoters and day-care mothers have frequently applied undue pressure on the Ministry to choose their relatives or friends, even though these individuals did not comply with established requirements, or have used their authority to pay local staff as an opportunity to exert influence or to demand payment of a small percentage of their wages as a fee. In addition, in the marginal urban sectors, especially in a city the size of Guayaquil, political activity is intense and the promoters and day-care mothers are often subjected to political pressure.

Effects on Women, Children, and Community

Since it began in 1979, the Preschool Child Care Program has been evaluated three times by outside teams, who emphasized the following results. First, both modes of preschool child care meet an evident need of the community. In the case of HCIs, for example, mothers can go out to work or look for work outside the home with the assurance that their children are being adequately cared for, fed, and protected from physical risks. In the case of CCIs, children have the opportunity to develop their intellectual, emotional, physical, and social potential. Such services did not exist in the community prior to the project. However, the demand for these services by the community is always greater than the program's capacity to respond.

The Preschool Child Care Program has had considerable impact on participating children's health and on their nutritional and psychosocial development. While updated information is not currently available, the testimony of care-giving mothers indicates that many children who came to the homes poorly nourished have made quick recoveries. Obviously, care, regular feeding, and prevention and control of diarrhea have all contributed to improving the children's nutritional status. The children from the homes and centers also have access to the Ministry of Health vaccination program.

While the most complex aspect, in terms of measuring the impact of the program on children, has to do with their psychosocial development, the children's improvement in the area of socialization is evident. They are less timid toward visitors and strangers and better able to share with their playmates. In the area of language development, the children are better able to express themselves. The environment of the homes and centers is definitely much more stimulating than their own homes, where preschool children's most frequent entertainment is watching television. (Most families in the suburbios do have televisions.)

For working mothers, the greatest benefit of the child-care program is the satisfaction and peace of mind that a mother feels when she leaves her child at a community home, where he or she will receive complete protection and care while she is at work. Something similar may be said of the parents whose children attend the CCIs. Parents interviewed report that, since their children have been attending the CCI, they are more alert and intelligent, less timid, and are becoming prepared for school. However, since the centers provide care for children for only half a day, they cannot effectively meet the needs of most working mothers.

As for the child-care providers, the two major advantages of participation for them have been the stipend that they receive (approximately U.S. $35 per week in 1988, or about 40 percent of the salary earned by a primary school teacher) and the opportunity to receive training in specific fields of social action. Another important incentive has been the opportunity to acquire higher status within the community.

One of the community home care sites in Guayaquil, Ecuador. *(UNICEF)*

Program Costs

An evaluation team (composed by the Ministry of Social Welfare, the National Development Council, and UNICEF) that analyzed the Guayaquil Project estimated that, by 1983, the cost of each HCI, serving fifteen children, included an initial investment of U.S. $210 and operating, supervision, technical suport, and monitoring costs of U.S. $1,850 per year. As for the CCIs, the investment costs were estimated at U.S. $876, while operating, supervision, technical support, and monitoring costs were estimated at U.S. $2,620 per year.

Regarding financial support for the program, initially UNICEF's financial input made up some 80 percent of the total cost, with national institutions covering the remaining 20 percent. A mechanism was provided for increasing contributions from national institutions so that UNICEF's input might gradually decrease. In general terms, this mechanism has worked well, but there have been difficult times, especially due to the slowness and inefficiency of public-sector funding mechanisms and the overcentralization of financial decision-making in the national capital. Despite these constraints, INNFA has now assumed full funding of the Women's Program, and the Ministry of Social Welfare is carrying 90 percent of the cost of the Child Care Program.

Looking to the Future

Since 1979, when the first community homes were founded, the Ministry of Social Welfare has been able to expand the program practically nationwide. As of 1987, there were 69 HCIs, 109 CCIs, and 10 Home Centers (a new model), serving a total of 55,222 children and 38,653 participating families in Guayaquil. The national government which took office in August 1988 announced its intention to expand coverage to 108,000 children throughout the entire country, thus creating a so-called Community Child Care Network.

Ethiopia: Providing Child Care within Farmers' Cooperatives

Background

The Melka Oba Farmers' Producers' Cooperative is located about 120 km. southeast of Addis Ababa, Ethiopia's capital. Accessible by road all year round, the cooperative is situated on a plain flanked by hills, dissected by the Awash River flowing from west to east. The area is hot and dry with very limited rainfall, making farming undependable for subsistence. Except for fruit trees and a few shrubs here and there, the land is completely deforested.

As part of Ethiopia's land reform program, 192 farmers and their families from the Harrarghe Region were resettled in Melka Oba by the government. Fruit growers by occupation, they were given 155 hectares of land that had formerly been owned by a private enterpreneur. The settlers—103 men and 89 women farmers, 124 children up to 9 years of age, and 34 children between 10 and 15—organized themselves as a producers' cooperative and began growing fruits and vegetables for the local market.

Agricultural tasks on the cooperative are carried out in groups. Cooperative members are divided into six teams to carry out farming activities: two teams in the orchard, two teams in cereal production, one team in growing vegetables; and a team that serves as sentinels against thieves and wild animals. A cooperative organizer, a home economics agent, and one development cadre from the Ministry of Agriculture's Woreda District office provide assistance to the cooperative. The average monthly income of a cooperative member is Birr 120 (approximately U.S. $58). Payment is based on work points earned for seven hours of daily work, six days per week.

Identifying the Need

An assessment of the situation in Melka Oba prior to the start of the daycare project revealed that the women were overworked in comparison to the men. Their tasks on the farm and in the house left them little time for relaxation. No maternal-child health services were available and children lacked proper care. The community did not have a clean and safe water supply and environmental sanitation left much to be desired. The result was that most of the children suffered from common health problems such as diarrhea, gastroenteritis, conjunctivitis, malaria, and ear and respiratory infections. The infant mortality rate was reported to be very high.

In the cooperative, as mothers received only 45 days' leave after delivery, they soon went back to work, primarily in the fields, for the entire day. This practice resulted in a dramatic decrease in breastfeeding. Also, when the mothers returned to work, their children were often neglected, not having a conducive environment for sound physical, social, and mental development. In the absence of mothers and fathers, young children were, in most cases, left to fend for themselves, or elder sisters and brothers were charged with the responsibility of caring for their younger siblings, including infants. While an elementary school was situated about six kms. away from the farm, the absence of a day-care center had forced the community to turn their 6–10-year-old children into babysitters instead of sending them to school.

Worse still, some parents would lock their houses when they went to the fields, so the children could not stay indoors. With the river so near to the houses, young children could easily drown; as wild animals and snakes roam about, the children were continually exposed to danger. The children also were not fed on time or properly. Overall, the absence of day care, inadequate clinic services, absence of pit latrines and refuse pits, lack of clean and potable water, all contributed to putting children and women in a hazardous situation. The community's attitude towards women was traditional, the men considering child care to be solely the women's responsibility, something they were expected to do in addition to carrying out time-consuming and often arduous domestic chores and fulfilling their duties on the farm.

Taking Action

In 1982, the cooperative requested assistance from the district administrators to establish a day-care center. It was willing to do everything within its means to realize this goal, provided it could receive the necessary technical and material support. The situation of women and children in Melka Oba was brought to the attention of the Integrated Family Life Education Project (IFLE), a semiautonomous agency supervised by the Ministry of Labour and Social Affairs and mainly financed by UNICEF. It has been running integrated, non-formal, and action-oriented family life education programs for many years.

In January 1983, IFLE established an Interagency Committee composed of the National Children's Commission, the Ministries of Health and Agriculture, and UNICEF, with IFLE servicing as secretariat. The purpose of the Interagency Committee was to identify the needs of the Melka Oba Cooperative and to seek solutions that would improve living conditions there.

Establishment of a crèche and a kindergarten were considered urgent interventions that would also serve as entry points for further initiatives in child survival and the promotion of social services. The goals of the project were to develop a program that would: (1) ensure the safety and proper care of children while mothers are away at work; (2) allow mothers time off for breastfeeding; (3) provide regular immunization services; (4) develop a program that would monitor the normal growth and development of children; (5) provide broad-based family life education programs to men and women of the community in the areas of health, child care, nutrition, family planning, environmental sanitation (waste disposal, construction of latrines, etc.); (6) alleviate some of the burdens women face in providing water and fuel and in food processing, cooking, etc.; (7) ease farmers' burdens through provision of appropriate (basic) technology, such as wooden wheelbarrows, to transport fruits to collection points; and (8) train traditional birth attendants.

Implementation

The strategy adopted was an interagency approach with responsibilities allocated among various organizations. IFLE took up the responsibility for coordinating and implementing the program with Birr 36,100 (U.S. $17,388), provided by UNICEF.

The first phase of the project was to establish a comprehensive child development program that would eventually be managed by the cooperative itself. The cooperative set up, from among its members, a children's affairs committee that would eventually be responsible for the management of the crèche and kindergarten. The funds provided by UNICEF were used to:

- Employ a local consultant for eight months to train child minders and establish the day-care center;
- Cover the cost of training child minders, who would be members of the community selected by the cooperative members;
- Purchase raw materials needed to make educational and play materials required during the training period;
- Equip the crèche and kindergarten with indoor and outdoor equipment;
- Buy basic tools needed for production of play and educational materials by the child minders.

Children in Melka Oba, Ethiopia, now attend the cooperative's crèche and kindergarten. *(UNICEF)*

Training, Organization, and Management

The cooperative provided a spacious villa to serve as the office for the executive committee of the cooperative and to house the crèche and kindergarten. The National Children's Commission provided the necessary policies and guidelines related to child care and development. The Commission also helped to identify a trainer who would come to Melka Oba to work with the potential child minders.

———

Aster Wolde Giorgis, the child-care trainer, is a woman in her mid-thirties. After being a preschool teacher for a number of years, because of her special skills in the production of play and educational materials, she became involved in a UNICEF-assisted pilot project to train preschool teachers. When the need for training semi-literate day-care mothers in Melka Oba arose, Aster was selected as the lead trainer. Aster's ability to adapt to Ethiopia's different regions and cultural groups helped her to easily gain the confidence of the local community. Her training in modern psychology, child development, nutrition, and health were helpful in encouraging the community to change some negative child-care practices. At the same time, Aster was able to build positively upon local traditions by selecting appropriate children's stories and songs from the cooperative members respective regions. Aster also was able to transfer her special skills in the production and maintenance of play and educational materials made from locally available materials using simple basic tools.

During the training, Aster lived with the trainees in the community. She organized day and night classes for the child minders and conducted discussions for cooperative members on topics such as nutrition, personal hygiene, home economics, and day-care management. Aster became a close friend as well as a teacher to the day-care mothers and had the respect of the community.

In addition to her special skills in day care, Aster possesses a dedication to her work, a down-to-earth personality, and the ability to adjust easily to local living conditions. She has played an important role in the promotion of day care in rural Ethiopia.

Child minders were selected from among the cooperative members on the basis of their interest in working with children and their educational level, which ranged from bare literacy to sixth grade. Training was conducted on site and lasted about eight months. The curriculum included creative work/materials production, child development, language development, number concepts, nutrition and hygiene, environmental studies, music, traditional dancing, and art.

In all, eight child minders (six female and two male) were trained. A young woman, 22 years of age, who had completed eighth grade and was trained at the National Institute for the Training of Day Care Teachers, was assigned to head the day-care center. She manages the day-to-day affairs of the center and appears to be committed and enthusiastic about her responsibilities. The cooperative supports the day-care center through a fund set aside for social development.

The Child-Care Program

Initially the day-care center started with 100 children. Children aged 45 days and above are cared for in the crèche. The kindergarten looks after children four to six. The center's hours are flexible, trying as much as possible to coordinate with the working hours of the mothers. Mothers with infants are now able to visit the crèche several times each day to breastfeed their children, thus allowing breastfeeding to continue for a longer period than when children had to be left at home. A typical day at the center includes various indoor and outdoor activities. Daily lesson plans generally follow the national preschool curriculum, and the center provides immunization and health care services.

Other Activities

Prior to establishment of the day-care center in 1983, there were no social services in Melka Oba. The existence of the day-care program has had a profound effect on the cooperative, making members aware of the need for other services. The Ministry of Health has assigned a health assistant, who is assisted by a Community Health Attendant trained for six months in a nearby farmers' training center. The MCH unit of the Ministry of Health, the Family Guidance Association of Ethiopia, and IFLE have provided training to members of the cooperative in family life education and family planning, and a health program is now being carried out by the Melka Oba cooperative. IFLE still provides some support to the cooperative and occasionally supervises community activities.

Effects on Women, Children, and Community

During the initial stage of project development, the Interagency Committee, particularly IFLE and UNICEF, agreed to have appraisal meetings on site and, as circumstances dictated, to have an evaluation of the program. In 1985, Dr. Andargatchew Tesfaye, Associate Professor at Addis Ababa University, visited the project site and interviewed staff of the implementing agency.

Highlighting past conditions and problems of child care, Dr. Andargatchew pointed out that the establishment of the crèche and kindergarten at Melka Oba was a great relief to parents and, especially, to working mothers. All of those interviewed by Dr. Andargatchew stated that they had witnessed noticeable changes in the health of their children since the program began, a view that was further corroborated by the Health Assistant and the Community Health Agent regularly serving Melka Oba.

Production, too, has increased because women are better able to concentrate on their tasks without worrying about their children. Absenteeism from work has fallen dramatically because of the reduced need to take sick children to health clinics. In addition to providing a relatively healthy environment and a balanced diet, the day-care experience is meeting children's developmental needs and stimulating learning in all areas (physical, social, emotional, and intellectual). This foundation provides for a smoother transition to and better performance in school.

In fact, a critical problem faced by the community was the placement of children from the preschool in regular primary school once they completed kindergarten. The nearest school was about six kms. away and young children could not walk that distance in extremely hot weather. Having received preschool training, parents were anxious that their children continue their education, so they put pressure on the Ministry of Education, and an elementary school has now been established in Melka Oba. In addition, a functional literacy program for adults has also been started.

Problems Encountered

The first and most difficult job was to sensitize the community at large, and men in particular, to the idea that child care is not the sole responsibility of the mother, that parenting involves a partnership between both parents and with the community at large. Prior to the start of the project, when queried about the need for day care, the head man of Melka Oba told the IFLE representative that there was no problem with child care in the community—the women take care of it!

Replicability

IFLE and UNICEF built upon their experience as advocates of child development and survival initiatives to implement the integrated program in Melka Oba. In less than two years, IFLE assisted in establishing another child care program within the Yetnora Agricultural Producers' Cooperative located in Dejen District, Gojjam Region.

—————————————— Lessons ——————————————

1. **Any attempt to adequately address the need for child care must take into account the needs of three groups: working mothers, infants and young children, and child-care providers.** The needs of these three groups are not contradictory. Rather, they are inextricably intertwined, and only when they are addressed in tandem will the result be programs that positively address the developmental needs of children, enable women to be more effective earners (in terms of increased time available and reduced anxiety), and provide the means for women, and communities, to become more effectively involved in the welfare of their children.

2. **To realistically meet the needs of working mothers, child-care services must meet four criteria;** they must be: (a) easily accessible; (b) available during the hours women must be at work; (c) offered at a cost that women can afford to pay; and (d) conducted in a manner that assures the woman that her child is being well cared for.

3. **To provide high-quality care for children, programs should exhibit the following characteristics:** (a) appropriate curriculum that

includes child-initiated learning within a supportive environment; (b) careful selection and training of staff and provision of an ongoing strategy for in-service training; (c) keeping the staff/child ratio at an appropriate level; (d) strong administrative support with linkages to comprehensive services such as health and nutrition; and (e) effective monitoring and evaluation of children's progress.[17]

4. **It is important to differentiate between the needs of mothers with very young and older children.** For example, to the extent possible, care for infants should facilitate the ability of mothers to continue breastfeeding.

5. **Home care and community-based programs are particularly effective in that they enable women to specialize: Most women become mothers, but one group of mothers can take on the job of child-care provider**—sometimes on a rotating basis, as in Nepal. Training local women as day-care providers not only offers them a source of employment, but increases women's sense of self-esteem. It also offers an opportunity for them to develop a solidarity with other women that can be translated into social action for change. The potential power of women, once they come together in groups, can change their own and their children's lives.

6. **Once trained, providers need to be appropriately compensated and appreciated,** not only in order to maintain quality care but to avoid high levels of turnover in personnel. They also require assistance from well-trained field staff. As projects expand, they need to build up technical expertise and make skilled personnel available who can supervise, encourage, and advise local women.

7. **Programs that actively involve parents and the community in the planning and day-to-day operation of day-care programs develop the community's capacity to meet its own children's needs,** thus increasing the potential for sustainability when outside funding is phased out. Community provision of buildings, food, toys, etc., and the employment of local people as care-givers, helps keep costs low; participation in the organization and operation of such programs increases self-confidence and the community's commitment to providing for the needs of its children.

8. **Successful community-based child-care programs can serve as the gateway for the introduction of other development activities within the community,** such as parent education, health care, sanitation, nutrition education, adult literacy, and income generation. Quality

child care/preschool programs also can greatly enhance the probability that children will be able to cope with, and thus remain in, school once their formal education begins. Removing the need for older siblings to serve as child minders also enables more children (mostly girls) to remain in school longer.

9. **Use of appropriate training methods and materials suitable to the educational level of the child-care providers is a critical element in the successful implementation and operation of a community-based child-care program.** Teaching needs to be learner-centered, recognizing the strength of traditional childrearing practices and respecting what women already know and have achieved. The focus should be on developing practical, common-sense, problem-solving skills and encouraging the growth of self-confidence.

10. **It must be recognized that there is no one solution to meeting the need for child care.** Given the wide variation in women's work patterns, and the conditions under which women must work, no single model is going to be sufficient. Provision of child care on a large scale must be developed in such a way that flexibility to respond to the particular needs and circumstances of each community is maintained. The issue of "going to scale" must be approached carefully. Rather than attempt exact duplication of a successful "model" program (that may well be the result of a unique blend of people and circumstances), a more effective approach might be to establish mechanisms whereby local groups are able to share common resources, such as access to training and supervision or cooperative purchasing of supplies.

11. **While community-based child care offers the best possibility of self-sustainability once outside funding is withdrawn, the need for continued follow-up and support of local child-care providers must be taken into consideration.** On the other hand, the problem of excessive regulation that often accompanies significant expansion of programs must be avoided. Unrealistic standards, however well-intentioned, can both drive up the cost and reduce the supply of child-care services. In most settings, ensuring the quality of care provided must be contextually judged and is generally best left in the hands of the mothers and the community.

12. **Making quality child care available to meet the needs of working mothers cannot be accomplished without political commitment.** Policymakers must recognize the substantial economic contribution made by women and the indisputable link between women's ability to work and their need for child care. They need to understand the impor-

tant role that early child care can play in preparing future generations to meet life's challenges, and they must come to recognize the valuable contribution made by child-care providers and seek to ensure that they are adequately compensated for their work.

Notes

1. UNICEF, WHO & UNESCO *Facts for Life* (Oxfordshire, U.K.: P&LA, 1989).

2. Daisy Dwyer, and Judith Bruce, eds., *A Home Divided* (Stanford, CA: Stanford University Press, 1988).

3. Joanne Leslie, and Mayra Buvinic, "Introduction," in Leslie and Paolisso, eds., *Women, Work, and Child Welfare in the Third World* (Boulder, CO: Westview Press, Inc.).

4. Cynthia Lloyd, and Anastasia J. Brandon, "Women's Role in the Maintenance of Households; Poverty and Gender Inequality in Ghana." Paper presented at PAA, Washington, D.C. March 1991. (New York: The Population Council, 1991).

5. Marianne Schmink, "Women in the Urban Economy of Latin America," in Schmink, Bruce and Kohn, eds., *Learning About Women and Urban Services in Latin America and the Caribbean* (New York: The Population Council, 1986).

6. The Ford Foundation, *Letter,* v. 21, n. 2, Summer 1990.

7. *The World Almanac and Book of Facts.* (New York: 1989).

8. Beverly Winikoff, Michael Latham, Giorgio Soliamano, et al., *The Infant Feeding Study.* A report submitted by the Population Council to USAID in fulfilment of Contract No. AID-DSAN-C-0211, 1985.

9. Dwyer and Bruce, 1988.

10. Kathryn Tolbert, "Availability and Need for Day-Care Services in Mexico City." Report to the Ford Foundation. (Mexico City: The Population Council, May 31, 1990.)

11. Tolbert, 1990.

12. Cassie Landers, *Innocenti Global Seminar Early Childhood Development: Summary Report.* (New York: UNICEF, Consultative Group on Early Childhood Care and Development, October, 1989.)

13. Janine Anderson, and Nelson Panzio, "Transportation and Public Safety: Services that Make Service Use Possible," in Schmink, Bruce and Kohn, eds., *Learning About Women and Urban Services in Latin America and the Caribbean.* (New York: The Population Council, 1986).

14. Tolbert, 1990.

15. Tolbert, 1990.

16. Jorge Mejia, Memo to Cassie Landers, January 28, 1991. M. Whitebook, C. House and D. Philips, *Who Cares? Child Care Teachers and the Quality of Care in America.* National Child Care Staffing Study. (Oakland, CA: Child Care Employees Project, 1989.)

17. Landers, 1989

AFTERWORDS

From Nairobi to Beijing: The Transition from Women in Development to Gender and Development

Caroline Moser

As the Women's Development Decade (1985–1995) ends and women worldwide focus on the upcoming Beijing meeting, it is important to reflect critically on both the remarkable achievements and the disappointing failures of the past decade. Obviously, neither can be viewed in isolation, and they must also be examined within the context of such historic political shifts as the fall of the Berlin Wall, the end of the Cold War, and the subsequent emergence of nationalist and ethnic conflicts; the drastic and painful economic crisis of stabilization, adjustment, and reform that has resulted in some economists' referring to the 1980s as a "lost decade"; and the emerging global development policy focusing on environmentally sustainable development.

Set against these broad and sweeping global trends and events, the specific focus on employment/income-generating activities found in *Seeds 2* illuminates an important microcosm. The case studies graphically illustrate and evaluate some of the important shifts and changes in development practice necessary to meet what are now widely identified as *practical gender needs*—the needs women identify in their socially accepted roles in society—as well as *strategic gender needs*—the needs women identify because of their position in society. The case studies contain significant insights relating to the underlying reasons for success, as well as the causes of failure. This knowledge is critically important for everyone involved in, and committed to, the slow processes of structural transformation in the nature of gender relations—whether working as policymaker or activist, whether woman or man, whether in the North or South.

WID to GAD: Moving from Rhetoric to Practice

During the past decade, there has been widespread acknowledgment among policymakers and practitioners of a shift from women in development (WID) to gender and development (GAD). This reflects growing recognition that women are not a special interest group but an integral part of every development strategy. Getting this point across, however, has not been easy. First, it was essential to convince entrenched interests that "women in development" was not a failure. The case had to be made that, just as in past decades paradigms for economic development have shifted (from earlier modernization or basic needs models, for example), so, too, views about women's essential contribution to the development process have undergone fundamental changes.

It must be noted that this change in perspective has resulted largely from the efforts of local women themselves, pressure exerted from the "bottom-up" for participation in development processes, as against passive acceptance of "top-down" welfare or efficiency-based priorities of policymakers and planners. Local women are capable of being agents of their own development; they are able to exercise choice and set their own agendas (Elson 1991, 14).

In the discourse of NGOs, government, and international agencies alike, however, the dramatic semantic shift from "women" to "gender" to date has been far more rhetorical than practical. A focus on gender, rather than women, requires recognition of the social relationship between men and women (in which women have systematically been subordinated), and the way in which male-female relations are socially constructed (Whitehead 1979). This understanding has proved remarkably difficult to translate into planning practice, not only because of technical constraints, such as inappropriate planning procedures, but also because of wider political constraints—entrenched interests that vigorously resist the emancipation of women and their release from subordination (Moser 1993, 7–8).

Within the Seeds case studies, we can trace the evolution of this changing conceptualization: the shift away from women-specific, "anti-poverty," income-generating projects described in the earlier volume (such as bus services in Kenya and handicrafts in Bangladesh)—the limitations of which Buvinic (1986) has aptly critiqued—to more mainstream efforts that seek to integrate women into a major economic activity (such as milk production in Thailand and agricultural production in Zambia). The newer case studies address the changing nature of gender subordination through the category of income generation, documenting the way in which more equal access between men and women to productive resources such as land and agricultural animals provides women with monetary income. The extent to which economic independence empowers women to "start asserting themselves in dealing with a broader range of problems" (Sarin 1993, 1) is one of the most critical issues running through the case studies. This highly complex issue, which is difficult to measure or evaluate, is most explicitly addressed in the SARTHI case study from India in which control over land resources is directly linked to empowerment.

The Struggle to Mainstream Gender Issues

As part of the effort to move beyond the rhetoric of gender to practice, feminists over the past decade have broadened their focus from separate, small-scale projects to the arena of broader policies and larger programs. In the new case studies, increasing recognition has been given to the important relationships between local women's organizations and governments and international agencies. Political strategies available to women include the use of "voice"—confronting those who have power—and also "exit"—withdrawal and the creation of alternative solutions. For practitioners, the emphasis has moved beyond the design of policies and programs to the identification of the most effective procedures to ensure implementation. Equally important is the identification of the appropriate types of institutional structures—mandates, resources, staff patterns, decision-making processes, links with other organizations, and so forth—necessary to integrate gender concerns (Moser 1993).

Given this shifting agenda, it is not surprising that many of the Seeds case studies in this volume focus on programs affiliated, at least financially, with either an international agency or the private sector, and often with liaison if not an actual affiliation with some level of government: the Home Economics Section in the Ministry of Agriculture in Zambia; childcare programs in Nepal, Ecuador, and Ethiopia linked with UNICEF and national or local government; the program in Thailand supported by the Women's World Banking and, in the United States, WomenVenture's Business Development Program. Such case studies also provide detailed illustrations of the ways in which more rigorous planning procedures can contribute to success. In WomenVenture, the "Stepping Process" accesses financing; in Zambia, mobile training courses break traditional barriers and change attitudes about the gender division of labor around plowing; in Nepal, the home-based "Entry-Point" Program clearly identifies three stages in the planning procedures—training, supervision, and evaluation—that integrate women as child-care providers.

The Importance of Political Empowerment

Mainstreaming, however, means much more than a shift from small-scale projects of NGOs to large, government-run programs. The limitations for women of relying on the state when seeking to reduce their dependency on men have been made all too clear. A cruel but blunt example of the fragility and vulnerability of programs not controlled and self-financed by women themselves is the project in the suburbios of Guayaquil, Ecuador, described in the case study on child care and women's work. This project was part of a national program of preschool and crèche facilities operating at the community and household level. Managed both through the Ministry of Social Welfare and through the National Institute of Children and Families, the program provided child care to approximately 80,000 children. Then, in 1992, after operating for more than a decade, the national government decided to terminate this modest community-managed system of child care at one month's notice on the grounds of severe corruption. No consideration was given to the damaging impact this would have on the women participating in the program—who, of course were not consulted. For many of these women, closing the child-care facilities has meant that they have been forced either to give up employment or to leave their children unattended while they go out to work.[1] Nor is this an isolated example; a recent review by the World Bank states that in the former Soviet Union and Eastern Europe, the closing of crèches by governments and state enterprises is adversely affecting women's income-earning opportunities (World Bank 1994).

Thus, while success stories are important, so, too, are critical assessments of the very real problems that globally confront thousands of similar initiatives around the world that were intended to meet practical gender needs—let alone those that challenge the existing status quo by meeting strategic gender needs. Training is a crucial component in raising consciousness and sensitivity about gender issues, as well as providing the tools and techniques for translating such awareness into practice. But such training alone is rarely a panacea—an end in itself—and rarely is it sufficient to change entrenched cultural attitudes or challenge widespread bureaucratic resistance.

Ultimately, the wider political agenda cannot be ignored, for the prospect of female empowerment is still widely perceived as a threat to male privilege (Staudt 1990). Consequently, it remains "in men's strategic interests to resist the idea that gender inequalities exist, and that such inequalities might be socially constructed, rather than naturally given" (Kabeer 1992, 34). Today, with the emergence of democratic processes across continents, we are witnessing visible resistance to policies that genuinely distribute resources, such as land or housing, equally to men and women, in such diverse settings as South Africa, El Salvador, and the former Soviet Union. History appears to be rewriting itself, with women's position as dependent on men for access to resources once again reinforced.

As we near the close of a century, the challenge facing efforts such as those described in the Seeds series is not only to continue their important work, but also to shift even further to documenting and supporting new initiatives that seek to empower women through political processes so that they are able to negotiate the redistribution of power and resources within households, civil society, and the state.

Note

1. In May 1994 (fourteen months after closure), together with local women in Cisne Dos, Guayaquil, I undertook a micro-level questionnaire to follow up thirty mothers who had previously had children in three community homes. All had worked prior to closure; this number dropped to 60 percent immediately afterwards, and a year later only half the women were working—with severe implications for family income. Of those still working, 96 percent used other family, mainly grandmothers or elder daughters, to assist them; all expressed dissatisfaction with these arrangements.

References

Buvinic, M. 1986. "Projects for Women in the Third World: Explaining their Misbehavior." *World Development,* vol. 14, no. 5.

Elson, D. 1991. "Gender Issues in Development Strategies." Paper prepared for UN Committee for the Status of Women.

Kabeer, N. 1992. "Triple Roles, Gender Roles, Social Relations: The Political Sub-text of Gender Training." Institute of Development Studies Discussion Paper No. 313.

Moser, C. O. N. 1989. "Gender Planning in the Third World: Meeting Practical and Strategic Gender Needs." *World Development,* vol. 17, no. 11.

Moser, C. O. N. 1993. *Gender Planning and Development: Theory, Practice and Training.* London and New York: Routledge.

Sarin, M. 1992. *Wasteland Development and the Empowerment of Women: The SARTHI Experience.* SEEDS Series, vol. 16. New York: The Population Council. (See also this volume, Chapter 5.)

Staudt, K. 1990. "Gender Politics in Bureaucracy: Theoretical Issues in Comparative Perspective." In Staudt, K. (ed.). *Women, International Development and Politics.* Philadelphia: Temple University Press.

Whitehead, A. 1979. "Some Preliminary Notes on the Subordination of Women." *Institute of Development Studies Bulletin,* vol. 10, no. 3.

World Bank. 1994. *Enhancing Women's Participation in Economic Development.* Washington, D.C.: World Bank.

The Elusive Agenda: Mainstreaming Women in Development[1]

Rounaq Jahan

Nearly two decades ago, the global community affirmed gender equality as a central development concern, and a decade ago it adopted the Forward Looking Strategies (FLS) to accelerate women's advancement. It is time to ask: What have been the achievements so far? Have the various policies and measures adopted by international agencies and national governments been effective in promoting women's advancement and gender equality? Have the world's women witnessed significant improvement in their living and working conditions in the last twenty years?

Evidence suggests a mixed record. On the one hand, sustained advocacy has led to greater understanding and awareness of gender issues. Women's organizations and networks have multiplied. The women's movement has gained in strength. A women's agenda has been more clearly articulated—equality, empowerment, and the transformation of existing development paradigms have emerged as critical issues. States and international agencies have adopted various mandates and policies and implemented a variety of actions. Protest movements and grassroots initiatives have shown alternative paths to development.

On the other hand, data also indicate that the inequalities between the North and the South and between the rich and the poor have grown. In the last two decades, more women have joined the ranks of the world's poor in countries both North and South, primarily because cutbacks in social services—as a result of structural adjustment policies—hit poor women the hardest. Women's responsibilities as sole or primary income earners have increased; their labor force participation rates have grown; but the workplace has not made significant changes in its rules and conditions to accommodate women's needs. Primarily it has exploited women as cheap labor. Economic desperation has led to unprecedented female migration and growing trafficking of women and children worldwide.

Why has progress been so elusive for women? What explains the contradictory trends—heightened advocacy and awareness of gender issues, on the one hand, and the growing poverty of the world's women, on the other? Where have the policies and measures failed?

The experiences of the last two decades indicate that the operational approaches of states and international agencies to promoting women's advancement fell short in four critical areas. First, no serious attempt was made by agencies and states to identify clearly the core elements of a women's agenda and shape various policies around that agenda. Policy objectives were articulated in a broad and diffuse manner. Process-focused objectives—e.g., "integration" and "mainstreaming"—were highlighted, which detracted from the substantive agenda—e.g., gender equality, women's empowerment, women's well-being, and so on. The distinction between ends (e.g., gender equality) and means (e.g., mainstreaming) was not clarified. Within agencies, concerns over means often took precedence over ends, resulting in priority being given to institutionalization of gender issues in agency processes and procedures rather than to the design of policy and program level innovations and the tracking of progress in moving a women's agenda forward.

For example, most donor agencies and national governments introduced women in development (WID) efforts either by establishing specific institutional structures (e.g., WID offices in donor agencies, women's bureaus or ministries in national governments, etc.) or by adopting guidelines for institutional behavior (e.g., WID guidelines or checklists for project design or WID sector guidelines). Their operational efforts were primarily limited to development of WID projects rather than policies and programs geared towards the creation of equal opportunities or the elimination of gender-based discrimination.

Though many WID projects were innovative and promoted women's income generation, literacy, or health, they generally tended to be *ad hoc* and experimental. They did not necessarily lead to national replication or influence policy/program changes at the national level. However, international agencies and national governments were preoccupied with monitoring adoption of institutional mandates, structures, and projects. Rarely did they attempt to assess whether these interventions were in fact contributing towards the achievement of the substantive objectives of the women's movement. Thus, agencies and governments tracked progress in increasing the number of female staff (due largely to affirmative action measures) or WID projects; they did not track progress in designing gender-responsive policies that would entitle women to productive resources—such as land or credit—or that would eliminate gender-based discrimination in the workplace or in civic/political organizations.

Additionally, operationalizing the goal of "mainstreaming" was difficult because it was conceptualized in different ways by different participants. Some emphasized an "integrationist" approach to mainstreaming; that is, addressing gender issues within existing development paradigms. Others preferred an "agenda-setting" approach that transforms an existing development agenda from a gender perspective.[2] Broadening women and gender concerns across a broad spectrum of sectors is the key to an integrationist approach. The overall development agenda does not get transformed, but each issue is adapted to take into account women and gender concerns. A good example of the integrationist approach is designing WID "components" in major sector programs and projects. Women are "fitted" into as many sectors and programs as possible, but sector/program priorities and assumptions do not change because of gender considerations. In contrast, under an agenda-setting approach, women's participation as decision makers in determining development priorities is the key. Women participate in all development decisions and through that process bring about a fundamental change in existing development paradigms. In this case, the women's agenda gets recognition from the mainstream. A good example of an agenda-setting approach is prioritizing women's health issues in health sector policy planning.

Generally, international agencies have tended to claim that they simultaneously pursued both approaches—that they followed integrationist strategies in order to be able to set the agenda. But this dual focus often introduced internal contradictions within agency strategies. For example, many WID projects or WID components of projects perpetuated or even worsened women's unequal work burdens, thus working counter to women's empowerment. On the whole, international agencies spent more time and energy in spelling out the details of operationalizing the integrationist approach than in working on the agenda-setting approach of mainstreaming.

Second, agencies and states rarely established measurable goals, targets, and timetables to achieve their stated objectives of gender equality and women's advancement. Though targets and incentives were used as planning and programming tools in other sectors (for example, population and family planning and environment), agencies and states were reluctant to use these techniques widely to promote women's advancement. In the absence of measurable goals, it has been difficult to track progress and hold agencies and governments accountable.

Third, agencies and states did not pay sufficient attention to designing a financial plan to achieve a women's agenda. For example, though data about gender gaps in human development were well known, international agencies and national governments did not work out a budget to achieve gender equality in human development. Planning, programming, and budget allocation for promoting women's advancement were generally done *ad hoc*. It was assumed that, with greater integration and mainstreaming, women would increasingly gain access to normal budget resources.

Finally, though progress was achieved in the last two decades in undertaking policy analysis as well as designing analytical methodologies and planning and programming instruments, development of operational tools often lagged behind changes in agency priorities. The 1970s were spent in gathering evidence from research and field projects and designing tools to address gender issues in the context of projects. In the 1980s, efforts were launched to undertake policy analysis from a gender perspective and develop new operational tools as agencies started emphasizing policy- and program-level interventions rather than projects. The gender-differentiated impact of structural adjustment programs (SAPs) was documented and special program components were designed to buffer the adverse impact of SAPs on women.

However, gender policy, analysis, and program development have only recently begun to function. Policies and programs in only a few sectors (for example, health, population, agriculture, and microenterprises) have been analyzed from a gender perspective. Gender issues in a wide range of macroeconomic (for example, trade price, taxation, etc.) and social and economic sector policies still remain relatively unexplored. For example, the development of policies and programs to reduce gender disparities in poverty, human development, decision making, and entitlement to productive resources lags behind. This constrains a consideration of gender issues in policy dialogues which have emerged as major forums for shaping the development agenda.

Though there is much discussion by feminists both within and outside development agencies about the need to transform the development agenda, as yet there is no road map, especially in terms of where cost shifting would be required to bring about a transformed agenda. For example, it has been apparent for a very long time that the sexual division of labor prevailing in most societies has resulted in women's greater responsibilities for unpaid reproductive work, and this has limited their participation in remunerated productive work and in paid and unpaid community and public service. Women activists have demanded greater sharing of responsibilities by men in child care and household maintenance, and stronger social policies to ensure the provision of public- and private-sector services for maternity benefits, child care, and care of the sick and elderly. But in the last twenty years, there has been very little progress in state or private-sector policies. Indeed, with structural adjustment programs and the collapse of the communist states, there has, in fact, been an erosion of commitment to provide for public-sector services to alleviate women's reproductive burdens.

Since the beginning of the Decade for Women, three key constraints to achieving gender equality have been highlighted by the women's movement: women's unequal burden of social reproduction (e.g., care of children, the sick, and the elderly, household maintenance, and provision of basic needs); gender-based inequality in entitlement to factors of production (e.g., land, credit, capital, technology, information); and a lack of women's voices in decision making. But up to now international agencies and states have generally just tinkered with these constraints. They have yet to come forward with bold policies, adequate budgetary allocation, and the institutional mechanisms necessary to overcome these obstacles.

Notes

1. This article is based on the author's forthcoming book: *The Elusive Agenda: Mainstreaming Women in Development* (London, Zed Books, 1995). The study reviews the progress achieved in making gender a central concern in the development process. It evaluates the women in development (WID) policies of selected donor agencies and aid recipient countries and addresses a key question: Why has progress been so elusive for women?

2. Rounaq Jahan, "Mainstreaming Women in Development in Different Settings," presented at a seminar on Mainstreaming Women in Development organized by the OECD/DAC/WID Expert Group, Paris, May 19–20, 1992.

Women's Income Generation Activities in Latin America and the Caribbean: A Commentary

Mayra Buvinić

*"The only thing I have is this training and I don't want to
be another baker; I have other dreams for my life."*
**—Reina, a female ex-combatant and
community leader in El Salvador[1]**

The conference signalling the end of the Decade for Women in 1985 found
the countries of Latin America and the Caribbean in a downward spiral
fostered by economic crisis and the stabilization measures enacted in
response by the International Monetary Fund. Poverty was rising, from a
conservatively low estimate of 26.5 percent of the population below the
poverty line in 1980 to 31 percent in 1989, and inequality was deepening
(Psacharopoulos et al. 1993). Regional economic reforms have now followed, including privatization of state assets, such as in banking and
telecommunications; shrinking the role of the state in providing services;
and substituting outward-oriented development strategies (those that seek
to open markets and emphasize exports) in place of the import-substitution
models (those that limits imports and emphasize domestic production) of
preceding decades.

These economic upheavals have had substantially more impact on
women's economic responses and income generation activities than have
development projects specifically designed to improve their economic

well-being. During the past decade, women in Latin America and the Caribbean have increased their participation in self- and wage employment, both to offset the poverty of their families and in response to new opportunities in export-oriented industrial and agricultural sectors. This "added worker" effect—that is, women entering the work force in times of economic downturns in order to compensate for declining family income—was alive and well in the 1980s in countries such as Chile and Costa Rica, Argentina and Brazil (Buvinic and Lycette 1994; Moser et al. 1993). The demand for female labor also increased significantly along with export-oriented industrial and agricultural growth. Women predominate in employment in manufacturing in the export processing zones (EPZs) of the Dominican Republic and Mexico, for instance, and in the processing and packing of fruits for export in Chile, Costa Rica, and Guatemala, among others.

In the region today, there is more employment for women, and this is an inherently beneficial, although unintended, result of economic restructuring. The problem is that, like traditional female work, this new export-led employment is low-paid, with few or no benefits or possibilities for growth. Discrimination in wages by sex remains pervasive throughout the region and has not been altered by the new jobs opened to women.

In counterpoint to the impact of economic policies, the effects of development projects in enhancing women's income-earning opportunities have been negligible at best, and perverse at worst. Many projects for women have ignored the lessons of the Decade for Women and continue to "misbehave," as the epigraph to this commentary suggests. Reina and her female ex-combatant colleagues in El Salvador were trained in breadmaking, while the men were trained in raising cattle and other animals for sale in agricultural markets, repeating the persistent pattern of training women in what are considered female-appropriate and, therefore, unprofitable skills. Fortunately, in this case, Reina received a monthly stipend for attending the training; at least she had not volunteered her time. The perverse effects from such poorly conceived income-generation projects for women are magnified when not only are the women unable to generate income as a result of the training, but the training itself has imposed additional demands on their time, thus negatively affecting the welfare of both the women and their children.

Within the region, the exceptions to such lackluster project performance are two: provision of credit and other assistance to the smallest businesses, known as microenterprises, and public works programs. Credit to microenterprises, mostly through intermediary organizations such as the affiliates of Acción and Women's World Banking, are well known in the region for effectively reaching women and promoting their enterprises by giving them access to loans on reasonable terms. The usual limitations of these projects—their inability to take deposits, to operate as commercial banks, or to graduate clients into the formal banking system—are being addressed through a new generation of interventions in which intermediary agencies have actually transformed themselves into commercial banks. The most striking example is BancoSol in Bolivia, which makes very small loans of about U.S. $100–200, uses personal rather than real guarantees, charges a 4 percent monthly interest rate, and has a zero default rate. BancoSol records 60,000 clients in its current portfolio, 75 percent of whom are women, mostly operating small enterprises in commerce, industry, or services (such as the clients featured in many of the Seeds case studies—street and market vendors, tailors, tradespeople, etc.).

In the case of public works programs, such as those designed and run by the government in Chile and Peru in the 1980s to buffer the effects of the economic crisis on the poor, there was an unintentional consequence of increased income-earning options for women. While these programs were explicitly set up to provide temporary work for unemployed males, it was women who leapt at the opportunity, making up 84 percent of those employed by the PAIT (Programma de Apoyo de Ingreso Temporal) in Peru in 1986, and 72.6 percent of those employed by the PEM (Minimal employment program) in Chile in 1987. Both of these programs hired poor people to do menial work, such as the cleaning of streets, beaches, and municipal buildings (Buvinic forthcoming).

Again, the limitations of these public works programs were poor working conditions and very low wages: they did nothing to improve the quality of employment for women or to reverse patterns of discrimination by sex. What they did was to provide an income-earning option for poor women in times of economic crisis. Ironically, the new generation of compensatory interventions in the region in the 1990s—the demand-driven social funds through which the government finances projects (that provide jobs or generate income) executed by both profit and nonprofit firms, which bid for contracts and awards—have reversed the pattern of these public works programs by providing employment for men and social welfare for women. This is happening to a large extent because the public sector institutions that manage the funds, the executing agencies that formulate and undertake the projects, and the donor agencies that underwrite these programs still do not see women as economic agents. Therefore, executing agencies design welfare programs for women to be financed by these funds, but do not target women as recipients of jobs and other productive resources.

The obvious lessons from the experience of the last ten years in Latin America and the Caribbean are that economic trends and policies that affect employment and income are not gender-neutral and have pervasive influences on women's employment. Awareness of gender issues, therefore, has to extend beyond the design of projects, to development of policies as well; and policy formulation and policy reform need to be informed by gender considerations. Within the domain of project development, the lessons of the last two decades regarding the problems of traditional income-generation projects for women need to be more widely understood and assimilated by those who design development projects. There is little justification for continuing to make the same old mistakes. The immediate challenges for both policies and projects are to upgrade the quality of women's economic activities and to begin to overcome the barriers of sex discrimination in the world of work. Then, perhaps, Reina can realize her dreams.

Note

1. Murray, Kevin, Ellen Coletti and Jack Spence. 1994. *Rescuing Reconstruction: The Debate on Post-War Economic Recovery in El Salvador*. Cambridge, MA: Hemisphere Initiatives.

References

Buvinić, Mayra. Forthcoming. "Promoting Employment Among the Urban Poor in Latin America and the Caribbean: A Gender Analysis." Geneva, Switzerland: ILO Working Paper, prepared for the Employment and Development Department, International Labour Office.

Buvinic, Mayra, and Margaret A. Lycette. 1994. "Women's Contributions to Economic Growth in Latin America and the Caribbean: Facts, Experience, and Options." Prepared for the InterAmerican Development Bank.

Moser, Caroline O. N., Alicia J. Herbert, and Roza E. Makonnen. 1993. "Urban Poverty in the Context of Structural Adjustment: Recent Evidence and Policy Responses." Transportation, Water, and Urban Development Department Discussion Paper. Washington, D.C.: The World Bank.

Psacharopoulos, George, et al. 1993. "Poverty and Income Distribution in Latin America: The Story of the 1980s." LAC Technical Department Regional Studies Program, Report No. 27. Washington, DC: The World Bank.

Mainstreaming Gender in Development from UNICEF'S Perspective

Misrak Elias

Over the past four years, Seeds has collaborated with the United Nations Children's Fund (UNICEF) on the production of two editions of the Seeds booklet series: "Child Care: Meeting the Needs of Working Mothers and Their Children" and "Supporting Women Farmers in the Green Zones of Mozambique" (both of which appear in this volume). Here, Misrak Elias, Senior Adviser for Gender and Development at UNICEF, comments on the emergence of that agency's concern with issues of gender in development, their current approach to bringing women into the mainstream of development, and the relevance of Seeds case studies to their work.

Within UNICEF, development programs for women initially were focused on women's roles as mothers—not surprisingly, given UNICEF's mandate as an agency primarily concerned with the survival and development of children. However, it soon became apparent that, in addition to their role as mothers, women in their own right are central to the entire development process. Research and experience have shown that the more women are empowered in their own lives, the more their children and other members of their families benefit.

For UNICEF, a major turning point in conceptualization came at the end of the Decade for Women (1985), when, for the first time, the agency clearly articulated its interest in women as individuals in their own right, in addition to their maternal role. As a result, the agency began to address women's needs in areas such as health and education, and to reconsider their economic role, including the possibility of providing support for income-generating projects.

By this time, however, it had become apparent within the field of women in development that, due to the relatively small number of direct beneficiaries of many income-generating projects, the overall impact on the social and economic situation of women and children had been modest. This has particularly been the case when external ideas have been superimposed on groups, rather than projects being based on the reality of what women were already doing. By the late 1980's the emphasis within the field was clearly moving in the direction of "mainstreaming" women's participation in development. Given this understanding, UNICEF faced the challenge of how to translate this more holistic view of women's lives into actual program activities.

Mainstreaming Women in Development at UNICEF

There are several definitions of mainstreaming in terms of gender. Rounaq Jahan's definition (see her afterword in this volume) provides both a conceptual and a practical distinction for action and policy: (a) *integration* within all development sectors, and (b) *agenda setting* to establish women's active participation and decision-making roles in defining what development activities are to be undertaken.

While we in UNICEF recognized the value of mainstreaming as agenda setting, we realized that we needed to begin with integration. Therefore, gender issues and the specific needs of women and girls are now integrated into programs from the onset. The first step is ensuring that gender analysis is an integral part of the process of preparing the situation analysis study (an assessment of strengths and weaknesses according to a variety of measures) of women and children in each country. The next step is determining how to integrate these concerns within UNICEF's main program areas (health, nutrition, education, and water and sanitation).

At first, there was talk of putting everything about women into a separate chapter in each situation analysis. With such an approach, however, information is not linked to the other chapters on the economy, on health, etc. This underscores why mainstreaming as integration is so essential. All factors have to be integrated: even though UNICEF works in the social sector, we *are* in fact talking about the economy, about the gender division of labor, about ownership, about patriarchy, and so on, not to mention the issue of women's political empowerment.

The path to mainstreaming, however, has not been simple or easy. Often there were wide gaps between stated objectives and concrete actions. For example, at first some people argued that the existence of integration supersedes the need for women's empowerment as a separate issue. When asked what had actually been integrated within programs, the reply was that women are included everywhere in programs: in health, in education, in agriculture, in nutrition classes—where they learn how to cook food for men! Clearly this was not our vision of integration. Integration (mainstreaming) has to mean more than the simple presence of women.

Therefore, in 1992, UNICEF started a program for building the capacity of its programs for integrating gender issues, with the aim of improving the understanding of gender issues among UNICEF staff and their counterparts in governments, NGOs, and local communities. This effort aims to build commitment and determine accountability for integrating women's concerns within development programs. UNICEF has also adopted a Gender Equality and Women's Empowerment Framework.[1] This is a conceptual and operational tool designed to reduce, and in time to eliminate, gender gaps between boys and girls, men and women, in its programming. The framework postulates that women's development can be viewed in terms of five levels of equality, namely: welfare, access, awareness raising, participation, and control, with empowerment an essential element at each level.

UNICEF is also moving toward the goal of mainstreaming as agenda setting by seeking to increase women's participation in the decision-making process by building up women's leadership capacity. For example, at the community level, there are health committees, water committees, etc., that implement UNICEF programs. Women's representation on these committees is enhanced through special efforts designed to increase their confidence and leadership skills.

Today, mainstreaming is one of the three operational approaches to women's empowerment being used by UNICEF. The other two are promoting gender-specific program activities targeted at girls and women and giving special attention to girls. Generally, the three approaches overlap within country programs contributing to the overall objectives of eliminating gender discrimination and improving the status of women in the context of UNICEF-supported programming. Income-generating activities are one important element of women-centered activities in UNICEF. These are aimed specifically at women in poverty and include actions to improve the access of women to credit and productive resources. However, while these projects have provided opportunities for women to improve their economic status, as stated earlier, their overall impact to date has been limited.

Adopting a Life-Cycle Approach to Gender and Development: The Initiative for Girls

A positive step in integrating a broader concern for women as individuals occurred in 1990 with the introduction of UNICEF's Initiative for Girls, which mandates equal opportunity for all children regardless of gender. There were several motivating factors behind the creation of this policy. First, in any discussion about equality, parity among children must be considered. As a children's agency, UNICEF has the responsibility to ensure that all people—men and women, boys and girls—are treated equally, whether in health care, in nutrition, in education, or in the overall opportunities they get as human beings. Secondly, we came to realize that unless efforts are made in the earliest stages of women's life cycle to gain equal opportunity, any subsequent assistance becomes remedial.

At first, the newly introduced concept of priority for girls and the life-cycle approach to women's empowerment and gender equality did not gain acceptance within women in development circles. One concern was that women and children were again being lumped together, with women being considered exclusively as mothers. But, from our perspective, this policy represented a concern for each individual woman's *own* early stages of life.

Within UNICEF, childhood is defined as being from birth to eighteen years of age. This stage of life is further divided into three subgroups: birth to age five (within which there is a subclass of birth to age one), followed by six to twelve, and then thirteen to eighteen. We believe that, from birth on, equality of opportunity is essential in health, nutrition, and education, since during early childhood a person forms a sense of identity.

Children from six to twelve years of age experience differences in workloads and disparities in education, depending on their sex. During this stage, many girls begin to drop out of school. Even when they stay in school, their performance often lags because of their increasing workloads. In most settings, girls work twice as much as boys, whether in paid labor or in the household. Therefore, an effort needs to be made to ensure that working does not limit their educational opportunities. In some cases, informal educational approaches become very important. For example, in UNICEF, we support the approach of BRAC in Bangladesh (a project profiled in the first volume of *Seeds*), which has organized educational programs for working children, most of whom are girls. In the few hours they are able to devote to their studies, these girls manage to learn at a pace on par with or even exceeding students in the formal educational system.

At the age of thirteen and beyond, choices become even more critical. At this time, girls get sent to the ghetto of limited choices. They drop out of the educational system to get married, to help their families for economic reasons, or because of pregnancy. As these girls become adult women, all of these factors will have a critical impact on the kinds of choices they will be empowered to make in their lives.

The Seeds Case Studies

The Seeds case studies are, I believe, particularly useful for those developing economic programs for women, because they show the *process*—not only the activity itself, but the steps both the organizers and the women have worked through and the lessons they have learned. As we look at these successful programs, certain qualities emerge. First, the projects documented are built on what women already do as their mainstream activities—women farmers are not being asked to crochet, for example. Next, the projects generally meet the needs both of women and of their communities—i.e., since products are not being produced for export, women have more of an understanding of and ability to respond to fluctuations in their market.

And third, many of these initiatives recognize that women have other needs, such as responsibility for children, and that they already have too much work to do. In these successful programs, economic goals are merged with real-life demands. The Green Zones project is a good example of a business venture in which women can work and at the same time have their children taken care of in the cooperative crèche or in school. In the case study called "Child Care: Meeting the Needs of Working Mothers," one sees that programs to assist working women in meeting their needs for child care can also provide other women in the community with an opportunity to earn income. In this way, what is a service for one woman becomes a business for another.

While our program is not primarily in economic development, wherever we can, we try to support women's economic empowerment through credit systems, through training programs, and through projects such as Green Zones in Mozambique. Women's empowerment goes hand in hand with other aspects of improving the lives of women and children.

With patriarchy based primarily on the division of responsibility and property, most of the world's women still do not have access to or control of property and related resources. This basic discrimination creates a problem for women in getting into any kind of paid employment or small business. This is true in both urban and rural areas, where, even if women are farmers or cattle herders in their own right, they still have to work through a male, whether a husband, father, uncle, or son. This has to change—and one way of bringing about such change is by developing projects that help women gain direct access to resources and to credit. Projects which both enhance women's economic status and increase their ability to make decisions—without a male—are, therefore, desired. Of course, this has to go hand in hand with structural changes in legislation.

Other factors ought also to be taken into account. One is that the number of households supported by women is increasing. Since many more women now have sole responsibility for families, they must be empowered economically. Furthermore—and this is one reason why UNICEF was so interested in this area—we know that a large proportion of women's income (a significantly higher percentage than men's, regardless of the amount earned) goes for the improvement of the lives of family members, especially children.

Lastly, political awareness is very important, because it is not enough to provide women with the opportunity to earn income. To be truly empowered, a woman needs to have the awareness that she can make choices and that, by joining forces with other women, she can create opportunities for change.

Note

1. The Framework was developed by Sara Longwe.

Planting *Seeds 2* in the Classroom

Kathleen Staudt

One clear outcome of the United Nations Decade for Women (1975–1985) is the internationalizing of women's studies. In the decade since the 1985 Nairobi Conference, women have aimed to "mainstream" and "transform" governmental, international, and non-governmental organizations into women-friendly institutions. The process has begun as some of these Seeds cases demonstrate, but we have a long way to go.

During the Decade's conferences at Mexico City, Copenhagen, and Nairobi, women from diverse cultures, classes, and political systems began the building and sustaining of relationships. They talked about women's struggles in the household, the community, and the larger society. Seeds cases make prominent the activities and priorities of grassroots women from around the world.

The field dubbed "Women in Development" is an important part of internationally-oriented women's studies and development studies. This field, drawing on a variety of disciplines, has embraced two approaches. First, it has examined the effects of the state, laws, economic strategies, public policies, and programs on women, men, and the relations between them. More recently, practitioners have called this type of approach Gender and Development (GAD). All too often, as studies have documented, women's circumstances have worsened in the course of the seemingly progressive or benign process of development.

In a second approach, studies document women's experiences as they vary by class and culture. Such experiences have often been rendered

229

invisible in typical mainstream approaches to understanding development. In reporting women's experiences, studies also reveal the ways in which women's or gender issues affect this process called "development." We need to learn much more about women's experiences, in all their intricate variations, so that they can serve as models to women elsewhere.

For this reason, *Seeds 2* is a welcome addition to the classroom. These real-life cases are an inspiring contrast to the grim record of many development projects. Frequently, development projects fall short of goals, aggravate income inequalities, and tie people more tightly into national and international political economies in which they can exert little control. Projects usually ignore women or the gender inequalities that the projects themselves may help to foster. With so many negatives, instructors, students, and activists might very well throw their hands up in despair. Fortunately, many women have not wanted to give up to despair.

As the Seeds cases show, women struggle in a variety of ways, achieving mixed successes. In women's efforts to achieve a better and fairer return for their labor, they challenge the sexual division of labor and rewards, as in India and Mozambique, or temporarily accommodate themselves to that division, as in the child-care programs in Nepal, Ecuador, and Ethiopia. Organizationally, some women join hands with men, as in Zambia; they share capital, resources, and risks, as in Mozambique; or they employ themselves, tapping credit or technical assistance as in the United States and Sudanese programs.

Whatever the country or cultural context, women in these development projects have joined forces in *organizations,* thus controlling the decision-making processes to some degree. Through collective strength, they challenge barriers to and violence against their participation, mobility, voice, and control over gains from their labor.

Several key issues rise to the surface in the consideration of the Seeds cases as a whole: *development, empowerment,* and *feminism.* I can think of virtually no course on women in development that doesn't (or shouldn't) touch at least one of these topics. Are Seeds projects examples of development, and how is this value-laden term defined and operationalized? To answer these questions, comparisons of several schools of thought can be useful. One might contrast capitalist and socialist strategies; nationalist self-sufficiency and international integration; and reformist variations within capitalist growth strategies such as "growth with equity" and "basic human needs" approaches.

Are women *empowered* in these types of organizations? Importantly, participants will need to consider what they mean by power and how it might be measured, implicitly critiquing mainstream approaches to understanding power in a public sphere alone.

And finally, are these efforts *feminist?* Participants many want to discuss whether there is either a single standard by which to judge feminism (in its various ideological hues as socialist- liberal- or radical-feminism), or a coexistence of multiple feminisms. As Gita Sen and Caren Grown for DAWN (Development Alternatives with Women for a New Era) have stated: "There is and must be a diversity of feminisms, responsive to the different needs and concerns of different women, and *defined by them for themselves.* This diversity builds on a common opposition to gender oppression and hierarchy. . . ." (Sen and Grown 1987, pp. 18–19.)

In this brief essay, I outline some of the classroom uses to which *Seeds 2* might be put. *Seeds 2* can be planted in courses on women (or gender) and development or on development in general, or development administration—to name only a few among many kinds of related courses in various disciplines. Seeds cases are written in reader-friendly ways, a welcome relief from academic treatises that obfuscate more than they clarify.

Seeds Cases in Their Contexts

To grapple with the big questions—development? empowerment? feminism?—course participants will need to situate the Seeds case studies in their national and international contexts. For example, civil war in Mozambique and Sudan has its lingering legacies for crushing national trust, displacing populations, and creating refugees. Environmental crisis, as in India, pushes people to devise new ways to nourish and sustain the common lands. Changing forms of international assistance compel governmental downsizing. As governments trim their supposed "fat" in these structural adjustment programs, cuts occur in health and education (rarely the military), as the two-volume UNICEF study, *Adjustment with a Human Face,* reveals so well (Cornia et al. 1987). Changes in larger policy priorities shift support away from women and children, as the child-care cases show, or undermine the idea of public support for children, leaving their responsibility fully in women's (unpaid) hands. The *Human Development Report* (HDR) regularly shows the low priority both governmental and international agencies give to human priorities (UNDP 1993, 1994). Why isn't public money—spent in huge amounts—doing more to support women's self-help efforts?

Of particular interest in political science courses are the varying stances women take toward politics. In most cases, silence about politics screams at us from the pages. The case from India, however, shows women whose land rights were threatened *engaging* with the political process to hold village *panchayats* accountable. (See Nelson and Chowdhury 1994, on political engagement.)

Governmental bureaucracy is part of the whole political process, and the disengaged may be marginalized. What is it about elections and political parties that creates general unease? What links exist between politics and bureaucratic policies or staff? Do female leaders, women's organizations, or women's bureaus connect any links on this chain? Under what *political* conditions are Seeds nurtured?

Seeds projects have operated in capitalist or so-called free-market economies, about which great debates have been generated in terms of their conduciveness to women's emancipation. To what extent are markets "free" for women, with both reproductive and productive responsibilities? Classroom participants may well want to carry on those debates, speculating about how women's conditions might change in transition toward "people-friendly markets" (UNDP 1993) with equalized access to credit and reduced burdens on women's unpaid labor. Ultimately, participants might want to assess the worth of different types of organizational strategies—developmental and/or political—under market economies. Income inequalities should be discussed as well, at national and international levels (UNDP's HDR has illuminating tables). Mozambique's *$13/month* minimum wage level is wretched. Can feminist outcomes occur with obscene levels of income inequality?

Seeds projects also operate in states where men virtually dominate political and bureaucratic decision-making processes. Multilateral and bilateral assistance organizations are similar in that regard. (For institutional analyses, see Staudt 1985 and 1990). In the Seeds cases, readers should take note of the extent to which development resources were channeled to men. Credit, with or without subsidized interest rates, has historically benefited men, as alluded to in the Sudan and U.S. cases. Even though the women of India work in natural resources and forests, *all* the forest extension workers in the project area were men, who not only were unaccustomed to working with women but verbally and physically abused them on occasion. In the past, administrators have conveniently fallen back on handicraft projects or welfare as a solution, though such projects tend to be time-consuming, offer little return for labor, and/or are threatened with budget cuts during hard economic times. A student project might involve checking the *development plan* of a particular country for how and where women actually and potentially fit in.

Clearly, the women in the Seeds projects struggle in environments of considerable constraints. Whatever those constraints, however, women have confronted fundamental aspects of the organizational process. They have fused personal and political concerns and realities, which makes for fascinating possibilities in the transition from subordination in *any* kind of political-economic system.

Once confronted, how were organizational and policy matters resolved? Virtually all Seeds projects faced the chronic issue of how to distribute incentives and rewards for labor; this is not an uncommon question, from debates in Chinese communes to those in the United States Congress over tax policy. Women are asking these basic, time-worn questions: To each according to her merit (merit being defined as labor time, productivity, capital contribution, talent, or some mix)? To each according to her need? Or to all in equitable parts?

Determining management structure is another recurring challenge, but all too often the development mainstream assumes that some universal standard exists for "good management." Defying Western management techniques, do women spread responsibility to all members, regardless of educational achievement, in order to avoid potential abuses of power by the literate? Among Indian women, democratic participation standards could offer a model to many governments around the world. Those who have followed the history of the U.S. feminist movement will recognize some familiar *process* themes.

Seeds 2 in Specific Course Content

Seeds 2 will be ideal in the many kinds of courses offered in international studies and development, from anthropology and economics to women's studies and management. The projects illustrate the ways women are central to development activities in such areas as health, water, and environment. The projects also are a testimony to the enormous difficulties posed in any and all development efforts, from a lack of transportation to insufficient capital; these difficulties often are more problematic for women due to their limited resource base, time-consuming household responsibilities, and the conventional (male?) wisdom that women's development efforts cannot succeed. In the first volume of *Seeds*, readers probably never forgot the taunts that Mexican women faced in a waste recycling project—"crazy women playing with shit."

One feature I particularly like about the Seeds series is its frank discussion of problems encountered and lessons learned. This represents a marked departure from the project histories/evaluations written in many development agencies, which tend to be superficial, glossing over mistakes to protect the image of the staff or their prospects for funding. Moreover, evaluations tend to be number-oriented, consulting only the staff and document files rather than, in agency language, the "beneficiaries or the targets" (one hopes, not lethal!). In the real world of projects in development, numerous problems are encountered that can be overcome with participation and flexible management.

Still, a top-down, pre-planned mentality prevails in many development agencies and among governments, requiring designers to determine precise goals, implementation strategies, and evaluation indicators before the project even begins (the "blueprint approach"). Designers usually work either in capital cities, far removed from rural participants, or in headquarters of bilateral/multilateral foreign assistance agencies. Implementation of projects designed in this way is virtually destined to fail owing to coordination problems, data inadequacies, delays, and human error, their rigidity making them inimical to participation from the very people who are supposed to benefit from the project.

In contrast, a "learning process approach" embraces the idea of learning from trial and error; ideally, projects pass through stages of learning to be effective, to be efficient, and to expand. This approach, also called "social" or "people-oriented" development, has a literature almost a decade old (Korten 1984), but its techniques defy the standard operating procedures of most large development agencies.

The Seeds project permits a perfect hybrid. With a learning process approach in mind, students might role-play alternative scenarios for further project development. After researching the political-economic context, students could take on the roles of organizational members or government and other officials to address the question: Where do we go from here?

The Seeds cases raise specific issues for classroom dialogue, such as: How are projects initiated? What is the optimal balance between leaders' and members' participation? Can women join forces across class lines? What is the nature of outside intervention, by women or by foreign governments? What role can women's advocacy organizations play? Should they initiate projects? Broker resources from other agencies? Advise or monitor other governmental agencies? Nurture women's political constituencies? How do the projects enrich the "conventional administrative wisdom" that assumes that only large-scale projects can spend significant sums efficiently? In the Sudanese and U.S. projects, large numbers of small loans could be moved without high administrative overhead. Project services are taken to the people, without forcing people to track down services in an abusive bureaucratic maze.

Personnel issues are also worthy of discussion, since little incentive may exist for government staff to serve women well. Management tends to work to please those to whom they report, who are *rarely* project participants. This is why the Zambia case is so important. It shows the slow, but significant, process of turning around bureaucracies that privilege men as employees and users of services. Why can't this become more common?

As more and more international assistance becomes policy- and program-, rather than project-oriented, women will need to find ways to transform their governmental bureaucracies through strategies as in Zambia, or through non-governmental organizations (NGOs) which press public officials to make government more people-friendly. We see, in many of the Seeds cases, examples of healthy civil society in NGOs and NGO coalitions. Perhaps we should heed Vina Mazumdar's plea in the first volume of *Seeds*: "My only request is that we do not treat politics as a dirty word, but rather recognize the inherently political aspects involved in any process of change" (1989, p. 217).

Sample Course Projects

The Seeds cases lend themselves to a variety of writing assignments, loosely organized around project design and evaluation. Students might read *Seeds 2* to acquire advanced technical knowledge on project design. Students can also write compare-and-contrast essays, evaluating Seeds cases on different criteria. Ideas from *Seeds 2* can be applied to hypothetical problem situations, which is what I have done in examinations: Students were asked to put themselves in the position of the project representatives and to consider "What happens next?"

In my development management course, students designed development projects over the semester through a staggered set of assignments, broken up into manageable parts. A useful companion book dovetails well the institutional, political, sector, and technical issues to know and to critique (Staudt 1991). Students first do background research on the country, culture(s), and policy area of their choice, culminating in an administrative strategy which charts the various people and institutions they need to mobilize. Students then prepare a draft of the entire project design, complete with implementation schedule, evaluation plan, budget, and participation strategy. They then present this plan to the class for feedback and to me for written comment. Completed projects are then placed on library reserve, and the final examination consists of peer review of projects, using a project evaluation sheet with this bottom-line question (after scores for each criterion are tallied): Would you fund this project? Student reviewers are also asked to evaluate the likely impact of the project on women. Armed with two Seeds cases, as well as a thoroughly women-integrated course, students consider complexities that go beyond how many women are involved or what resources come women's way, such as alteration/reinforcement of the sexual division of labor, increased/decreased labor time, increased self- and partner-respect, provision of support networks, and more.

Discussion about issues such as these throughout the course permit a workshop-like session on project evaluation techniques. I outline the evaluation guidelines used by the U.S. Agency for International Development—a formidable chart on which designers outline goals, outputs, inputs, objectively verifiable indicators, methods, and assumptions. Although this demanding exercise requires the designer to think through the many dimensions of the project, it can promote—even if unintentionally—a form of "blueprintism" that often develops in large-scale organizations. Seeds cases offer a way to critique and expand these kinds of evaluation techniques.

Bringing Development Home

Students can apply the women's experiences that have been collected for the publication of *Seeds 2* to development problems in their own communities, or to women in transition from subordination. Students might also consider the kinds of government policies that support and deter international, and specifically women's, development. For course wrap-ups, Seeds cases can generate the kind of dialogue necessary to bring development home, both in terms of addressing analogous issues in the students' own communities and in supporting the kind of development assistance which empowers women all over the world.

References

Cornia, Giovanni et.al. 1987. *Adjustment with a Human Face.* Oxford: Clavendon.

Korten, David, & R. Klauss, eds. 1984. *People-Centered Development.* W. Hartford, CT: Kumarian Press.

Mazumdar, Vina, 1989. "Seeds for a New Model of Development: A Political Commentary." In Ann Leonard, ed. *Seeds: Supporting Women's Work in the Third World.* New York: The Feminist Press.

Nelson, Barbara, and Najma Chowdhury, eds. 1994. *Women and Politics Worldwide.* New Haven: Yale University Press. Contains 43 country chapters authored largely by women from those countries.

Sen, Gita, and Caren Grown. 1987. *Development, Crisis and Alternative Visions: Third World Women's Perspectives.* New York: Monthly Review.

Staudt, Kathleen. 1991. *Managing Development: State, Society and International Contexts.* Newbury Park, CA: Sage.

Staudt, Kathleen. 1985. *Women, Foreign Assistance and Advocacy Administration.* New York: Praeger.

Staudt, Kathleen, ed. 1990. *Women, International Development and Politics: The Bureaucratic Mire.* Philadelphia: Temple University Press.

UNDP (United Nations Development Programme). 1993, 1994. *Human Development Report.* New York: UNDP.

Notes on the Contributors

Ruth Ansah Ayisi is currently working as an information officer for UNICEF in Mozambique. Before joining UNICEF, she worked in Mozambique for four years as a free-lance print and radio journalist and for three years in Zimbabwe as an editor for a women's feature service of Inter Press Service (IPS).

Mayra Buvinić is a founding member and current president of the International Center for Research on Women (ICRW) located in Washington, D.C. As president of ICRW, she manages a program of research, technical assistance, and educational activities that seek to improve the economic, social, and health status of poor women in developing countries. Her current research focuses on the feminization of poverty in developing countries. Mayra Buvinic received her Ph.D. in social psychology from the University of Wisconsin at Madison and a degree in psychology from the Catholic University of Chile.

Martha Alter Chen is research associate at the Harvard Institute for International Development (HIID), a lecturer at the Kennedy School of Government, and director of a program on non-government organizations at HIID. An experienced development practitioner, planner, and researcher, she lived and worked for a number of years in Bangladesh and India. Martha Chen has specialized in and written extensively on gender, poverty, and the non-governmental sector. She received her Ph.D. in South Asia regional studies from the University of Pennsylvania.

Misrak Elias is currently the senior advisor for Women's Development Programmes at UNICEF, New York. Her areas of professional expertise are management, policy formulation/program development, and training, with special emphasis on issues of gender and women's economic development. From 1988 to 1992, she was based in Nairobi, Kenya where she held the same post for UNICEF's Eastern and Southern Africa region; from 1980 to 1988, she was senior consultant and WID program coordinator at the Eastern and Southern Africa Management Institute (ESAMI) in Arusha, Tanzania. A citizen of Ethiopia, Misrak Elias graduated from the College of Business Administration at Addis Ababa University where she subsequently taught and served as head of external relations. She received her MBA in international business and industrial relations from the Graduate School of Business, Columbia University.

Sara K. Gould is the founder and director of the Economic Development Program at the Ms. Foundation for Women in New York City. Through her leadership, the foundation created both the annual Institute on Women and Economic Development and the Collaborative Fund for Women's Economic Development. Sara Gould has worked with low-income women's and other community-based development organizations for over fifteen years on project planning and organizational development issues. She holds a master's degree in city and regional planning from Harvard University.

Eve Hall is a specialist in small enterprise development for women. She is currently employed by the International Labour Organization as chief technical advisor to a project which assists poor urban women in Addis Ababa who collect and sell firewood for sale to find alternative sources of income. She has worked in a similar capacity in several eastern and southern African countries, and as an independent consultant in West Africa, and in South and East Asia.

Rounaq Jahan, currently at Columbia University, was previously a professor of political science at Dhaka University in Bangladesh. From 1982 to 1984, she headed the Women's Programs of the United Nations Asia Pacific Development Center in Kuala Lumpur, Malaysia and from 1985 to 1989, she directed a similar program at the International Labour Organization in Geneva, Switzerland. Rounaq Jahan received her Ph.D. in political science from Harvard University. She has published several books and numerous articles on the subject of women's economic development. She was also founding president of Women for Women: Research and Study Group in Bangladesh; served on the Board of Trustees of the Population Council (1982–92); and is currently on the Advisory Councils of *Human Rights Watch: Asia, Asian Survey,* and *Asian Thought and Society: An International Review.*

Janice Jiggins is an independent consultant based in the Netherlands. Her work includes program development in agricultural research and extension (primarily in sub-Saharan Africa and South Asia) and women-centered analysis of the links among population, agriculture, and environmental concerns. She is also senior program advisor to the International Women's Health Coalition in New York and visiting professor, Department of Rural Extension Studies, University of Guelph, Ontario, Canada. From 1993 to 1994, Janice Jiggins was president of the International Association of Farming Systems Research and Extension. She has also lived in and still travels frequently to South Asia and sub-Saharan Africa and has published extensively in the area of women and agriculture.

Cassie Landers is a consultant with the Education Division, UNICEF, New York. As a specialist in early child development, she provides technical expertise in the design, development, and evaluation of child development programs for UNICEF country offices in Africa, Asia, and the Middle East. Most recently she has been involved in the development of a media-based parent education initiative. Cassie Landers holds both a master's degree in public health and a doctorate in human development from Harvard University.

Ann Leonard is an associate in the Programs Division of the Population Council working primarily in the areas of family, gender and development, women's economic development, quality of reproductive health care, and AIDS and sexually transmitted diseases. Prior to joining the Population Council, Ann Leonard was involved in information, education, and communication (IEC) activities related to family planning and international development at The Ford Foundation and subsequently as an independent consultant.

Paul Maimbo is a training and extension specialist working in Western Zambia. During the period of the women's extension program, he served as provincial director of agriculture in the Western Province.

Mary Masona is a livestock specialist and former animal husbandry officer in the Western Province of Zambia. She was head of the Women's Extension Program from 1986 to 1992 and, subsequently, was appointed to the senior staff of the Department of Agriculture in Mongu.

Katharine McKee is currently transition director of the Community Development Financial Institutions Fund, a new federal agency created to provide capital and other support to community-based lenders across the United States. From 1986 to 1994 she served as associate director of the Center for Community Self-Help in North Carolina. Prior to 1986, she worked with The Ford Foundation in its West African field office and in the Rural Poverty Program in New York. In addition to developing programs focused on enterprise creation and credit, she coordinated The Ford Foundation's women's programs overseas. Katharine McKee holds a master's degree in public and international affairs from Princeton University.

Caroline Moser is a social anthropologist/social planner who is currently senior urban social policy specialist at the World Bank, Washington, D.C., where she is completing a research project on gender and urban poverty in the context of adjustment. Previously she was a university lecturer, first at the Development Planning Unit, University College, London, and then at the London School of Economics and Political Science. She has spent the last decade teaching, training, and writing extensively on gender planning and development.

Aruna Rao is an international consultant working primarily in the areas of gender analysis, training, and institutional change. For five years she was the coordinator of the Population Council's Women's Roles and Gender Differences in Development Program in Asia, based in Bangkok, Thailand. Currently she heads a team working on gender training and organizational development at BRAC (the Bangladesh Rural Advancement Committee). Aruna Rao received her Ph.D. in educational administration from Columbia University and currently resides in Dhaka, Bangladesh.

Madhu Sarin is an architect cum development planner who, since 1980, has been working on natural resource management issues with a particular focus on women's empowerment. At present she is program advisor to the National Support Group for Joint Forest Management (JFM) at the Society for Promotion of Wastelands Development in New Delhi, India. JFM involves development of partnerships between local institutions made up of both women and men forest users for the sustainable management of state-owned forest land. Madhu Sarin is currently working with JFM on issues of gender equality within this program.

Kathleen Staudt is Professor of Political Science at the University of Texas at El Paso. She has published articles on agricultural policy and women's politics in various journals, including *Development and Change, Comparative Politics, Rural Sociology,* and *Women and Politics.* Her latest books are *Women, International Development, and Politics: The Bureaucratic Mire* and *Managing Development.* Her current research projects involve informal economies on both sides of the U.S.–Mexico border, institutional accountability to women in donor agencies, and gender-balanced political representation worldwide.

The Feminist Press at The City University of New York offers alternatives in education and in literature. Founded in 1970, this nonprofit, tax-exempt educational and publishing organization works to eliminate stereotypes in books and schools and to provide literature with a broad vision of human potential. The publishing program includes reprints of important works by women, feminist biographies of women, multicultural anthologies, a cross-cultural memoir series, and nonsexist children's books. Curricular materials, bibliographies, directories, and a quarterly journal provide information and support for students and teachers of women's studies. Through publications and projects, The Feminist Press contributes to the rediscovery of the history of women and the emergence of a more humane society.

New and Forthcoming Books

Always a Sister: The Feminism of Lillian D. Wald. A biography by Doris Groshen Daniels. $12.95 paper.

A Rising Public Voice: Women in Politics Worldwide. Edited by Alida Brill. Foreword by Gertrude Mongella. $17.95 paper, $35.00 cloth.

The Answer/La Respuesta (Including a Selection of Poems), by Sor Juana Inés de la Cruz. Critical edition and translation by Electa Arenal and Amanda Powell. $12.95 paper, $35.00 cloth.

Australia for Women: Travel and Culture, edited by Susan Hawthorne and Renate Klein. $17.95 paper.

Black and White Sat Down Together: The Reminiscences of an NAACP Founder, by Mary White Ovington. Edited and with a foreword by Ralph E.Luker. Afterword by Carolyn E. Wedin. $19.95 cloth.

Changing Lives: Life Stories of Asian Pioneers in Women's Studies, edited by the Committee on Women's Studies in Asia. Foreword by Florence Howe. Introduction by Malavika Karlekar and Barbara Lazarus. $10.95 paper, $29.95 cloth.

The Castle of Pictures and Other Stories: A Grandmother's Tales, Volume One, by George Sand. Edited and translated by Holly Erskine Hirko. Illustrated by Mary Warshaw. $9.95 paper, $23.95 cloth.

Challenging Racism and Sexism: Alternatives to Genetic Explanations (Genes and Gender VII). Edited by Ethel Tobach and Betty Rosoff. $14.95 paper, $35.00 cloth.

China for Women: Travel and Culture. $17.95 paper.

The Dragon and the Doctor, by Barbara Danish. $5.95 paper.

Japanese Women: New Feminist Perspectives on the Past, Present, and Future, edited by Kumiko Fujimura-Fanselow and Atsuko Kameda. $15.95 paper, $35.00 cloth.

Music and Women, by Sophie Drinker. Afterword by Ruth A. Solie. $16.95 paper, $37.50 cloth.

No Sweetness Here, by Ama Ata Aidoo. Afterword by Ketu Katrak. $10.95 paper, $29.00 cloth.

The Slate of Life: More Contemporary Stories by Women Writers of India, edited by Kali for Women. Introduction by Chandra Talpade Mohanty and Satya P. Mohanty. $12.95 paper, $35.00 cloth.

Solution Three, by Naomi Mitchison. Afterword by Susan Squier. $10.95 paper, $29.95 cloth.

Songs My Mother Taught Me: Stories, Plays, and Memoir, by WakakoYamauchi. Edited and with an introduction by Garrett Hongo. Afterword by Valerie Miner. $14.95 paper, $35.00 cloth.

Streets: A Memoir of the Lower East Side. By Bella Spewack. Introduction by Ruth Limmer. Afterword by Lois Elias. $19.95 cloth.

Women of Color and the Multicultural Curriculum: Transforming the College Classroom, edited by Liza Fiol-Matta and Mariam K. Chamberlain. $18.95 paper, $35.00 cloth.

Prices subject to change. Individuals: Send check or money order (in U.S. dollars drawn on a U.S. bank) to The Feminist Press at The City University of New York, 311 East 94th Street, New York, NY 10128. Please include $4.00 postage and handling for the first book, $1.00 for each additional. For VISA/MasterCard orders call (212) 360-5794. Bookstores, libraries, wholesalers: Feminist Press titles are distributed to the trade by Consortium Book Sales and Distribution, (800) 283-3572.